Story of Water and Fire

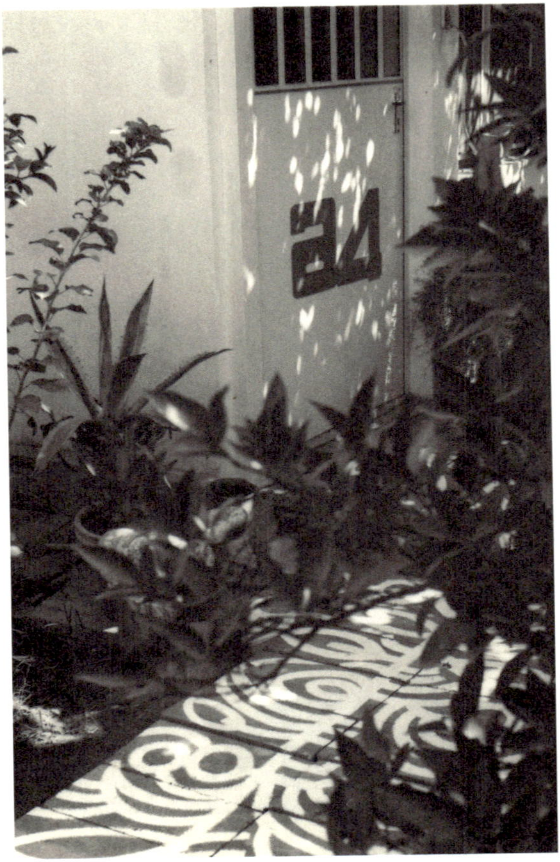

Story of Water and Fire

May Muzaffar

HATJE
CANTZ

Foreword

It is our pleasure to introduce May Muzaffar's book, *Story of Water and Fire*, which provides a captivating insight into the lives of two prominent figures in the Iraqi art world. May Muzaffar and her late husband Rafa Nasiri were pioneers in their respective fields of poetry and painting and print making, and their story is a testament to their passion for art and dedication to their craft.

The book takes the reader on a journey through the couple's life before and after they met each other, providing vivid descriptions of the art scene in Baghdad from the 1960s until the early 1990s, as well as their travels during these and later periods. The book also details their years of exile from 1991, when they resided in Jordan and Bahrain. This rare glimpse into the personal lives of these two great artists offers a rare glimpse into their position and relations with both the Arab and international art scenes.

This book serves not only as a tribute to the remarkable careers of May Muzaffar and Rafa Nasiri, but also sheds light on the rich artistic heritage of Iraq and the broader Arab world. We hope that their story will inspire future generations of artists and art enthusiasts to continue pushing the boundaries of creativity and artistic expression. The book includes photographs of the art scene in Baghdad, adding a visual representation of the couple's legacy.

In addition to being a compelling portrait of two influential Iraqi artists, May Muzaffar's book serves as an invaluable guide to the archival materials that al Mawrid Arab Center for the Study of Art at New York University Abu Dhabi has digitized and will make available to researchers.

Al Mawrid is dedicated to the study and the preservation of Arab art and culture, it is uniquely positioned to serve as a bridge between past and present. Through its research, pedagogy, and archival work, al Mawrid plays a vital role in documenting the rich artistic heritage of the Arab world, promoting contemporary scholarly work on Arab artists, and fostering cross-cultural dialogue.

We express our gratitude to May Muzaffar for her invaluable cooperation in writing this book. Her first-hand accounts and personal insights have enriched our understanding of Iraqi art and culture. We also extend our appreciation to Maher Kayyali from the Arab Institute for Publishing and Research, publisher of the Arabic edition from which this book was translated.

Salwa Mikdadi
Director, al Mawrid Arab Center for the Study of Art
New York University Abu Dhabi

Preface

Rafa's departure from this world left a tremendous gap, and nothing, nor anyone, could have pulled me from its depths. Nothing, that is, but preserving his presence by my side. When friends and family took their leave late that first night after his funeral, I closed the door behind them and withdrew alone with my new reality. Loneliness enveloped me like the walls of a deep, dark well as I faced a looming question: How could I continue our journey alone, and assume the duty of preserving his legacy, his name, his great contribution to art? I'd long aspired to work on a project documenting our shared life, one that was filled with love, harmony, and unity rarely found in cultural circles. I once shared this idea with him and it pleased him; he said he wished that I would. Now, I found, the time had come to carry it out, for this is what would keep us together.

Rafa was passionate about documenting his artistic practice and maintaining his work from all its stages, beginning with his studies at the Institute of Fine Arts and through to the final year of his life. He produced remarkable photographic documentation of everywhere he went, and kept notebooks of various sizes in which he recorded his thoughts, poetic literary texts, and visual ideas. His need to write, and to create an outlet for his feelings, increased after we left Baghdad.

Rafa kept his correspondence with his father and siblings from his four years of academic studies in Beijing, China, as well as other letters from friends. In his final years, he revisited his past and shared memories of it whenever he had the opportunity to meet or speak with his siblings. He even made a voice recording with his mother, who spoke of his springtime birth and his tenderest years. Rafa often spoke of his childhood, of playing in the open spaces of Tikrit and summers spent on the riverbanks, all of which he documented in his delightful autobiography *Rihlati ila al-sin* (My journey to China, 2012). Relying on his active memory, he wrote of his upbringing, his life's path and artistic journey, and his family's move to Baghdad. He later added additional thoughts and memories, which I published in his final and posthumous book, *Fifty Years Between the East and West* (2019). As such, I chose not to include a chapter on Rafa's childhood and early life in this book. I did, however, dedicate a chapter to myself, to shed light on aspects of my life and youth that even those close to me do not know.

With the exception of the first and second chapters, I relied foremost on my memory in the writing of this book. I'm blessed with a highly present and detailed memory, even of my early childhood.

Yet, for the first and second chapters I relied on diaries in which I'd recorded details of my every meeting with Rafa, from the time we met and throughout the two years before we married.

Completion of this memoir took about six years, from 2014 to 2020, during which I was forced to take occasional breaks to focus on other tasks and responsibilities. Numerous reviews of each chapter also delayed its completion, and I still do not feel that I am finished. Throughout this difficult journey I conversed and consulted with two close friends, journalist and publisher Amel al-Sharqi, and writer and translator Bahira Abdul Latif, each of whom carefully and lovingly read my words. They both know me and Rafa well, and for each of them I am grateful.

The Arabic edition of the book was designed by my dear nephew, Mohammed Namir, with the completion and final touches to take it to press coming from artist Ala Younis. Thank you to photographer Haitham Aziza for assisting me in enhancing the quality of the selected photographs.

For this English edition of the book, I am deeply grateful to al Mawrid for their translation of the book into English and for including it in their digital archive, thus ensuring its accessibility to a wider audience. I am also indebted to Salwa Mikdadi for her initiative to translate the book, and to Ala Younis for her editorial effort and management of the publication process. The generous support of New York University Abu Dhabi is also gratefully acknowledged. Finally, I would like to express my heartfelt appreciation to Jennifer Peterson for her excellent translation of the book, and to my dear friends and family who have stood by me throughout this journey. Together, we have ensured that Rafa's legacy and contribution to art will be remembered and celebrated for generations to come.

May Muzaffar
Amman, Jordan
March 2023

Introduction

We were having breakfast on a bitingly cold winter's day, Rafa sitting in his place facing the wide window overlooking the valley, gazing out into the open space, when he said, "Look at the sky. . . . What pure blue it is!"

Thus, he began his morning, leaving me unable to look at the sky without seeing his face in it.

A letter to Rafa:

> In order to fill the dreadful emptiness created by your absence, and so as to be with you, in your company, I'm going to start writing the story of our life together over forty years. I told you one day, when you'd regained some energy, of my intention to write such as book. Your handsome face lit up as you softly said, "I wish you would."
>
> Starting today, I'll record every thought and scene passing before me from the store of memories I have of the years we lived together.
>
> I'll continue speaking to you, and with you, so that you remain present with me, my love and companion. I'll follow the footsteps of that rebellious young man we met in the Paris home of Etel Adnan and Simone Fattal during the summer of 1979. Do you remember?
>
> At the time, we'd just completed our stay at the Moussem culturel d'Asilah in Morocco.[1] For about a month, we'd attended its second season, made rich by the attendance of cultural actors and artists, both Arab and not. We'd attended enchanting plays and concerts, and a poetry reading by Adonis and Mahmoud Darwish. Mornings had been allocated for seminars open to the public, while the evenings were filled with cultural activities, meetings, and convivial gatherings held in the open air amid stunning land- and seascapes. You were pleased you'd begun working in the graphic art studio that you'd set up with your friend Mohammad Omar Khalil, and you'd produced a captivating collection of prints. A highlight for you had been meeting your Portuguese colleague David de Almeida, of whom you'd often spoken. During that season, we met many people, including Tayeb Salih, who was a regular guest at the festival. We grew close to some, including Charbel Dagher and Pierre Abi Saab.
>
> We'd planned to go from Morocco to France and roam its southern coasts. Etel Adnan and Simone Fattal were among the festival participants that year, and we'd previously met them at the

1974 Al Wasiti-Fine Arts Festival in Baghdad. We told them of our intention to head to Paris, and they offered for us to stay in an apartment attached to their Parisian home.

We traveled by plane from Tangier to Nice and rented the Renault 5 we so loved. We bought a map and decided to take the rural roads. My job was to follow the map, but I'm not good at reading one; in my childhood I struggled to draw the map of Iraq. And so we got lost—you'd refuse to seek the help of anyone to guide us, and I was a bad guide. You'd get irritated and upset as you circled through farmland and forests. We'd stumble across a lovely hotel and spend the night, and then resume our way in the morning.

Our trip took ten days, during which we visited the most beautiful of the coastal cities and enjoyed their gorgeous beaches, stopping at Monte Carlo, Saint-Tropez, Juan-les-Pins, and Antibes, where Pablo Picasso had lived and produced his gorgeous ceramics kept in the Musée Picasso. We avoided the main highways and penetrated deep into the green environs, intoxicated by the scent of the land and greenery. But with continually getting lost, we eventually had to resort to the highway to follow its clear signs. We visited Aix-en-Provence and were lucky to attend a Kandinsky exhibition at Château des Baux de Provence, spectacularly situated on a mountaintop. From a distance one can see Mont Sainte-Victoire, which Paul Cézanne had prolifically painted. When we reached Avignon, we found it filled with tourists attending its famed theater season, and unfortunately it wasn't possible to stay over as no accommodation was available, not even for just one night.

Finally, we reached Paris, stopping at the first rental office to hand in the car, and there I contacted Simone. Breathlessly she asked, "Where are you, we were worried about you! Etel woke up this morning crying because she dreamed that you wouldn't be coming to Paris!" Oh, Etel and her tender heart!

We headed to their address in Saint-Germain, 27 rue Jacob, and entered a large courtyard shaded by a linden tree, with which Etel conversed and to which she dedicated a splendid volume of poetry. There we met the handsome and rebellious young Frenchman whom Etel had met by chance and taken pity upon. He rejected any kind of constraint, including formal education, and had left his parents' home to live alone in a small abode allocated by the state for the homeless. His voraciousness for independently selected reading, and his revolutionary ideas, meant he could not commit to any methodology other than that which he chose for himself. He was nineteen years old and possessed knowledge comparable to that of leading intellectuals, knowledge that qualified him to engage with philosophy, poetry, music, and the arts. Yet, he was rigid in his chaotic and extremist opinions on life and art, and often angered Etel with the anger of a mother fearing the ruin of her son. He lived on meager assistance from the state that was insufficient to cover his basic needs, including his bills for electricity, which got cut off. And so Etel provided him with food and a comfortable place to read after the public libraries closed their doors.

After we'd settled into their pretty upstairs apartment, we sat to rest and drink tea, and were joined by this young man. Whenever we'd succeeded with a segment of conversation—which took place in English, Etel helping him to grasp whatever was difficult for him to understand—he'd slip away to stand at the window, pulling from his attire a thick notebook in which he'd scribble something, and then return to us. Etel told us that he wrote anything and everything he encountered or that crossed his mind, and had done so since he was six years old. He recorded all his thoughts and everything he witnessed.

Today, I find myself recalling the image of that young man so fully immersed in himself, his thoughts, and his engagement with the world.

I see him as a model to follow so I can be fully engaged with you.

May
Amman, Jordan
December 22, 2013

1 It was our second visit to the coastal city of Asilah, Morocco, and I will speak more of it in the chapter on our trips.

The Beginning

Our friendship was born in autumn, and autumn remained the season dearest to our hearts.

A letter to Rafa:

A year ago today, you were sitting on the sofa opposite my desk in our new studio in Lweibdeh [Amman, Jordan]. Soft sunlight bathed your face, and your eyes had surrendered to its magic as you listened to Bach cello suites. Perhaps you were immersed in a close, yet unattainable, dream.

"When will I go back to painting?" you asked. "Will this weakness continue to drain me of my energy?" You said this although—and despite the frailty that had rapidly undermined your previous vigor—you'd recently accomplished your purest work yet in terms of brevity, clarity, and transparency: *Beside the River*. It was your latest attempt to locate an alternative homeland.

Alone, I am today in a world desolate but for your spirit shadowing me, lingering with me wherever I am. I subsist on memory that returns you to me, and see you sitting nearby, each of us listening to the sounds within us. My conversation with you will not end, and your image will not disappear. I'll bring our story back, here, on these pages, just as I promised you.

Over forty years ago, during one of my visits to the home of our friend the writer Jabra Ibrahim Jabra, I was halted near the entrance by the sight of a translucent painting in white and blue bearing no signature by the artist. It enchanted me as much as it confounded me: Was it a wave in a turquoise sea, or the body of a woman in a state of passion? I asked Jabra whose work this was, and he replied in surprise, "Rafa Nasiri, how can you not know him?"

I conjure you up and see that handsome young man sneaking glances at me from between paintings hung in the National Museum of Modern Art (Gulbenkian) in early 1971. I still hadn't met you. I wondered that day who was pursuing me with those stolen glances, and why he didn't speak to me directly. Then I learned from Dia [al-Azzawi] that you were the artist whose paintings had enchanted me, an artist who'd dared in that exhibition to turn square frames into rhombuses, and painted clear swathes of color, sometimes horizontally and sometimes vertically, separated by lines of gold. That young man was Rafa!

Amman, Jordan
March 23, 2014

The first exhibition of the New Vision group in March 1971, the vanguard of Iraq's modern art movement, provided my entrance into writing on visual arts. I attended with the aim of viewing its works and meeting Dia al-Azzawi, to interview him for the journal *Mawaqif* (Positions) at the request of [poet] Adonis. I approached him with a carefully reverential demeanor, for it was not easy for a beginner in the arts like me to hold a competent conversation, for a well-established journal, with an artist whose name was dazzling Baghdad and Beirut at the time. Yet, my careful reverence dissipated, or nearly so, before the friendly welcome al-Azzawi gave me. Dia was extremely close to the literary scene, and always sought to create lively interaction between artists and writers, building support for the visual arts movement through serious writing based on knowledge that went beyond the style commonly used in journalism at the time. I didn't know Dia personally, but I'd seen him when we were students at the College of Arts [in Baghdad], and I knew him to be among those who worked during their free time in the college's open studio run by the artist Hafidh al-Droubi. Dia asked me to first view the exhibition's works, and then set another appointment for the interview.

As I summon the image of Rafa, I see him beside me now with his glowing, childish face and hesitant smile, while underlying it was worry and a curiosity as to what I was thinking as I stood before his work. As for me, I was drowning in confusion, seeking someone to guide me in this world that seemed impenetrable and bewildering at the time. Over the years, I grew to understand that this worry clung to Rafa at all of his exhibitions, even to his last exhibition in Manama, Bahrain, in February 2013. This worry churned beneath a tense silence only broken after the exhibition's opening, when he'd leave with his own personal convictions. He'd take a deep breath and let out the ringing laugh so unique to him, as he announced the start to a celebration of victory. Yet, these worried, curious looks of his were how we first became acquainted.

My relationship with artists developed after that meeting, for we met at the Society of Iraqi Artists in al-Mansour where I attended various cultural activities. Dia and Rafa were members of the board, from 1971–73, headed by sculptor Ismail Fattah. At the time, the society had a program of cultural activities and was a meeting place for the New Vision group, which included Dia al-Azzawi, Saleh al-Jumaie, Hashim Samarji, Ismail Fattah, Tariq Ibrahim, and Mekki Hussein. I'd receive invitations to attend its events, for they came to me at the company I worked in since the autumn of 1970 [the Iraq Reinsurance

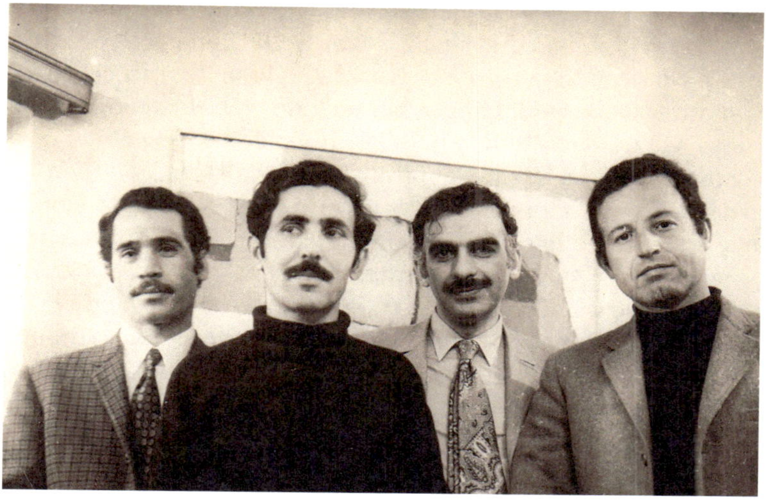

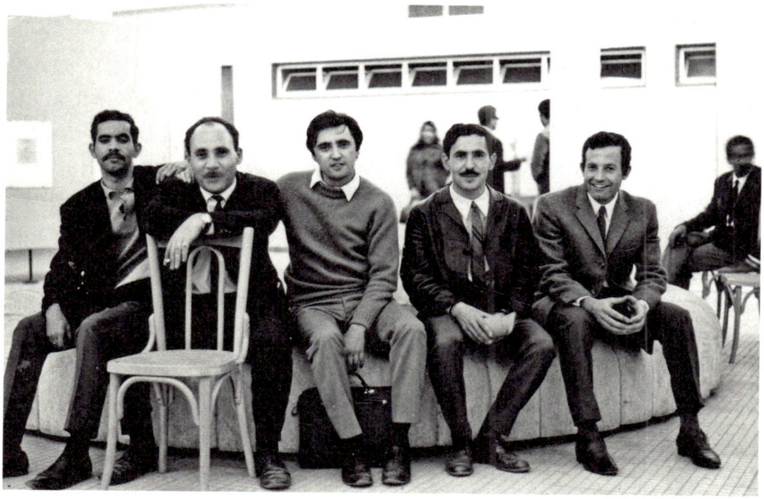

Top: New Vision group: Saleh Al Jumai'e, Dia al-Azzawi, Hashim Samarchi, Rafa Nasiri

Bottom: Ibrahim Zayer, Yousef as-Sayegh, Sadeq as-Sayegh, Dia al-Azzawi, Rafa Nasiri, 1970

Company] via the information desk, and I was taken by the beauty of their modern designs. After we met, Rafa would come to my office to deliver invitations in person, either with Dia or on his own.

Sometimes Rafa would linger, but he didn't speak much, and I'd get flustered as I tried to fill the gap left by his silence. He avoided looking me in the eye. Once, he didn't appear at all for a while, and then returned with a new invitation, saying he'd been on a trip to Ljubljana to take part in the Biennial of Graphic Arts. He said it as if I were knowledgeable of such artistic gatherings, though I'd never heard of the city nor knew what graphic arts were. I was somewhat embarrassed and didn't know how to continue the conversation, although I wanted to know more. Nor did he linger, excusing himself and saying that he'd be expecting me at the exhibition.

My office was on the ninth floor of a modern building in which Rafa and Dia had previously been commissioned to create two murals symbolically representing safety and security on the eighth and ninth floors. Dia had worked in his studio, while Rafa had had to work on location in the evenings due to the mural's large size. He'd treated the concept in his abstract style, pure colors, and wavy lines. The elevator hadn't been ready to use at that time, and for months we climbed the stairs to the ninth floor. Every day I would follow the mural's developments without ever meeting the artist. One day, my mentor Najib al-Mani‘, who was assistant director of the company, spoke to me of Rafa's brilliance and the steadiness of his hand in controlling large swathes of space. He had seen him at work.

Rafa continued to diligently bring me invitations. He'd come to the office and sit with me for a while, drinking his coffee, his eyes always wandering to the large window overlooking al-Jumhuriya Street behind my desk, with the minaret of al-Ghazel Market in the distance, across from the Latin Cathedral. As he was prepared to leave from one of his visits, he said to me, "It doesn't befit you to sit at a steel desk. They should make a diaphanous desk for you."

I shared the spacious office with my friend Anan Sami Fattah. We'd become colleagues after I'd recommended her as manager of the general director's office. She didn't have any prior experience, and so I helped her at first, and she became brilliant and meticulous in her work. Later, a presidential decree prohibited female employees from working in offices adjacent to those of department heads.

Anan was a cheerful person, and I'd had a relationship with her and her sister Siham since our childhood, thanks to our mothers' friendship. She had a strong influence on my personal and social life with

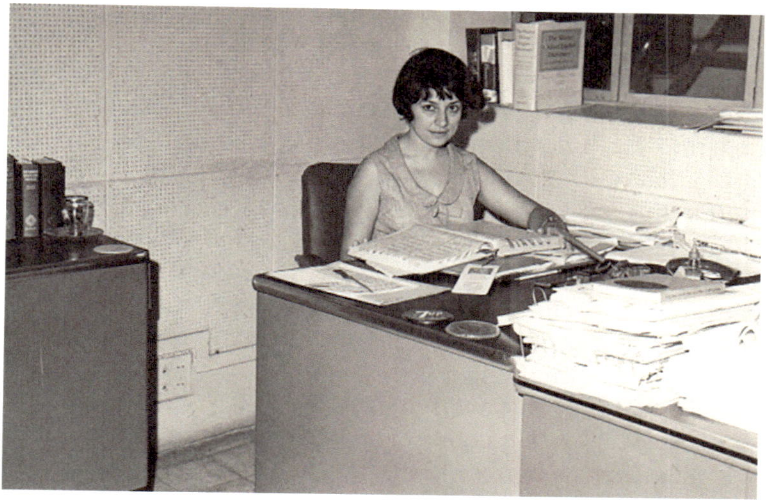

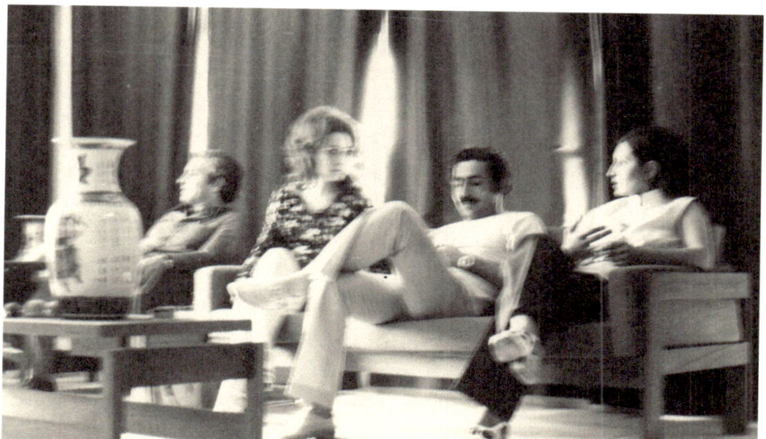

Top: May's office at the Iraqi Reinsurance Company, Baghdad, 1968

Bottom: Lunch at Rafa's family house with Dr. Ferdous al-Abbasi and Dia al-Azzawi, 1971

her open-mindedness, vivaciousness, beauty, style, and good humor. She was also in dire need of a friend to confide in about all that she bore within, and to speak of her wishes for a future beyond the disappointments she had suffered. We had an exceptional friendship that lasted until the unfortunate end of her life due to cancer—a friendship that remained strong, our conversations never losing their effusiveness.

She liked Rafa from the very beginning, and he too felt comfortable with her. She grew increasingly impressed with his likeable nature and found him suitable for me when she innately realized he was infatuated with me. After hearing Rafa's comments to me, she said, "I've never heard of such flirtation!"

I said, "The words of an artist and poet," and she replied laughingly, "Whoever climbs nine flights of stairs to deliver an invitation that could have been left at reception is not just using language. Open your eyes!"

Baghdad, Autumn 1971

We met one evening at the Society of Iraqi Artists, at one of the gatherings we were accustomed to attending. The society formed an ideal cultural space and had become a meeting place for writers, artists, architects, and musicians. I felt a strong need to belong to cultural circles, and was comfortable with this group, having seen the sophisticated behavior of its members that allowed to me move freely among them, something difficult to find in the literary scene at the time. They seemed to accept and welcome women in their gatherings. Dia al-Azzawi spearheaded the group, and was the connecting point between writers and artists, active with a zealous energy and vitality that he maintains until today. I could tell Rafa was the closest to him, and that they shared ideas and ambitions despite the differences in their personalities.

That evening we were in a large group. I noticed Rafa looking at me from afar, and then he changed his place to sit beside me. Friends were speaking of general topics, interspersed with laughter and mockery of just about everything, whereas Rafa remained silent, hardly participating at all. He leaned toward me and whispered, "I'm bored with this gathering. Can we go somewhere else where we can speak at our ease?" I agreed without hesitation, for I harbored a desire to get to know him.

I sat beside him in his old Opel and didn't ask where we'd go. I knew there were few places I could go in the company of a young man, for Baghdad was not as liberal as Beirut. He complained he'd been irritated by the gathering and its repetitive talk, as though he needed to justify his invitation to leave. I paid no mind, for so much in our encounter exuded a sense of comfort—the calm atmosphere, his handsome face, his polite behavior. I felt at ease, as though I'd known him for years. This was my first bold departure from my usual cautiousness in Baghdad.

I could tell he was accustomed to speaking with women in a relaxed manner. And I knew a little about him: his blue painting with its enchanting connotations, my entrance to his beautiful world of art that had so confounded me; and that he was spoken of in Beirut two years earlier, as well as what I'd heard that summer about his astonishing exhibition and his escapades in the city of beauty and freedom. It had shocked me when I discovered that the young man sneaking looks at me between paintings, pursuing me as I turned away, was that very same daring young lover.

We stopped at an outdoor restaurant in east Baghdad that I didn't know. Men and a few women were seated around its tables, and in the center was a dance floor with live music by a group of young men singing English and Italian songs popular at the time, including "Strangers in the Night." We sat in a quiet corner, where we quickly exchanged a few words about the place and then fell silent. Rafa was mirthful, but equally flustered. He asked if I'd mind if he ordered a glass of beer, and I didn't, as I was accustomed to social clubs where alcohol was served. I asked for a juice, and we conversed on general topics before he asked me to dance, which I politely declined.

I noticed his discomfort and the shaking of his hand as he held his glass. He thanked me for accepting his invitation to join him, as he felt a need to speak privately. Then he exploded, expressing his dissatisfaction with Baghdad, its stifling atmosphere, and its restrictive life. He spoke of his desire to be freed of this world, and to find avenues allowing one to be true to oneself. I understood how he felt, given how my brother had suffered upon returning from eight years of study in London. Rafa had spent four years in China, and had recently returned from Portugal, where he'd spent two years training in graphic arts and printmaking. He'd visited several European cities and spent months in Beirut. He said he wanted to leave Iraq and was thinking of completing his studies in America.

I was a good listener; I understood his distress and his pressing desire to flee. Then he told me something more like a confession: "I'm a failure of a lover living his crisis. I say a failure because I know no better description." Surprised, I asked, "You? But that's different from what I've heard. It's said that you're an unrivaled lover." He was stunned by this and laughed in cheerful embarrassment, as he'd now found the way paved for conversation. Yet, he remained self-conscious and didn't ask me what I'd heard, or how.

In the summer of 1969, I'd gone with my mother to Beirut as always. We stayed in a hotel in Raouché and got in touch with our friends. We often sat in the Dolce Vita Café, which was beside our hotel and the most beautiful of the cafés overlooking Raouché. I'd met a number of Lebanese writers, and by good coincidence the poet Lami'a Abbas Emara was there with her son, staying in the al-Manara Hotel in Ras Beirut, where Rafa also resided. She'd come visit us with the writer Daisy al-Amir and the poet Habib Sadiq, and occasionally the poet Khalil Hawi. I'd met them at the Arab Poetry Festival and the Arab Literary Convention held in Baghdad that year. When we were alone, she'd speak of Rafa's artistic news and personal adventures, conveying them lightheartedly with a mixture of wit, admiration, and a sense of pride in him. I hadn't met Rafa, because his exhibition had ended before we arrived. That summer I also saw Adonis, who'd also attended the poetry festival, and through him I met Samir Sayegh, Munir Akash, and Riyadh Fakhouri, and my relationship with them grew closer during subsequent visits to Beirut.

And, thus, I found the door to conversation flung wide open, for Rafa had a close relationship with the poets and artists of Beirut. We spoke in a continuous flow, Rafa gradually losing his reserve. His tense hands relaxed and his discontent dissipated. The sense of absolute comfort and ease between us inspired within me a sense of delight with the atmosphere and the gentle October breeze. It was a clear and moonless night filled with intimate, effusive conversation, and I listened to Rafa with interest and pleasure. I wasn't swept away by his tide but remained steadily on the shore, observing the flow. For the first time, I realized how one could be both within a moment and apart from it. It was one of the few instances in which I'd felt satisfied with myself and confident about what I wanted.

We sat across from each other. At one point he drew close and whispered with glistening eyes, "You're different; you're splendid." I smiled and was overcome with a sense of responsibility toward him, a feeling for which I couldn't place a source. I liked the idea of being his close friend. He continued to complain of his work and home environments, of troublesome relations and the scarcity of places to go. I, too, felt some of what bothered him, especially the feeling of failure. And I also felt oppressed by the restrictions of Baghdadi society and my familial obligations.

He spoke to me of the last thing he'd painted: death embodied in blue. I don't know why I didn't take him seriously. It seemed like the words came from his mouth, not from the blazing depths of his being. Death! What death could lurk in that raging vitality? I was facing a small genie who'd broken his bottle and taken off. He was troubled, filled with discontent of known causes, and a restlessness needing a woman's company. I was a safe shore for him that night, and he confided freely.

This man so often silent around me, only rarely speaking, was now conversing without restraint. He was a spirit rebelling against everything constraining him, including feelings he saw as a tie to others, no matter who. In the dim light his eyes seemed to shine with vigor and conviction. As I listened, I compared him to everyone I'd known and perhaps admired, and no one was equal to this shimmering soul. I wanted to hear everything and anything. I felt the life pulsing through my veins, a sense of satisfaction filling me; I was utterly at peace and felt I was who I'd always wanted to be. "You're different." I'd been told that on numerous occasions, but it had a different ring under that night's sky.

We stood briefly at the door to my house. He seemed happy and at ease, with just a tad of the discomfort that never left him. With a nervous hand he grasped mine and kissed it with gratitude and decorum. I wasn't sure of my feelings toward him at the time, but I was certain that he'd left with me a part of himself.

When I woke up the next morning, the previous night's meeting felt like a fresh breeze, a splendid and spontaneous encounter in which I'd gained an incomparable friend. Perhaps it was a passing fantasy not to be repeated.

The On-and-Off Stage

I don't know how to describe this period that lasted about two years. It was filled with the sweet and the bitter, with hope and a sense of threat, with connection and separation. Rafa was neither an ideal I aspired to, nor the person I dreamed of, but the light that he sparked within me melted away all other images and conceptions, stripping me of any desire to withdraw. Rafa kept making me feel like our relationship was temporary, always remaining uncertain and hesitant. He clung only to his freedom and was preoccupied only with fleeing to the far reaches of the earth that allowed him to create art as he aspired. Something prevented him from living in harmony with Baghdad and its restrictions. And, despite this, I found myself utterly swept away with love for him.

After that special first evening we spent together alone, he told me he'd be away from Baghdad for a few days on a short trip. Yet, he surprised me the next day by opening the door to my office and standing before me, his eyes drifting to the open space beyond the window. I was delighted by his unexpected appearance. Without my asking, he explained, "I cut my trip short because I forgot some papers."

Then he added, "And I also returned for another reason," and fell silent. I didn't ask him what it was. Silence ensued, and then he hesitantly asked if I could visit his studio to see his latest work. His request was quite a surprise, if I don't say odd, for I knew his studio was in his family home. "One day," I replied, "why not?"

Many days passed before I heard from him again and he asked to meet. When we did, I found myself facing a different person. He was provocative, tumultuous, and aggressive. I felt as though I were being tested, that there was something contrived about his behavior. I kept calm and ridiculed his trifling talk.

We continued to meet, both in groups and alone. Baghdad's many cultural events also brought us together, and we spent much time conversing on the phone. Whenever he'd draw close to me, he'd then distance himself, and his behavior perplexed me. His calls would start off cold and indifferent, which I'd ignore and go on talking, and then he'd take off in lively enthusiasm. I never understood his hearty laughter, and as for his contradictory statements, they could raise to me to a peak and then crash me to the deepest depths. We had long conversations in which I purposely focused on his work and projects, what each of us were reading, and what we were doing. As we listened to each other, we happily discovered the points where our taste converged on the smaller details of life. I grew certain of his uniqueness among everyone I'd ever known.

I wanted to hear more from him and discover who he was, and the telephone was the best way to pull him into speaking. Through our conversations I learned that he suffered from states that worried and confused me: discontentedness, hesitancy, and an indifference toward everything. Nothing was clear to me in the beginning.

Once he spoke to me of a blue painting crossed with a line of red. Then he complained of his excessive use of blue. "Using it again means it's turned into a phenomenon, and I have to figure out the reason for it."

"What does the color mean to you?" I asked.

He replied that he didn't believe in naming colors. "Blue implies sorrow, or failure."

I reminded him of the diaphanous blue pulsing with life in the painting hung at the entrance to Jabra Ibrahim Jabra's home, without mention of its sexual innuendos. He was delighted by the praise and laughed softly. Somewhat provocatively, I asked, "Is it comparable to Picasso's blue phase?"

"No," he said, "the journey remains a long one."

That evening I wrote a poem, "Drawing Lines in Blue and Red," in which I envisioned red sweeping away the blue.

A few days later, he called and inundated me with loving words. With childish joy he proclaimed, "The rule's been reversed! I've been freed of blue, and my painting has turned red! Red has triumphed. And I want to see you."

"When?" I asked softly.

"Now, at this very moment."

"But it's very late. We can speak for a while, but . . ."

"No, no. I want this now." He let out his mighty laugh and I got flustered. I had to control myself before I could control him without dampening his enthusiasm. "Do you really see it as appropriate for me to go out with you at such a late hour?"

"Of course."

"Can you convince my family?"

After a moment of silence, he whispered, "No, most certainly not."

We ended the call. I was unsettled; half of me was overflowing with joy and longing, and the other half was asking where I was going with this man who was wild to the core. "Whims, whims, whims, I'm all whims," he'd said. "I eat when I want, sleep when I want. I leave the house and don't know when I'll return . . . I hate restrictions of all kinds . . . I was created to live without them."

How could I keep up with this flow when I was a person who made a thousand considerations for every step I took? I'd always sought a tender heart to reassure me, not to daunt me. Yet how could I resist the charm of this sweeping tide?

We chose a small table in a quiet and cozy corner of a Karrada café, far from prying eyes. He asked me what I feared.

I looked into his eyes. They were sharp, showing no tenderness. Rather than expressing fear of my fate with him, and his mood swings that bewildered me, I expressed fear of the misunderstanding that often dominates human relationships, the eternal conundrum of people misunderstanding each other. Perhaps what I said was a bit strange to him, and more like a philosophical dilemma.

"Wonderful, that will lead you to utmost confidence! But if you want to understand me, you'll have to enter the world of madness."

I don't know why I didn't take these words seriously: "enter the world of madness." It was most likely contrived, a flexing of muscles and a performative call by the likes of those holding that all poets should resemble Rimbaud or Dylan Thomas, that all artists were bohemians freely roaming the earth without inhibition. I'd always made fun of Dylan Thomas's often-quoted reply to a girl who'd asked him, "How can I become a poet?" He told her to be a prostitute.

What I found loveliest in Rafa was a sincerity he could not hide; it was his most splendid characteristic. Yet, at that time, I still hadn't been able to determine where I stood with him: I had no doubt fallen for the artist, and now was falling for the person, but I hadn't made a decision. I found him churning within my depths like a storm moves through a deep valley, tearing everything from its place. He changed so much within me as I followed his lead. In our conversations, we often reached the pinnacle of understanding as we discovered the points of strength and weakness within us.

"You wouldn't be doing what you are now without me, if it weren't for my invitation and my instigation," he bragged. I wasn't comfortable with the arrogant tone in his voice. In utter confidence I replied, "That's not true, this was my decision. I wanted to be with you."

On another occasion he asked me, "Do you cry?" I told him, "Crying melts the soul and purifies it."

"When do you cry?"

"When a feeling raises me to its extreme. Yesterday, for example, I was listening to Spanish flamenco, with Nati Mistral reading and singing the poetry of Lorca. There was fire and sorrow in her voice, a life force as present as that found in the poetry of Lorca. Beauty is

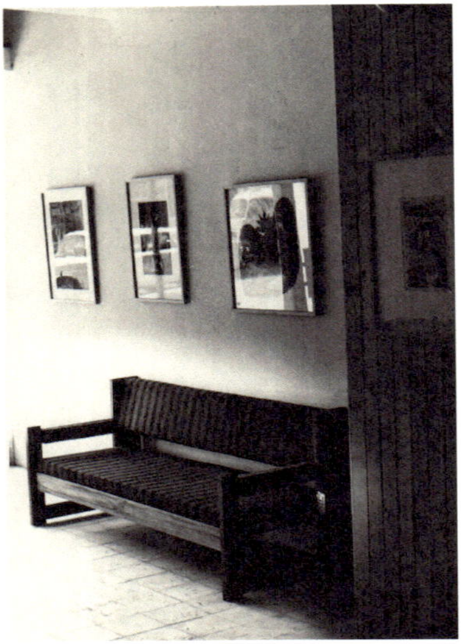

Rafa's solo exhibition at EA Gallery, Baghdad, 1966

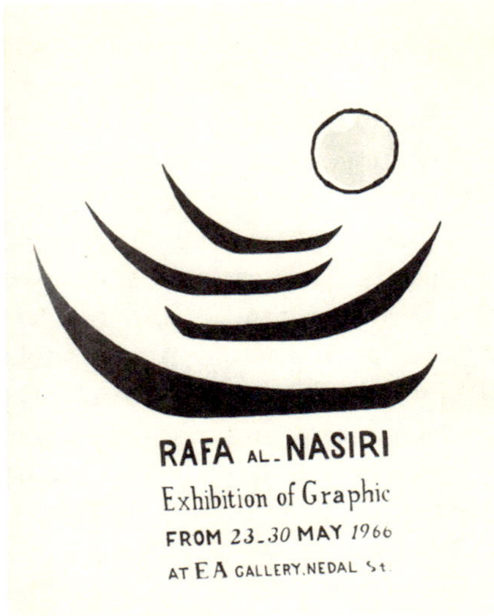

Poster for Rafa's graphic art solo exhibition at EA Gallery, Baghdad, 1966

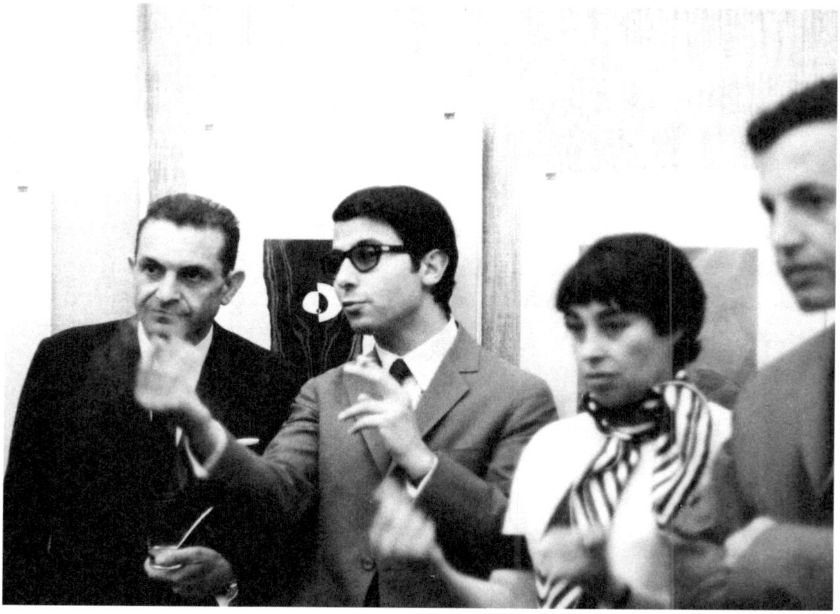

Graphic art exhibition
at The Gravura, Lisbon,
1968

poetry, in that it's the spirit that kindles life in anything. And this is how, in my isolated life, I experience moments of intoxicated rapture that stir me. I'm swept up by it, and then awaken to find myself trapped between walls, consumed by loneliness and impotence. And so I cry."

When I spoke to him of beauty, he'd listen intently, his eyes shining captivatingly. Having connected with something in his fiery soul, I'd find him calm, compliant, and free of affectation or contriteness. We shared a lot about ourselves. He spoke to me of his travels and of his relationships with places, events, and women in Beijing, Lisbon, and Beirut, and we'd discuss them both seriously and in jest. He enjoyed speaking freely with me, devoid of any self-consciousness. Once I tried to speak similarly of myself, but he placed his hand over my mouth. "I beg you, I don't want to hear about it. I know you better."

He began insisting that I visit his home studio in his father's house, and I was eager to enter his art world, so I went with him. It was the second time I'd been to their spacious home. The first time I'd been invited to lunch with friends: Dia al-Azzawi, Tariq Ibrahim and his wife Dr. Fardous, Mekki Hussein, and Saleh al-Jumaie. On that visit I'd admired the modern style of their home designed by architect Hisham Munir, and we sat in the reception area with its comfortable, modern furniture designed by architect Rifat Chadirji and made by Abdel Amir al-Najjar. Rafa had supervised the construction of their family home, and the furnishing of the dining and reception room.

In the mid-1960s, after imports had been banned, the locally produced furniture in Baghdad's markets sorely lacked for taste. Rifat Chadirji opened EA Gallery, offering Scandinavian-style furniture alongside exhibited paintings, although a year later it was split into two separate showrooms. The Orozdi Bak storerooms, which had been purchased by businessmen, also offered modern furniture at that time, and were under the supervision of Soad al-Omari.

Their house was extremely tasteful and stylish, especially as the walls had been hung with artworks by Rafa and others. In the reception area I was drawn to a somewhat abstract painting in black and white that occupied an entire wall and suggested a woman's disheveled bed. I asked whose work it was, and Rafa tersely replied, "A [female] Lebanese artist."

On my second visit I gazed intently at this painting, my admiration for its abbreviation, innuendo, and powerful execution increasing. Rafa had brought his paintings down from the second-floor studio to the living room so I could see them. We spoke a bit and then began

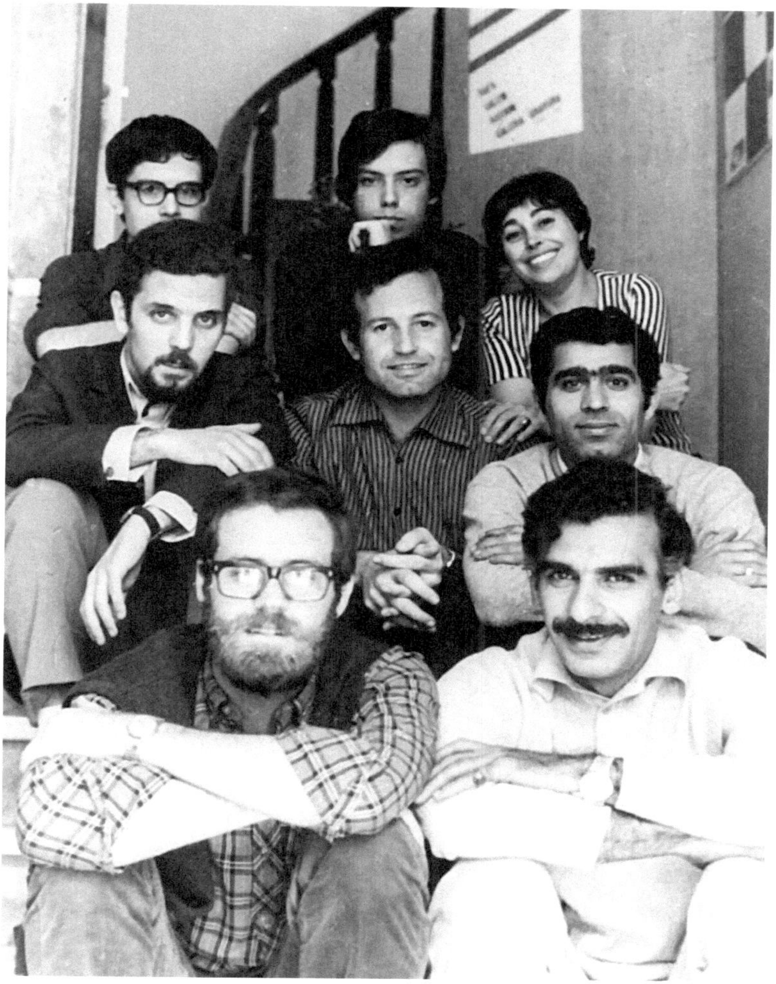

Hashim Samarchi, Salim Al Dabbagh with Rafa Nasiri, The Gravura, Lisbon, 1968

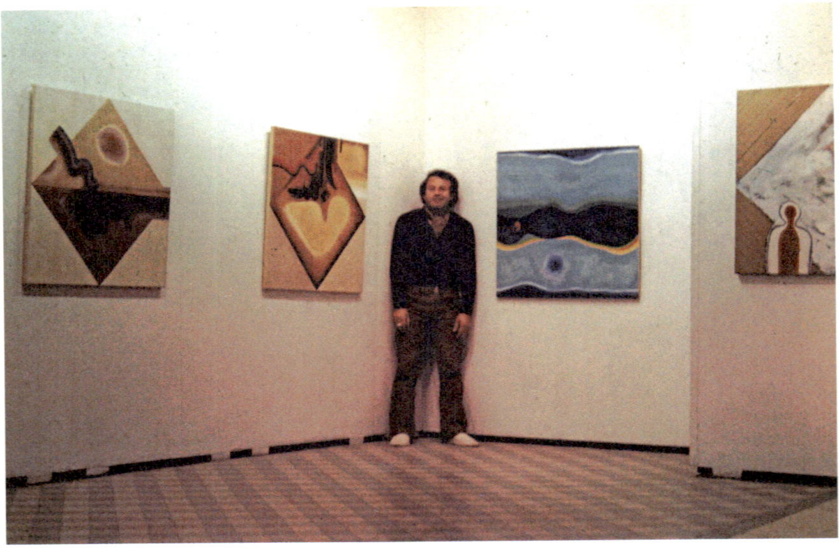

Rafa at the New Vision group exhibition, Museum of Modern Art (Gulbenkian), Baghdad, 1974

our viewing. Rafa watched me with worry and curiosity in his eyes.

I saw the blue painting that had kept him up all night, pointing it out and smiling. It was beautiful, like the others, and nearly all were minimalist in their elements and colors. They were mostly of an almost geometric nature, and I found in this somewhat of a sternness. I perceived a kind of rigidity in the repetition of forms and parallel swathes of color, whether vertical or horizontal, and recalled the astonishing works I'd seen in the first exhibition of the New Vision group (in 1971). Following some consideration, and a bit of hesitation, I said to Rafa, "Don't you think there's some rigidity in the work? Where's your fire and vitality, your freedom and madness you boast of?"

I expected he might be angered by my observation. But he replied with a calmness that surprised me. "I don't know. This is where I am now: standing in a void."

I wasn't comfortable with his response. Perhaps it was an exceptional state, but I didn't know how I could help him. What I'd witnessed during our first meeting, in his outburst over love, death, and failure, was sufficient evidence of his inability to adjust to his life's present circumstances, his rejection of his lived reality. He repeated this with and without occasion to do so. I felt I could help him move forward with his life and work, and sensed the enormity of my responsibility toward him. First, however, I needed to arm myself with the knowledge I lacked so I could counter him and contain his outbursts, whether sincere or affected.

In a stormy conversation some weeks later, he was extremely tense and told me, "You'll suffer with me. I'll torture you with my behavior and moods."

I received his words with agitation at times, and indifference at others. I concealed my fears, exhibiting only calm and certainty, whether facing his outbursts or tenderness, his whims or evenhandedness. The road before me appeared rocky, and yet I intended to follow it. I'd acquired quite a bit of his energy despite its hidden dangers and ordeals.

He spoke of great pain awaiting me, pain that would affect us both. "I'll harm you as much as I may myself." He added, "Place me on the margins, and I'll do the same with you. You were a remarkable woman on our first meeting, but then your Iraqi behavior surfaced as being inseparable from your being."

"You're as Iraqi as I am. We both belong to this land."

"I'm not one of them; I'm different. I don't believe in society's trivial values. Women are so skeptical of men."

"Your residency in the West didn't make you one of them overnight. You have your own identity, and your history is here. We're not alone in this world; we have family and a society."

"Don't mix me up with others, I'm different and independent. I know that I need you, and that this need is mutual. Let things be my responsibility. You were incredibly close to me that first night, and I felt you were the only woman I wanted to speak to, the only woman able to get close to me. But we won't get anywhere if you're going to play the role of the shy virgin. Or do you see us as only a one-night stand?"

"I don't know why you drew close to me, or why you chose me, or why we went out. It really was spontaneous. Perhaps I found in you what I hadn't found in others, perhaps I was enchanted by something mysterious in your talent, in your hand as you steadily pulled a line across a canvas stretched on the wall where I viewed your work in my office building. Perhaps I thought you were to be trusted, after I'd lost trust in others and myself. But why then do you insist on meeting me? What do you find in me?"

"So, so many things. You're different from anyone I've ever known, and that's the truth."

He drew his face close to mine, cupping my shoulders with his hands and gazing at me in the candlelight. "You're astonishing. How I need you."

I didn't know whether to laugh or cry.

He didn't contact me again and we didn't meet. I decided to train myself to play this game. I swallowed my anger and protest, hiding them from him and ignoring behavior that didn't appeal to me to see where this would take us. Several days after his disappearance the phone rang, breaking the silence in the middle of the night. My heart trembled. The phone's rings felt like the stabs of a knife, and I decided not to answer. Silence again took reign, only to be overturned again an hour later. I was slow to answer and the ringing stopped. I wished I'd answered.

I truly began fearing an imminent breakdown due to the pressure I was under and my lack of self-confidence. I resorted to a kind friend who was incredibly compassionate with me. He found much of my behavior positive and urged me to stay on course. He advised me, "Men are like gypsies: if you pursue them, they'll flee."

I'd arranged to meet a number of writers, among the few whose polite behavior I was comfortable with. I told Rafa that we'd meet in the Society of Iraqi Artists' garden the next evening, and he asked who they were. "You'll know when you see them. Come join us."

"We might not let them in."

"They're coming in any case."

We were a group of four and sat in a small circle in the society's garden, and Rafa joined us. We discussed poetry and modernism, and whether we'd become a part of it or not. Rafa remained silent, not taking his eyes off me. Then he suddenly got up and excused himself, saying he was waiting for guests and sitting down at a nearby table.

As soon as I got home, he called and rebuked me, "Why did you leave so quickly? I wanted to take you home."

"It's better this way."

"Pretenses, pretenses. . . . Your gathering was all pretenses and a flexing of intellectual muscle, nothing more. It was not a friendly atmosphere."

I wanted to provoke him further and asked what he meant, but he suddenly changed the topic. "What are you doing? I want to see you."

"I can't."

"Why were you avoiding me?"

"I was afraid of being driven mad."

"And who could drive you mad?"

I loved the way he expressed his jealousy in a childish, lighthearted manner. But then his tone suddenly changed to one of cruel distancing, and I cut him off sharply: "I don't like you speaking to me in that tone."

"You always object to the way I talk."

"Although you're tender in person, you're suddenly possessed by a demon on the phone. It's only when we meet that my charm seems to overpower your drive to harm me!"

"And you're tender on the phone but then harmful when we meet. I'm going to put a phone in the car or hang one around my neck!"

He wanted to go on talking but I was tired, so I ended the call on a comfortable note. That day I became certain of his attachment to me, and that each of us had been doubting the feelings of the other. Days went by without us being in touch, but I resisted my yearning for him and held myself together. Then he called while I was at work.

It was the first time he'd called me during my work hours. He asked to meet, and we set a date for 6 p.m. But then he contacted me an hour beforehand, saying he had a problem with his car. He called me late at night, longing to speak, but I excused myself, complaining of feeling weak due to insomnia. "And you don't like weakness."

"Why do you think that? I often submit to weakness that I conceal."

"Conceal? Even from the one closest to you?"

Following a brief silence, he responded tenderly, "I love what you said. And it's lovely to hear it from you." Were we growing closer, and had the barriers between us begun to fall? That was my sense that evening.

He spoke to me of six sketches he'd completed, inspired by the poetry of Aragon and his passion for Elsa. "It's a great love, but a servile one. A person turned into a dog because of who he loves!"

"Love doesn't recognize such labels, that's purely Eastern thinking. Labels are placed by those who haven't been touched deeply by love. Remember this when you go through the experience."

"I had a deep experience and came out of it unscathed."

"Because it didn't touch your depths. And what about your last experience, and your failure, as you called it, or have you forgotten?"

He laughed in embarrassment and coughed, then changed the topic. "Where did you go today?"

"I didn't go out."

"But you're going out a lot these days."

"I escape from the house when I feel down."

"I used to flee the house every day. But then I started taking refuge in my studio and working. I'm working a lot these days. You're the one driving me to work."

"Don't you feel lonely?"

"Not at all, for you are present deep within me."

Another confession I heard from him for the first time. He'd previously surprised me one day by speaking of the senselessness of travel, and of the need to stay close to one's homeland. He held my hands between his and said, "Here, and here alone, can I give that which is most precious." His words slid gently into my heart. For the first time I heard him say, "I love you."

Over the next two days he contacted me to excitedly tell me about a new work of his, a painting in raucous colors. "It's called *Flight of the Last Pain*, but I hope you'll find another title for me."

I caught the contagion of his delight and wanted to fly through space and kiss him, to state in all frankness that I wanted to see it. But I sufficed with self-satisfaction and a sense of comfort with where we'd arrived. "I finished it at three in the morning. I was overtaken by madness and wanted to call you at the time."

"I wish you had."

"What kind of madman would call so late?"

"Haven't you said you're mad?"

He called again around two hours later. His voice was sluggish, lacking its former ring of intoxication. "Orange and green have overwhelmed me. I can no longer distinguish between colors, so I'm fleeing from color to you."

We spoke about the artistic process and how it developed. I asked him about practical matters in painting of which I was ignorant. It was a serious conversation, and I noticed that he enjoyed explaining. Then he said, "You speak of things telephones have never been witness to."

"Because I've found it's the best way to speak with you."

"We'll speak more when we meet."

"You choose silence when we meet, although we could speak at great length."

"Speaking is only for women."

"In the beginning, you were the one who spoke."

"Because you whet my appetite with your good listening. In general, I don't speak much. I'm from the crisis-ridden world of colors, and you're from another world. Clamorous colors, for me, mean brutal agony, fear, and madness. When I'm at ease, I turn to calm colors, and their harmony further soothes me. Then I can stay at home for a week content."

The conversation was seamless and lovely. I didn't want to impose upon it feelings of loneliness or discontent, those two beasts who destroyed my nights and threatened my being . . . my childhood filled with baffling fears . . . losing my father at a young age, and my youth lost to my early familial responsibilities . . . my fear today of him, and of a dark future clouding over my treasured time with him. . . . Should I speak to him of the agony of suppressing overwhelming feelings, feelings that have come to inspire creative energy?

Nearly six months had passed when I began feeling that we'd grown extremely close, and were now acting freely with each other, once the contrived outbursts had dissipated, or nearly so. About a month into the new year, he called one night to say his close friend from Beirut had arrived, and I calmly asked when. He forced a cough and said, as he caught his breath, "She arrived last night and surprised me by contacting me this morning. She said she brought me something from Beirut. I'll see her for just half an hour, no longer, she's on a work trip and will only stay two days. I'll call you later. What are you doing now?"

"I'm reading John Berger's book on Picasso."

"Then you won't be sleeping early, it's a good and useful book."

"As it seems."

He ended the call on a nice note, but I felt this was the most difficult test I'd encountered yet. Had he begun longing for his Beirut life,

I wondered, recalling what he'd told me that first night about the pleasurable times he'd spent in nightclubs and curious places. At the time he'd spoken to me of her mysterious glances and copious femininity, and it seemed to me she was a model of the freedom he demanded I adopt.

He disappeared for three days. The phone rang at midnight, and in a hesitant, hoarse voice, he said, "Good evening."

"Welcome back."

"Curse me out, hang up on me, be as angry as you want, but you maintain your place deep within me. How did you manage to tighten your hold on me so?"

"Be angry!? With whom, and why?"

I wasn't sure if it was me who was speaking or someone else. He, too, was surprised by my reply, and his voice relaxed and warmed.

"Did I wake you? I wish I could see you."

I laughed.

"I wanted to call you but didn't dare, and that tortured me greatly."

"Why the hesitation? Stop playing with my nerves, you know who I was with . . . aren't you angry with me?"

"What right do I hold over you? Aren't you free?"

"That's a fatal blow!"

"Good night. Enjoy your beautiful dreams."

He later told me they'd gone somewhere outside of Baghdad. It rained and his car tires got stuck in the mud. He'd told her about his attachment to me, or his "discovery of me," as he put it, and how I was different from all the women he'd ever known. But he didn't tell her my name.

"You've become fixed within me; there's no breaking loose. I love you greatly," he said, "but you'll drag me into the talons of fear. I've started to fear you, and for you. You'll harm me as much as I'll harm you. It's up to you to be mine or not. You're free in your choice, and I'm at your disposal. You're different, beyond any limits, you combine form and intellect. I've encountered other women I quickly got bored with, but no one could grow bored with you."

His words did not fall with a resounding ring in my heart, but rather slipped quietly in and settled without a ruckus, as if I'd heard them years before. Yet, what I heard from him was also an unprecedented confession, both contradictory and sincere. By then I'd grown absolutely certain that he only said what he meant. I saw the world open up before me with all its might, and felt I was living a beautiful love story. I wanted nothing other than to preserve this rare gem. I began feeling the synchronicity of our heartbeats, our hands falling into each other's, our intermingling breath and melting lips. My ears began hearing "I love you" as the morning's greeting and the evening's goodnight. And yet I became a bird of fire, drinking from yesterday's bitterness and awaiting tomorrow with concern. For he didn't speak of the future without also speaking of taking leave.

"We'll part ways, sooner or later. I don't like to feel besieged; I want to own my freedom fully."

Yet I'd persist stubbornly. "My siege will have another form," I replied, "a horizon that, the further you advance into it, the more it stretches and continues. A barrier that is simply an illusion."

"I worship such a restriction."

A new year began. We entered 1972 full of optimism. Rafa said he wanted to spend the first day of the year in my company; this was his wish for the new year. I wanted us to be happy, as we deserved to be and as we wanted. When I sat beside him in the car, his face was glowing with joy. He squeezed my hand, and I kissed the palm of his. He stole a warm kiss, saying "Happy New Year" between feverish breaths. We sat in our favorite corner and spoke a great deal. He made one confession after the next, and promised me love, happiness, and communication. His confessions were frank, revealing the insincerity of past episodes that had been negative and contrived.

"You're a woman to be loved, a blazing idea, a trusted friend. I felt an electric current hit me the first time I saw you, no longer aware of anything around me other than your face and the images it inspired, and which have never left my mind. There's an innocence in your face that could serve as a symbol. You're the most complete of women; you're the queen of all."

I'd accustomed myself to receiving his declarations, whether positive or negative, with calm, and not to display satisfaction, concern, or fear. With this frank confession he nullified all he'd previously claimed about wanting a woman who was mad and demonic and. . . . What he said pleased me as much as it befuddled me. Passion for him was being planted in my being like an olive tree, its roots digging deep into the earth. I wished that our secret meetings could be openly recognized, allowing us to live our lives freely. I could see in his eyes companionship and comfort; in his hand I felt his overwhelming love. Tears gathered in my eyes from intense emotion, and I despised the moment that did not bring us together.

The next evening, he called to say, "Forget everything I told you yesterday, I was intoxicated. We'll part ways sooner or later! To maintain the beauty of this relationship, each of the two parties must remain free."

He didn't contact me again for a long time.

We met by chance at an event at the Writers' Union. He was with Dia, and I sufficed with a greeting from afar.

The next day he stormed into my office and angrily placed a stack of books on the table. He sat near me, but turned his sullen face away to speak with Anan. He liked speaking with her, and enjoyed her light-hearted energy and amusing descriptions of people and incidents. As he was leaving, he turned to me and said in a soft but sharp voice, "I wanted to break your arm and nose last night."

I told him I'd be attending the Society of Iraqi Artists party by invitation of its president at the time, doctor and artist Qutaiba al-Sheikh Nuri. He asked if I really wanted to go and seemed hesitant, as though he didn't approve of my attendance. Calmly, I replied, "I'll be with friends and we'll spend the evening together."

We met there. The party was raucous and splendid, with a special, select group of people in attendance. The dance floor was filled beyond capacity. He joined us at first, and then left our circle. He was extremely flustered, disappearing amid the crowds only to return and whisper sweet nothings into my ear before fleeing again. An artist approached to greet me, and Rafa suddenly appeared from afar, raising his finger in the man's face and saying, "Don't you dare!"

It was embarrassing, but thank God it did not turn into a fight. Iraqi behavior of the first degree had exposed all his pretenses, and that night caused an earthquake in our relationship. I suggested we leave, and on the way home he rushed to excuse his awkward behavior and apologize for it. He spoke as if in a delirium: "It terrified me for us to appear publicly amid all those people we know. What should I do when I don't know myself what I want? I've never grown attached to a woman like I have with you, but I'd rather kill myself than make a commitment."

"It's our joint responsibility. I want only you, but you're placing me before the more difficult choice."

He looked at me in terror and buried his head in my palms. His forehead was scorching, and he was crying hot tears. I didn't think of myself; my concern was getting him to calm down and return home safely. The face-off had been bitter and humiliating, as though society as a whole was pointing at me and holding me accountable for what I was doing. I took refuge in my bed, wanting nothing more than to erase that wretched night from my memory.

He called me the next evening with a tired voice, wanting to check in on me. He was extremely worried and wanted to meet. It was like I'd entered an underworld, or a dark sea. I begged him to postpone the meeting and asked him to calm down and rest assured. A week went by with no contact between us, and I managed to regain some composure. He called to wish me a happy birthday, and I asked how he was. He rushed forth with an unreserved declaration: "I'll see you, and we'll speak. Tomorrow, I'll make you happy. Trust that I'll only do what I do for your sake."

His voice was sad, and a sense of impotence had enervated my body and drained my spirit. I reconsidered what he'd said, and his promises of a reassuring tomorrow. I detected a scent of calamity in the deep sorrow overwhelming his voice. Even his declaration of feelings seemed sad. He called again at midnight, and it was the longest phone conversation we'd had, lasting an hour and a half. He spoke with a weeping voice.

"You're magnificent, and will remain so. I'm the one who is nothing. You don't know what a lost child I am; I don't know what I want. I'm not fabricating this, I'm truly living it."

After the call, my eyes remained fixed in the darkness, unable to relax or close. I took two tranquilizers, but they had no effect. I sensed a rising tide of threat as I recalled everything that had happened between us since our first meeting. I felt depleted. I reached out for the tranquilizers and swallowed more, thinking perhaps they'd extinguish the erupted volcano of my thoughts.

In the morning, the first thing I sensed was my mother standing beside me, baffled to find me fast asleep and not getting ready for work. I was too weak to open my eyes to respond. I tried getting up, but dizziness prevented me. I was somewhere between sleep and wakefulness, and feared waking up and having to face more worry and questions. I considered the situation: my passion for the artist and belief in his talent, the pleasurable times we spent together, our lively conversations with no limits, his attachment to me despite the stops and starts, his jealousy, his sincerity, his nobility, his radiant spirit whose flame had touched me . . . what a beautiful life this could be!

I needed to overturn the scales and reconsider the years I'd spent both avoiding myself and shutting myself off. I rethought everything I'd wished for, imagined, and considered before knowing him. I'd met many people, but never in my life anyone as perfect as he. And I'd thus stepped out of my comfort zone, boldly setting forth with him in ways that were completely uncharacteristic of me. His worry perplexed and terrified me as much as it fostered within me a sense of challenge. One day I'd find him closer to me than my own hand, and another more distant than the stars in the sky. He was both reality and a mirage, clarity and obscurity, doubt and certainty. It was from this disoriented point in his life that we'd met, grown close, fallen in love, and become a team, exchanging ideas, dreams, visions, knowledge, concerns, and fears. I was the stability he was both seeking and fleeing from, that would entice him once and terrify him many times over.

Our appearance together at the crowded party that night had raised many questions. Our relationship became known and was whispered about by those who knew us from beyond our small circle. One of my mother's friends whispered to her about it. My mother was extremely distant from cultural circles, and when she asked me about it, I told her the truth. Of course, she did not accept it. I told her firmly that I knew better, that I would not give him up, and that I wanted no one other than him. My response was unequivocal, and threw her into a whirlwind of worry, placing me before an even greater responsibility, my worries and concerns increasing. My mother was a red line not to be crossed. She'd been my weak point throughout my life. Thank God my brother was far away, working for the Basra oil company, and had recently married. It would pain him if news of it reached him. I was the role model in our family, and I felt the scope of the burden beginning to weigh on me, producing contradictory feelings. Rafa left me no other choice than to withdraw.

"We've come so far. You now know me probably better than I know you, but I've reached the farthest point I can. We either continue life together or we part. Embrace your freedom as you like and leave me to my world. We'll remain close friends and continue to talk about the personal and otherwise."

We parted ways, and yet also did not part.

We stopped meeting alone and our phone calls dwindled to a bare minimum. And, thus, my evenings quieted down and the phone fell silent. I embraced the fire of my longing for him and resumed my life, reorganizing it and scheduling my time outside of work. Yet the emptiness was brutal despite how busy I was.

I wrote a great deal and read even more, focusing my attention on reading. I penned diaries of our relationship to distract myself, and wrote poetry, most of which was in vain. At the time I hadn't even completed a short story collection, and I didn't dare to publish my few poems in a volume. I wrote prose poetry that I also hesitated to publish; two of these poems later became Rafa's first art book, which he dedicated to me after our marriage. They still have not been published to this day.

The days passed by meaninglessly, even as my feelings were etched with a fiery coal into the depths of my being. I searched for a glimpse of him wherever I went, waiting for my office door to open and for him to appear behind it, searching for him at cultural events, concerts, and film screenings. I'd see him once and then miss him many times, becoming devoured by paranoia. Sometimes I heard the sound of his car outside our house at night. I'd resist my desire to go out to him, instead dreaming of sitting beside him, concealed by the car windows fogged with our breath. I didn't dare go out and sufficed with the overwhelming joy I felt with his presence and longing and slept in happiness. But then all of that ended.

In the spring of 1972, the first Al Wasiti-Fine Arts Festival was held in Baghdad. It was the first gathering of its kind in the Arab world, with exhibitions, roundtable discussions, and social gatherings, attended by leading artists from across the Arab region. I had no doubt that Rafa and Dia had worked endlessly to prepare for it. We began meeting in passing, in hotel lobbies or exhibition halls, and I was alarmed by his pale face and the harshness in his eyes.

Among the festival's exhibitions was a pottery exhibition held at the Academy of Fine Arts. Valentinos, the splendid Greek ceramicist so devoted to Iraq, and head of the ceramics department, invited me to attend, and I went with Anan, my constant source of support. In the university courtyard I encountered him sitting on a bench in the shade of a huge tree, beside him an attractive young woman. He greeted us icily and introduced us to his companion, who I realized was the artist of the white abstract painting I'd seen in his house. Despite the hot weather, I felt a chill pierce my body.

My friends suggested we take a trip to Beirut. Travel was good for me, an opportunity to rest and enjoy myself. I'd also been promised work at an insurance company there that my company had cofounded. It became me who was thinking of distancing myself from Baghdad, of fleeing from it. We were five women: Anan Fattah, Niran Maher, Wafa Lami, Nina al-Jamil, and me. Three married women and one engaged.

On our first evening in Beirut, in Hamra's Horseshoe Café, Rafa and I met face-to-face. He'd come with Dia al-Azzawi and Saleh al-Jumaie to open their group exhibition in Gallery One, which was next door. My heart pounded as I saw him approach us. At first, I detected longing in his eyes, but it quickly faded and turned to ice. He greeted us coldly in a passing manner and left, and I decided not to attend their exhibition for fear of receiving further blows. It was a stormy, depressing evening, and at about the same time we received news of the young artist Ibrahim Zayer's suicide in Beirut. I didn't know him personally but was aware of his talent and knew that Rafa thought highly of him.

My dear friend and mentor Najib al-Mani' was working in Beirut at the time, and came to meet us at the Horseshoe Café, which was our base we took off from and where we reconvened. With Najib I felt I had someone to support me, and he lifted the dreariness I felt. They were cruel days as I roamed Beirut's streets like a madwoman, crying alone, far from the eyes of my companions. We spent five days in the city. Najib invited me to lunch in Hamra one day and told me that approval for my transfer to the Arab company had been denied due to my work commitments in Baghdad. I sat in silence while he spoke effusively as always, for we regularly conversed on a multitude of personal, literary, and general issues. Then he commented in surprise, "You're neither eating nor speaking." I burst into tears, trembling. In alarm he cried, "What happened? All this because of a job you didn't get?" I didn't reply. I excused myself and left.

On our last night in Beirut, I was seated in a car among my girlfriends on our way to a Fairuz concert, and just before turning from the main road onto a side street, I saw Rafa in a car ahead of us. He was in the back seat beside his beautiful artist friend, his arm around her. Anan squeezed my hand, for she'd told me about meeting Rafa in the café and his speaking of his happiness in Beirut, and how he'd come back to himself in the city he loves. I listened to Fairuz calmly, as though the intense stabs of seeing Rafa had numbed me, and I'd submitted to my fate.

I don't understand the transformations that can take place in a person's body and mind. I woke up the next morning with a strange sense of strength, as though I were a different person than the night before. We got up early for our return to Baghdad and donned our new clothes we'd bought in Beirut. The fashion at the time was men's suits with ties, and we looked like a soccer team, all matching except for the different colors. We ran into Rafa, Dia, and Saleh ahead of us at the airport, and I saw Rafa sitting there at ease, without any sign of tension. He even welcomed me with a friendly, tender look, and I thought to myself, God be praised!

Nearly two months after our return he called, and my resistance collapsed. I agreed for us to meet. I wasn't thinking of anything at all; I didn't want to analyze, or make excuses, or judge what was to come.

We spoke frankly, as though we'd never parted. He spoke of our encounter in Beirut and said he'd been eager to talk with me and to invite us to the opening, but said, "I refrained, thinking your position would not be a friendly one. And that was confirmed when you didn't attend, although I was so eager for you to do so."

He spoke of the indifference he'd be struck with during that period, how in trying situations it had overwhelmed him and stripped him of any human feeling. He spoke of his suffering that night and how it had built up, and cumulated with the suicide of Ibrahim Zayer. He was cloaked in sadness as he recalled that evening, and I wanted to change the topic.

"I saw you in a car embracing your artist friend. We were driving behind you. Where did you go?"

Between shock and laughter, he cried, "What a coincidence!"

He told me how that evening had unraveled. An ex-lover of his was driving, and when she noticed how extremely close to each other they were, she stopped the car and demanded they get out. We laughed at length, stopping only when he continued in a serious tone: "I excused myself that night from my companion and roamed Beirut's streets alone, pursued by the image of you. I'd sacrifice my soul for you, yet feel as though I'm trapped, and don't want my decision to come from that place. I'd still choose suicide over commitment."

He called me the next morning. "I wish you'd erase everything I said last night. Let's start anew!"

That morning I stood gazing from between the curtains at the blue of a bright and clear sky. I found the world a beautiful place.

After having lost a common language with many of my girlfriends, I started avoiding them; Rafa had become my best and most complete friend, and our endless conversations were varied and enjoyable. We shared our news transparently; I spoke to him about what I'd accomplished, whether I was satisfied with it or not, and he told me about his work and my role in his competition with himself. Once I asked if he still wanted to travel abroad, and if he'd found a way to do so.

"It's the desire that prevails above all others."

"And you want to keep me as a stopover."

"You've never been that, and never will be. I fear I'll harm you; I don't know what tomorrow will bring, I can't foresee it. Shall I leave you hanging to a distant promise? I can no longer live without you, but is it right for me to commit to you for a period of stolen time? I fear for you as much as I love you. You occupy my entire world and every moment in it, you're my tie I cannot be rid of. But I know this wretched being of mine will only bring you suffering."

The new year arrived to find us gathered with friends. Our phone calls continued while we stayed physically apart, exchanging news of what we'd accomplished and what was happening in the world of art and culture. It was a relatively calm and balanced period lacking in tension, a sense of waiting, or stops and starts.

In March 1973, Rafa left on an extended trip with Dia and Saleh al-Jumaie to Damascus, Beirut, and Cairo for group exhibitions in the three capitals. Their trip lasted six weeks. From time to time, Rafa would send me letters and cards that were beautiful and creative, but extremely concise and abstract in their messages. I'd search for him in them, finding him once and not finding him many other times.

Long weeks of separation and silence passed. There was much talk circulating that suggested we'd reached the end he'd promised from the start. I was just as concerned about him as I was worried that I'd lost the opportunity of a lifetime, one rarely obtained. And yet I submitted myself to reality.

One night, we encountered each other by chance in al-Khuld concert hall at the monthly performance of the Iraqi symphony. I looked everywhere for him, as I did at every event I attended, and found him sitting behind me by two rows, his eyes pinned on me. It was a rare and beautiful moment that gave me strength and filled me with rapture. Rafa's message was clear, with no room for doubt. My tears flowed in time with the Schubert sonata played by a young woman French pianist performing in bare feet. When I returned home, I wrote Rafa a letter that I kept to myself.

Baghdad, Spring, 1973

Rafa,

A million words would not suffice to revive me the way my stolen glimpse of you did in a chance meeting. You were an inspiring moment of creation.

I want to speak with you of this rare moment in which I gained access to an entire universe of contemplation and rapture.

I can no longer speak with friends of a stolen moment of longing, not after the major and painful events that have taken place between us. It would become a source of mockery were I to speak of it.

I live in isolation and have lost all contact with the world. I want to at least speak with myself, to share with her that swelling moment that flashed like lightning, like that which strikes prophets with the shudder of creation.

Our eyes met for the first time after a lengthy absence that may be the last, and I found you fully absorbed in me. I'd never seen you with such fullness and depth. Were you becoming your destiny? Were you crushing a diamond mine between your ribs? Were you invading a planet never before discovered? I felt my faith rising like a fiery arrow, as though I myself were rising again from the rubble. I regained love for myself, for I'd come to possess a divine moment. If there had to be an end, let this be it, praying at the feet of this encounter.

We unexpectedly met again in a public space, in the company of friends. I could see he was tense and sullen. As the conversation swung between jest and serious discussion of various matters, Rafa suddenly exploded in anger, uncharacteristically turning into a strange and highly destructive being. He wrote me a long letter apologizing, and explaining his emotional state and tension:

My beloved May,

I'm suffering from compounded pain, and you know well that in this state I lose many of my qualities. I become aggressive and cruel with no clear feelings; I embody my issues. And so why do you prolong our parting and increase my pain? I fear for my love as never before; I get jealous over it (for it's all I possess). You know how I get jealous in silence, or perhaps you don't know, you don't know many of my feelings (as I've recently discovered). Trust that I love you to the point of pain. You've always been the queen of all women to me. I respect you to no limit, so why do you wound me, rendering me incapable of controlling my deepest self and offering it to you, in all its states.

All that happens is that, in the flash of a moment, I lose everything called feelings and become nothing but a pile of meat, bones, and skin. Everything escapes me, and I move, speak, and perhaps smile, but in a very mechanical way. I immediately get a headache, and this additionally paralyzes me from thinking about future outcomes.

So may you forgive me for what I've done, and may our friends understand (perhaps they didn't and won't). May we leave time to quiet down, and may we be silent in anticipation of speech. And may there be trust that we understand each other in all cases. (On Tuesday, May 29, between 4:30 and 5, I searched for you between al-Sa'adoun and al-Salihiya.) I was in a state of extreme clarity, and longed for you so. I didn't find you, but will certainly find you deep within me again.

A few weeks later he sent me another letter:

My May,

I've been living every moment with you, all this time, speaking to you and always seeking your advice (and pray you're satisfied with the simple works I've produced recently; they are few and wretched).

All of this compounded and materialized, and I felt you were sick without my knowing, so I rushed to meet you, and was alarmed and pained with all my heart when I didn't find you. Then I danced with joy when I spoke with you (they were surprised by this at home!), and I grew all the more eager to be reassured of your good health, but you rejected my feelings at their very peak.

You rejected, forever, my humanity (which is always under accusation), and since yesterday I haven't been able to see or hear a thing apart from your words. I hate myself completely.

I'm no longer optimistic, May, all my ambitions have collapsed and I can no longer cling to any of them despite having new and heavy responsibilities. They mean nothing to me, and this would be odd if circumstances were natural, but my love for you justifies what happened yesterday. Don't despise me so, my love. You're the most gracious person I've known, don't lose your graciousness and kindness in a moment of imbalance, or in other, future moments in which the spirit will grow like palm trees. You will always be my love.

In July of that year, I decided to spend my summer vacation in London with my mother. I intended to stay on, if I could possibly find work with the help of friends in the city. Another escape. I told Rafa, and he asked me to submit a portfolio for him to the Royal Academy of Arts.

I took his documents and prints, feeling as though I were transporting the most valuable part of him.

In London, I met my lifelong friend Issam El-Said, an architect, scholar, and printmaker. I spoke to him of Rafa and spread his works out before him. He went through them, expressing ever more admiration with each piece. In astonishment, he asked, "What does Rafa want from advanced studies when he already possesses such abilities?" I told him this was Rafa's desire, and that he was determined to carry it out, although I was also certain it was not from ambition for learning as much as an excuse to reside in the West.

The head of the Royal Academy's visual arts division was Issam's friend, and we went to show this English professor Rafa's works. The professor was surprised that Rafa had studied in China and suggested that further studies would not serve Rafa's artistic practice, repeating what Issam had said: "This is a talented artist and it would be worthier of him to devote his life to his art, unless he has an aim in theoretical studies."

I left with a sense of satisfaction and reassurance. Issam could tell from my enthusiastic talk of Rafa that this was more than assistance for a friend, and so I spoke frankly with him, just as we'd been accustomed to doing since our childhood. He appeared concerned when he saw my confusion and sorrow. I told him I wanted to remain in London if I could find work that would keep me distant from Rafa, and he did not comment. He pulled me by the hand, laughing, and said, "Let's go to the Tate Gallery." It was my first visit, and I wanted to see with my own eyes the work of Turner that had so impressed Rafa.

London was the first European city I'd ever visited and had done so alone, in 1968. Dr. Esmat El-Said, Issam's mother, had secured housing for me close to her and Issam. I didn't feel at all out of place in London; perhaps the sense of being a stranger comes first of all from not knowing a language. I was eager to encounter the world I had so deeply engaged with, first during my university studies, and then through my brother Namir, who'd spent eight years studying at the University of London and had developed extensive social circles there.

I was thirsty for poetry, theater, and concerts. In Baghdad, I regularly read *The Sunday Times*, which arrived in Baghdad's bookshops every Monday, and I'd follow the cultural events in its weekly cultural supplement. During this second visit five years later, I bought the *Times* newspaper every day; I'd read the cultural programs and make my way to events by following the bus map. I kept a busy schedule, while also closely following the job advertisements.

One day I found an Arab embassy seeking a secretary who could type and was fluent in Arabic and English. I wrote down the address and made my way, filled with enthusiasm for the opportunity. I had to change buses in Oxford Circus, and waited on the sidewalk for the bus that would take me to the embassy address. I looked around me and saw everyone rushing along; no one walked casually like we did in Iraq. Time, time, and then time!

I let my mind wander to the future, imagining what my life in London would be like. I saw myself rushing like these people in the morning and returning home exhausted in the evening. The secretary described by T. S. Eliot in his poem *The Waste Land* appeared before me, returning home exhausted to her dark room where she lived alone, to her loneliness and misery, her head still resounding with the rhythmic strikes of her typewriter. I compared this to my place in my family's home and my comfortable domestic life, wondering whether I'd truly be able to live in a manner that allowed me to enjoy a cultural life as I'd imagined. Would I be able to buy the books I loved and attend film screenings, plays, and concerts? Would I make enough income to afford that? This was not to speak of loneliness, being away from one's homeland, and long, cold, desolate nights. Strangely, I could only see the negative side, and then the face of Rafa appeared to me from amid the crowds rushing in every direction, observing me in silence but revealing nothing, only waiting.

The bus pulled up but I did not get on. I threw the embassy's address into the closest garbage bin and took off aimlessly roaming the streets.

Upon my return to Baghdad, I contacted Rafa immediately. We met in our quiet corner, and he seemed glad that I'd returned. I told him the opinion of Issam and the English professor, and he let out a deep breath. He seemed delighted and smiled with satisfaction. We spent a warm, quiet evening together.

Two weeks went by without my hearing from him. Then he called to ask when his mother could visit us. I couldn't believe my ears. Softly, I replied, "My mother is in Beirut now and it may be some time before she's back. Will you stick to your decision until she returns?"

He let out a soft laugh and did not reply. I felt I'd hurt him. "I almost stayed in London after I found a job opportunity," I told him.

"And so why did you return?" he asked in bitter agitation.

"Because my soul's attached to Baghdad."

On the eighth of October 1973, two full years after our first date, we were officially engaged.

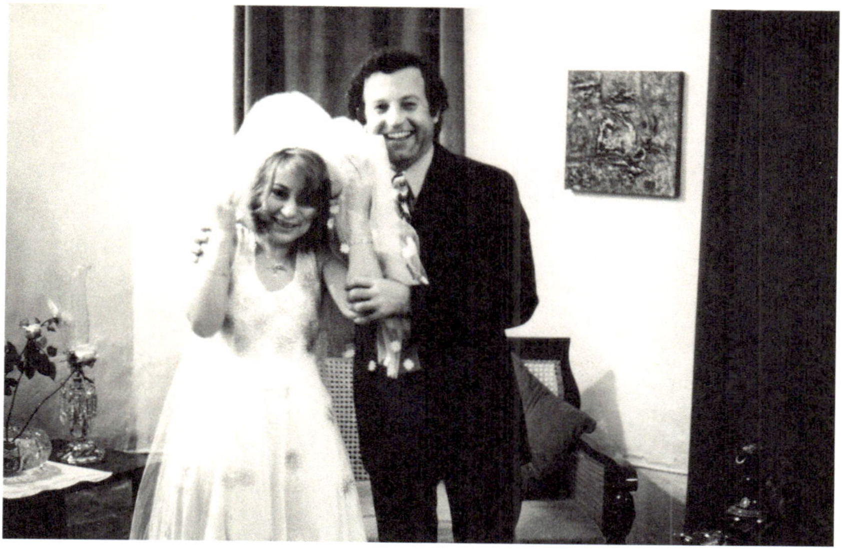

May and Rafa's wedding
evening, December 31, 1973

The Cottage (Al Koukh)

On October 8, 1973, Rafa and I were officially engaged under Islamic law, and it became possible for us to appear together wherever we liked. We agreed to follow the simplest of routes, far from the traditions of families and collective celebrations, and went directly to the court. This shocked my mother, who asked in wonder, "You're going to the court instead of a judge coming to the house?" Traditionally, judges were invited to the bride-to-be's house, the engagement legally registered in the presence of family members and close friends. I could see the bewilderment and disappointment on her face. Calmly, I told her that this was Rafa's wish, and she begrudgingly said no more. From that moment on, my mother gradually learned to accept our approach to life.

It was an exceptional day filled with contradictory feelings and questions. To be tied to Rafa was my dream, but what was this worry and confusion, even panic filling my chest with its smoke? I stood at length before my wardrobe, searching for a suitable dress to wear to the court, and chose a white one embroidered with small flowers, with long sleeves and a high collar, although the dress itself was short, in keeping with the fashion at the time. I didn't give a thought to this, for it was natural to unashamedly wear such clothing anywhere, even to work. At noon on Thursday, October 8, Rafa came with Dia al-Azzawi and Tariq Ibrahim, our witnesses, and together we went to the Islamic judicial court in East Karrada.

We all stood before the judge, and I felt as though I were a student facing a difficult examination. The common advice was to not immediately respond when the judge asked if you accepted so-and-so as a husband, but to wait until the question was repeated three or seven times. The judge, Mohamed Hassan Kashkul, sat at his desk, the file with our identification papers before him. He looked at me for a long time, and with some doubt and disbelief he asked, "The bride-dowry offered to you is only one dinar, are you satisfied with that?" I said, "Yes." He asked me, "Do you declare that?" Again, I said, "Yes." He asked if I'd received the sum. I said, "Yes." "Where is it?" he asked.

We both got flustered. I didn't have a handbag with me, and not even a pocket to put money in. As for Rafa, he was wearing tight white jeans and a white short-sleeved shirt. He awkwardly searched his pockets and turned for help from Dia, who was trying, like Ibrahim, to fish anything from his pockets. Then the judge laughed merrily and asked us the questions about accepting each other. I replied immediately, not waiting at all as advised, and we left laughing, admiring the judge's lighthearted manner and easygoing nature. I considered it a first sign of optimism for our future life together.

We returned home, where my mother had prepared a feast for us and our friends. I placed the certificate in her hands, and she read it fully before hiding it away among her few valuable possessions.

Rafa had spoken a lot to me of the private studio he was building to house the graphic art press he'd bought from the artist Sami Haqqi. He was eager to practice printmaking, which he'd discontinued in Baghdad due to the lack of workspaces except for those at the Academy of Fine Arts and the institute. He'd chosen a large room facing the spacious garden of his father's house, in which he lived. It had a private entrance, allowing him to live an independent life, as opposed to his bedroom on the second floor of the house. I was extremely eager to see this dream project of his.

I met all the members of his family residing in the spacious, two-story home. His mother greeted me with her sweet warmth and great generosity. She'd left a strong impression on me and my mother when she came to ask for my hand, accompanied by her daughters-in-law Dr. Etimad Al-Rawi, the wife of Sami, Rafa's oldest brother, and his cousin Hanaa Mohamed Saleh, the wife of Maath, their sixth brother. I liked his mother's shyness, simplicity, and the pureness radiating from her rosy face in everything she said and did. I told her that day how closely she and Rafa resembled each other. I approached her and kissed her hand in respect. She hugged me with overwhelming joy and in turn kissed my hand. I was embarrassed, but then I later learned that exchanging hand kisses was a form of greeting among the women of Tikrit.

At the spacious entrance to their house, where the garage connected to the kitchen, you were welcomed by colorful, circular ornamentation that Rafa had painted on the walkway. When I looked up, I saw a wide window, its glass painted in the same style as the path, and this clearly marked his studio. Having passed through the large, landscaped garden, we entered the house via the main door, and this entrance in turn led to two doors. One opened to the guest room in which Rafa had previously welcomed me and our friends Dia, Tariq, Fardous, Mekki, and Saleh. The other opened to a living room, where his parents sat with the rest of the family. I saw his mother dressed in her flowing, traditional gown, sitting cross-legged atop a wide traditional sofa in the center of the room, beside her a basket of medications and a copy of the Koran, which the pious *hajji* had studied in her youth and learned by heart. She maintained this setup as her place to sit until her death. There, I was introduced to Rafa's father, and quickly discerned in his face the purity found in the face of his life companion, the mother of his nine children. I immediately recognized how Rafa's face combined each of their features. He proudly welcomed me with a few kind and simple words, his tone soft and pleasant. He was bare-headed and wore a bright white dishdasha, the traditional men's gown.[1]

After they welcomed me and asked about my family, we fell silent, until Rafa asked about his cousin, who was responsible for building his new studio. He was told there was nothing new, and silence fell again. Hanaa, a kind and shy cousin, came in with a tray of tea and traditional cookies, followed by her husband, Maath, carrying their two-year-old daughter Lina. Then came in Talal, the youngest of the brothers and a student in the college of science. And so I met all the members of the family residing in their home, and saw their respectable treatment of each other, taking note of their short and sweet style of speech. In this first meeting I was able to identify all the voices that had kindly and politely answered my calls, including his mother's. Rafa later told me she'd called me the "sandpiper bird" when informing him who'd called. I met his sister and other brothers later.

Rafa gestured to me and we got up and went to the next room, which Rafa had chosen to be his studio. He'd added to it a section taken from the garden, doubling its size. The addition was still not roofed or floored; it was simply a frame. The space was enchanting, surrounded by apricot, apple, and peach trees whose leaves had changed color, announcing an autumn rich in hue. A little further away was a bountiful Barhi date palm, and Rafa took pride in offering its fruit of exceptional taste to guests. He said his mother had grieved when some of the apple trees were cut down to expand the house and had come down with a fever. I thus understood that she hid her feelings and sorrows from others, whether close to her or distant, as did Rafa's father. It was a noble trait that my beloved inherited from them with great aptitude.

The space had two entrances: an independent entrance from the garden, and on the opposite side another connecting it to the house, and it'd been allocated as Rafa's studio and workroom housing the printing press, as an alternative to his large room on the second floor. I loved the space. Ever since I was little, I'd loved small spaces, because they filled me with a sense of security and independence. I'd create refuges in small corners where I enjoyed my solitude with my dolls who kept me pleasant company. This studio presented me with a vision of a future life that was happy and peaceful. “Why don’t we live here instead of renting somewhere?” I asked. Rafa was surprised. “And you’d live with my family?”

“Why not?” I said, “They’ll be my family too. We can be independent and run our life as we like without imposing on theirs, and at the same time be with them and save the cost of renting a house.” Rafa seemed surprised but pleased. “As you like,” he said, but stipulated that a place be allocated for the press.

We decided to set our wedding date at year’s end so as to welcome in the new year with our new life. From the very start, we’d been clearly compatible in our views on life, our pleasure in small things, our surmounting of difficulties, and our perpetual optimism regarding that which was to come. We had two and half months to prepare this small space in a way that provided for our basic comfort and stability. As Rafa’s cousin was busy constructing a larger building, his work on our home went no further than laying the flooring and installing the windows. We had to put on the roof and take on all the interior finishings ourselves. We were at a loss, saved only by the initiative of friends. It was recommended to roof it in the simplest and cheapest of ways, a roof of tin and mud in the style of countryside cottages, finished off with an interior papyrus ceiling. This was the suggestion of Rafa’s sculptor friend Mekki, who did the work himself with his sculptor friend Selim Abdullah,[2] and together they built the roof in a convivial atmosphere of joy.

Once the walls were covered in white gypsum plaster and the lighting was installed, we had a tiny house of exquisite beauty and style that would become a source of delight and astonishment for all our guests. All that remained was painting the interior walls, which was Rafa’s responsibility, and which he kept putting off. When he finally began, I was ordered to not move about, and to remain silent until allowed to speak. He’d paint a small section of wall and then sit down to smoke a cigarette and contemplate what he’d done, as though it were one of his paintings he was working on. Or he’d stop, complaining of being tired, to continue another time. This small space took days to paint, and we really should have celebrated its accomplishment. We lived there for eleven years, and the space witnessed many memorable, intimate gatherings with friends.

The period in which we were destined to marry was a difficult time in Iraq’s economic history. Following the decision to nationalize the global oil companies in June 1972, Iraq underwent economic stagnation compounded by the pressures of its prior circumstances. There

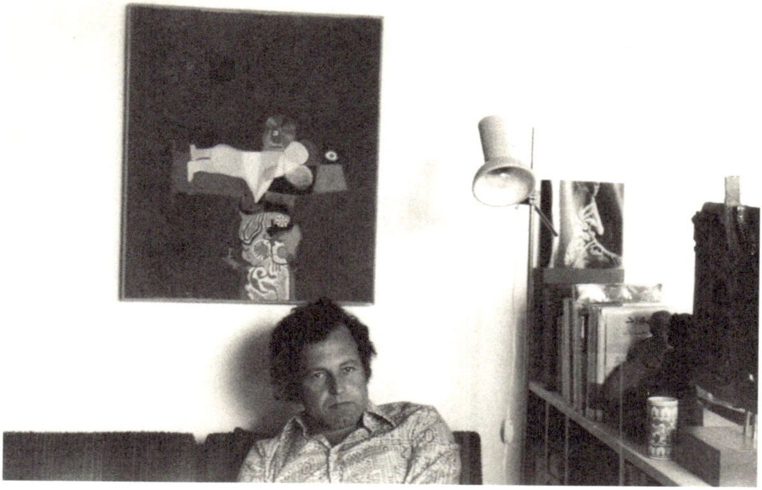

Rafa in Al Koukh
(the cottage), 1975

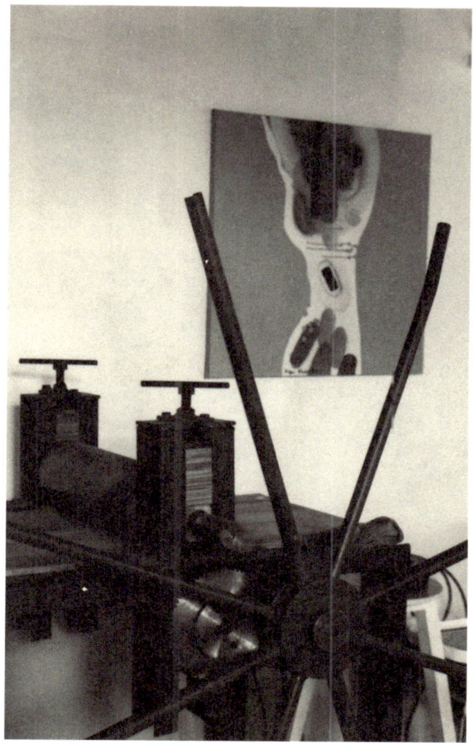

Graphic press in Al Koukh

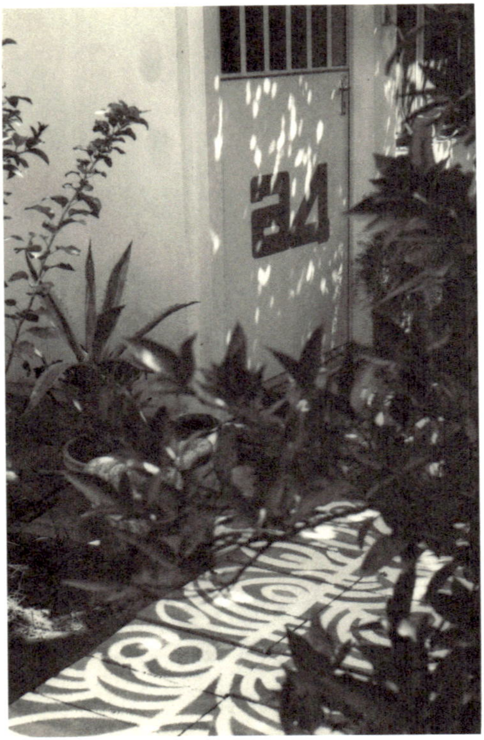

May and Rafa lived
at Al Koukh in
Al Qadisiyah between
1974 and 1985

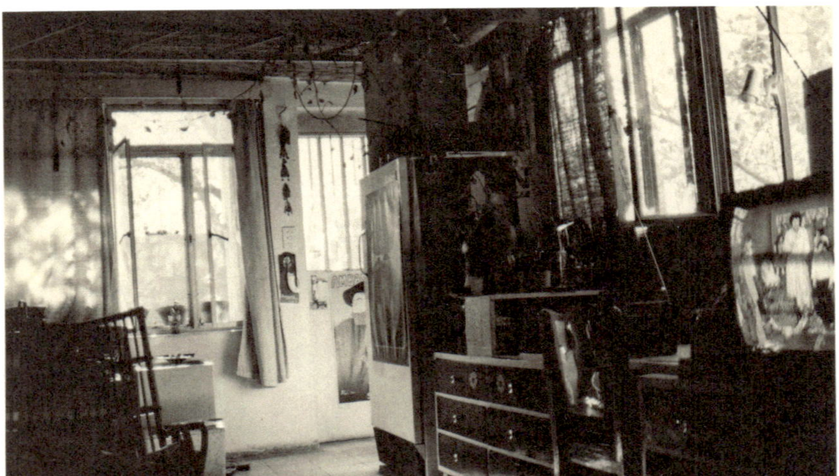

Interior of Al Koukh

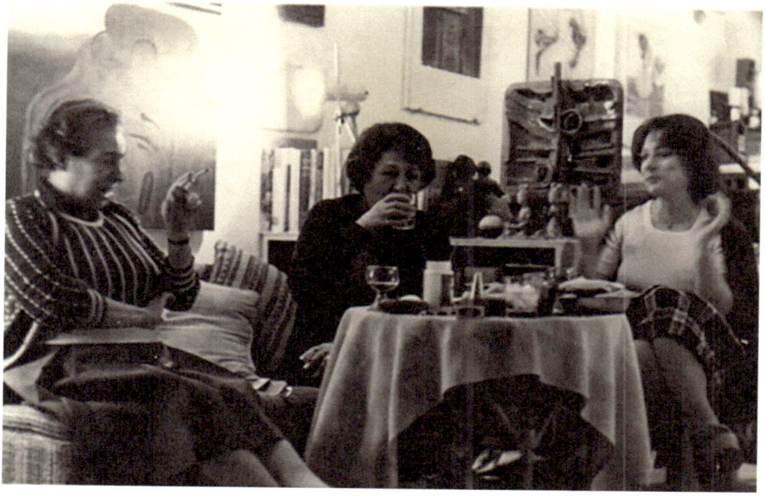

With Najla and Aida Al Saadoun in Al Koukh, Baghdad, 1975

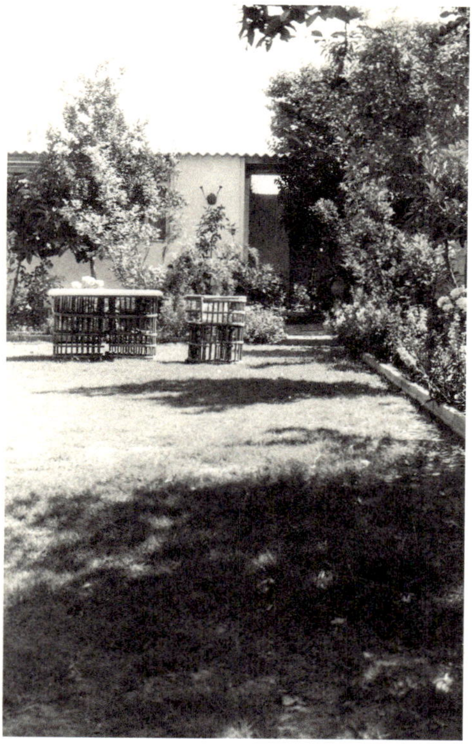

Kamel Al Nasiri's house in Al Qadisiyah, Baghdad

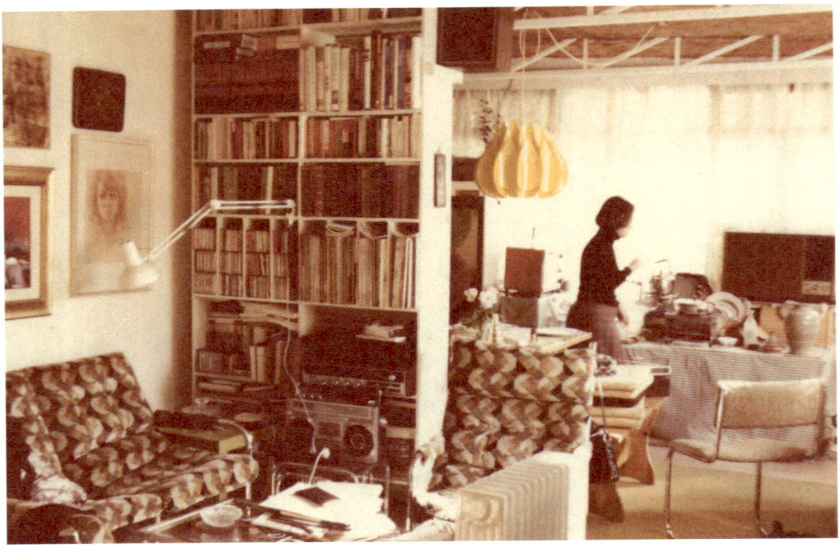

Al Koukh refurbished,
Baghdad, 1978

was a scarcity of imported goods, and local production was poor in quantity, variety, and taste. People's means were extremely limited and government jobs were the main source of income, although these modest salaries were compatible with the needs of daily life. The earth's bounty was generous, and government support included food staples and fuel subsidies, as well as free education and health services.

It was under these circumstances that we searched for furniture and clothes that suited us in price and taste, which was an extremely arduous task. We did not have many demands for filling our small space we'd decided to live in, and furnishing it required only a full bedroom set that we separated from the rest of the space by a wide bookcase supplemented with a plastic accordion-like folding door. We allocated a small space for sitting that only had room for five people, with a round table at its center, and this too was set off on the opposite side by another bookcase. The press took up the remaining space, which was larger than the area allocated for sitting. Beside the large window looking onto the garden, we placed long wooden shelves above two sets of drawers for storing papers. The empty space between the drawers was occupied by a small chair upon which we placed a twelve-inch television that was a gift from Rafa's sister Mekkiya.

This left a small space at the end of the cottage where we placed a one-by-two-meter wood table, upon which we put a small electric oven[3] and a plastic tub beneath a water faucet. Beneath the table we stored the few kitchen appliances we needed for our daily use. In the corner we placed a medium-sized refrigerator that was a gift from my brother. At the entrance to the cottage, which was shaded by a peach tree, Rafa painted the wall and ground with colorful symbols, circles, and numbers, and we placed a gas canister there for speedy heating. And now we had a complete home with a bedroom, bathroom (one square meter; it had been a laundry room), with a sitting area and an office, and floor space Rafa used for painting by leaning over the ground. In return for this housing, Rafa later had to give up his spacious studio on the second floor.

The cottage was still not ready to live in by the end of the year, and yet we insisted on spending New Year's Eve in celebration of our public and private weddings. We chose to hold our wedding at the Baghdadi Society, which was a beautiful club established in the mid-1960s by an elite group of intellectuals, architects, doctors, and lawyers concerned with protecting and reviving heritage buildings.[4]

It used to be the home of the former prime minister Hikmat Sulayman in al-Sleikh, and was a Baghdadi-style home situated within a lush garden of palm and citrus trees, eucalyptus, and night-blooming jasmine, crossed with irrigation streams and filled with incomparable fragrances. The architecture professor Rifat Chadirji had supervised its renovation, salvaging it from the negligent destruction of its beautiful features. Then an administrative committee was formed that set forth conditions for joining the society, and it began hosting art exhibitions, lectures, and art-house film screenings, in addition to monthly concerts of traditional Iraqi music.[5]

We celebrated our wedding at the Baghdadi Society in the company of my brother Namir and his wife Kholoud, our friend Anan Sami Fattah and her husband Rajih Muhieddin, and Niran Nu'man Mahir and her husband Ahmed al-Samara'i (Ahmed al-Hijjiya). We sat in a circle in the crowded hall, and ululations were heard from time to time, but we didn't know from where, as none of us knew how to howl in the Baghdadi style. At one point a man came up to us and, placing his hand on Rafa's shoulder, asked with glee, "It seems there's a bride and groom among you. Which one's the groom?" Glowingly, Rafa replied, "Me." The man shot him an apologetic look and quipped, "How'd you get implicated in this?" We all burst out laughing, most of all the happy, implicated groom.

When we returned to his father's home around dawn, our bedroom had not yet been prepared to sleep in; my mother was going to get it ready while we traveled to Mosul for a few days. On our way home I asked Rafa where we'd spend the rest of the night, and he nonchalantly replied, "I swear, I didn't even think of that!"

We had no option other than his studio. Quietly, we snuck up to the second floor and went in, overwhelmed by the mixed smells of painting supplies, piles of paintings in various states of completion, and bottles spread across the large table that took up half of the spacious room. Other than this workspace, there was only a sofa and an unkempt single bed. We only had four hours before our morning flight to Mosul, where we'd decided to spend a few days, and Rafa was exhausted from the long night and the excitement and tension of the emotional time. A bed, a place to sleep, and a plan, were all beyond the scope of his heart and mind on this day marking a transition from one life to another.

The room was incredibly cold, which was my foremost enemy, and I always suffered when sleeping in a new place, but I was intent on Rafa getting some rest in the few hours left before continuing our activities the following day. So, I spent the few remaining hours in a narrow space on the bed, gazing at Rafa, breathing in his breath and looking at him there before me within hand's reach. I was, without doubt, the happiest creature on earth.

I eventually nodded off, as I later awoke to a numb arm and extreme pain in my twisted neck. Rafa wasn't in the room, and I sat there not knowing what to do. After a few minutes that seemed longer than they really were, Rafa returned. He'd bathed and had a cup of his morning coffee. "My mother and family are waiting for you, why are you so late?"

His mother welcomed me in the kitchen with a beautiful song of blessing. I kissed her and had a cup of tea with her, along with a piece of hot bread and cheese, which helped me regain some warmth and energy before leaving for the airport. Rafa's mother seemed embarrassed. She regretfully explained that she'd been shocked to discover we'd spent the night in the studio, not knowing that our place wasn't ready and apologizing for not preparing it for us. She said that Rafa didn't allow them to enter his room except by invitation. This was the first of my family lessons in my new life.

The four days we spent in Mosul were indicative of the dynamics that would govern our marriage, and which we strove to maintain throughout our life together. During these four days, we overcame difficulties, practiced tolerance, respected the wishes of each other, and turned everything into a source of pleasure.

Mosul was similar to Baghdad in that it was impoverished in appearance and rich in content. I'd visited Mosul many times starting in my childhood, as we were tied to it through strong family friendships that went far back in time and had been transferred to the next generation. My remarkable friendship with Anan Sami Fattah was one of the wonderous fruits of these relations.

In the late 1930s, my father was appointed as a judge in Mosul, as it was standard practice at the time to appoint government professionals and administrators to serve in the provinces before being transferred to the capital. This was to ensure they would be well versed with the problems Iraq faced by having directly dealt with these problems all around the country. I later visited Mosul with my mother every time we spent the summer in northern Iraq; we'd always pass through Mosul and be hosted by friends who lived near the heart of the old city.

On the plane Rafa spoke happily of the harassment and tricks played between people of Tikrit and Mosul on the trains south to Baghdad or returning north. For although the cities are in geographic proximity, and the people's accents are quite similar, the people of

Mosul and Tikrit did not get along. We reached Mosul after a flight of about an hour, and made our way to al-Mahatta Hotel, which had been built by the British in the style of Basra's Shatt al-Arab Hotel. Its furnishings and fixtures were worn, but comfortable, and overall the hotel seemed to have maintained its status, intimate atmosphere, and service, including in the types and standards of its meals.

We had only enough money for our food and accommodation for these four days and toured the city by foot. It was my first experience traveling with Rafa, and I learned I must train myself to walk at a pace accommodating the camera always around his neck. I began seeing how he looked at his surroundings and discovered inconspicuous elements of beauty. I often asked him, as he was bent over a neglected corner, a decrepit building, or a group of people that he observed from afar, what he found in them. He also photographed fleeting moments in natural scenery, such as sunset on the Tigris, captured in perfect harmony with his composition.

The weather was extremely cold, and the delicious milk pudding sold by vendors on the streets helped us to counter the chill. We devoured it hot in glass bowls, the cinnamon sprinkled upon it filling the air with a warm and enticing scent that warmed our chests.

On our last night we were on Nineveh Street, the main commercial thoroughfare, and in one of the boutique windows saw a beautiful vest whose style seemed out of place with the market. We asked the shop owner about it and he said it was Italian, declaring its final price six dinars. We left the shop laughing. Rafa put his arm around my shoulder and did not comment. The money we had left was just enough to purchase our return tickets, four dinars per person, and hire a car from the Baghdad airport back home.

At the entrance to our hotel I ran into one of my colleagues, a pretentious braggart who Rafa didn't like. He congratulated us on our marriage, and asked when we were returning to Baghdad. When I told him the following morning, he offered to take us in his car rather than flying, as he was going to be leaving at the same time. I rushed to decline, knowing that Rafa couldn't stand his company, but was surprised to find him accept without hesitation. They agreed on a departure time of 8 a.m. Even more surprising was Rafa's apparent joy over this opportunity. He told the man, "And we'll have lunch at my uncle's home in Tikrit when we arrive there at noon."

I concealed my astonishment until we were alone and then asked him about it. Nonchalantly, Rafa said, "Why not? I love traveling by land and we'll pass through Tikrit . . . and I'd love for you to see it, even if in passing . . . and my uncle will be delighted to meet you. And how generous the people of Tikrit are with guests, whether a visit's scheduled or not." When we got to our room, Rafa suddenly excused himself and rushed back out. He returned shortly later with a bag, which he opened to pull out the vest, winking and letting out his thunderous laugh.

We left by car for Baghdad at 8 a.m., my colleague driving with his travel companion beside him, and Rafa and me in the back seat. To avoid engaging in conversation, Rafa spent the entire trip either sleeping or feigning sleep. I thus had to assume the duty of conversing, despite the fact that I love traveling by land to immerse myself in daydreams and contemplation of the landscape's endless horizons. At the entrance to Tikrit, my colleague remarked contentiously as he looked at Rafa in the mirror, "We've reached Tikrit!" Rafa stirred and raised his head. He looked around and said, "Look, May, this is Tikrit." Then he went back to sleep, or to feigning sleep. This became a joke that our "friend" would tell every time we met him.

We arrived home, welcomed by our cottage, just as lovely as could be.

1 Kamel Abdul Baqi al-Nasiri, Rafa's father, had been head of the Tikrit municipality until 1956, when their family moved to Baghdad. Rafa's upbringing and family history is covered in *Rihlati ila al-sin* (My journey to China) (Beirut: Arab Institute for Research and Publishing, 2012).

2 They both now live in Europe. Mekki Hussein is based in Germany, and Selim Abdullah in Switzerland.

3 This oven was one of the many wedding gifts we received, and one of the items remaining in the Novex warehouse belonging to Fouad Hassou, near Hafidh al-Qadi Square, when he was obliged to liquidate his stores. Fouad Hassou had been famous for the high-quality goods he imported, including Swiss watches and modern home appliances, belts and men's suits, and other goods he chose with style, taste, and expertise. He was one of the brothers who owned the Hassou Brothers shops in Bab al-Sharqi that set a precedent in providing American home furniture and appliances, including air conditioners. The activity of such outlets dwindled following the 1958 coup and the transformation of Iraq's economic policies.

4 Among the members of the society established in 1965 were Mohamed Saleem al-Radi (former ambassador), Rifat Chadirji (architect), Qahtan Abdullah Awni (architect), Nezar Ali Jawdat (architect), Mohamed Makhzumi (civil engineer), Khalid al-Qassab (surgeon), Salem al-Damlouji (doctor), Amin Abdel Karim (economist), Rifaat al-Haj Sirri (military official and Baghdad mayor at the time), Mohamed Abdel Wahhab (businessman), Siham Saieb Shawket (playwright and businessman), Nayera Munir Abbas (homemaker concerned with heritage). From Khaled al-Qassab, *Dhikriyat fanniya* (Memories of art), (Dar al-Hikma, Baghdad, 2007), pp. 149–50.

5 In the summer of 1968, the society was the target of an explosion while a film audience was watching a foreign drama. This affected the type of activities the association held thereafter, which ceased to be cultural. Under the new administration the association limited its activities to social events.

May

It was a moonlit night in Baghdad, and I was sleeping on the roof, where Iraqis used to spend the hot summer nights. It was the first summer we spent in my grandmother's house, where we'd moved following my father's death a few months earlier. I dreamed that I saw my father, wearing a traditional white gown, slip down from the shining light of the full moon. He landed on the rooftop and laid down beside my bed, raising his tired, burdened face, pained with illness, and said, "I'll continue to protect you."

He seemed frail and enervated when I'd snuck a final glance at him through the door of his private room in the royal hospital. He was surrounded by doctors, and they'd barred anyone from entering. He turned toward the door and saw me, and I ran off fearfully, his pained look haunting me to this day. He struggled with cancer and passed away on February 9, 1949.

I kept my dream a secret, fearful because his name had become taboo in our household, and we could only refer to him as "the deceased." That day, two of my paternal aunts came to visit, and when they saw my father's photograph hanging in my mother's bedroom, they got angry and threatened to tear it up if she didn't take it down. Yet the elder of my paternal aunts would always tell me about my grandfather and his library and great knowledge, and how the occupying British army had raided their home and taken his collection of old books. As for my maternal aunt, she enchanted us in the summer evenings by recounting her surreal dreams. She'd narrate them enticingly, blending reality with imagination, and recalling through them the heroic acts of her father, cavalry officer Mahmoud al-Basri. He'd joined the Arab army when Nuri al-Said, his colleague and personal friend, had asked him to join the Great Arab Revolt against the Ottoman Empire, led by Sharif Hussein bin Ali. He died at a young age from a blow to the head during a cavalry maneuver before King Faisal the First.[1]

We moved in with my maternal uncle and aunt—the middle sister—in the home of my grandmother, who had passed away two years before my father. It was a decision made by the husband of my older maternal aunt, for he was now head of the family in terms of his age and stature.[2] "A young widow cannot live alone with two children in an independent home," he declared.

It was a final decision leaving no room for debate. My mother's pleas to maintain the independence of her home and lifestyle that my father had accustomed her to were futile. My father was a modern man, the opposite of my maternal uncle, who was ten years younger.

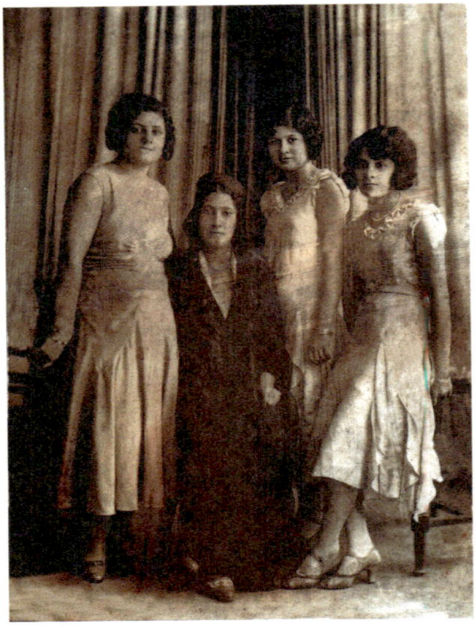

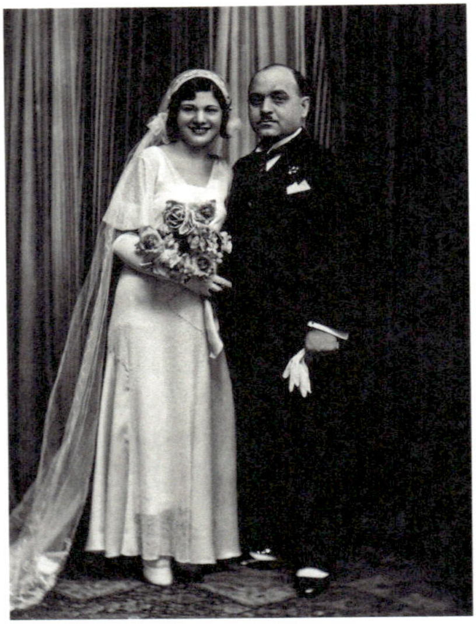

Left: My grandmother Nashmieh and her daughter, Baghdad, 1930
Right: My parents on their wedding day, Baghdad, 1934

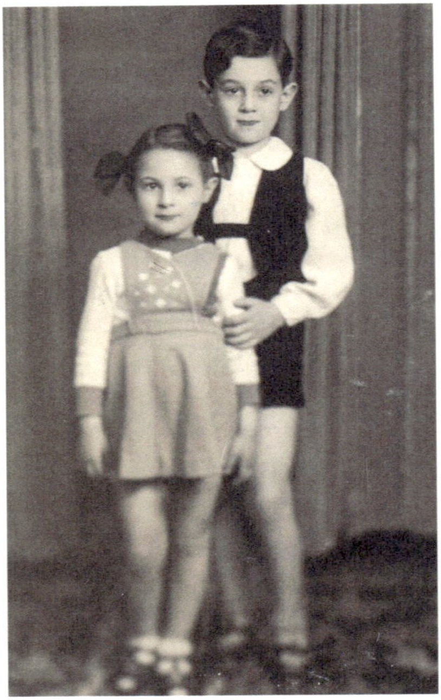

May with her brother, Namir, Baghdad, 1946

Yet, the mutual respect between the family members led my uncle to promise there would be no interference in her lifestyle. My mother was his youngest sister, and he was sorrowful for the plight she bore in the prime of her youth. He continued to miss his cousin, my father, who he'd always considered an older brother.

We were just two children, myself and my brother, who was two and half years my elder. My father's name was Abbas Muzzafar, which was a compound given name, and he decided to suffice with this title, including on the sign hung on the door of our house, dropping the family name al-Khalidi for purely personal reasons.[3] He came from a family that had migrated to Baghdad from northern Iraq and was traced to Haidar Chalabi, known for his donations in al-Mustansir Street near the Tigris, including the Haidar baths, one of the oldest public baths in Baghdad. My father managed his legacies until his death.

My father studied law in the 1920s and worked in the judiciary. He lost his mother as a young child and was raised by his eldest sister. He spoke Turkish, Arabic, and French, and was appointed at a young age as a translator in the royal court, continuing his law studies in the evenings. Like many of his peers in the middle class, his government job was his primary source of income. I don't know much about my father except what I recall of his tenderness; he handled me as though I were a porcelain plate. He married my mother, who was much younger than he, through his right to wed his beloved paternal cousin after waiting for her to complete her intermediate studies. My great love for and attachment to my mother made me feel that losing my father was more merciful than losing my mother, who was like the oxygen I breathed.

My brother and I were different in all ways except for our love for one another. I was calm and mild-tempered, while he was rebellious and impassioned like his friends, which irritated my mother. Yet, my father viewed his youthful energy as a sign of vitality and natural male behavior. The difference in their child-rearing theories was that between the thought of a modern, educated man, and a young woman still lacking knowledge and experience, not to mention her unfamiliarity with the male being in general.

My brother was well known at school and in our neighborhood for his strong personality and fierce face-offs and was a master of imaginative play with his friends. We were opposites. Everyone feared him, and I feared everything including my own shadow. I was in awe of his intellect and superiority in everything, and always saw myself as far behind him. My father stipulated that I accompany him wherever he went, believing that the presence of a girl among boys would keep them polite and rein in their unruliness.

Starting in first grade, the art teacher at Sa'adoun Exemplary School, Fawzia Naji, included me with my brother in the student program she broadcast Friday mornings on Baghdad Radio. We both had good singing voices and were capable of performing. Art was no stranger to our home; my father had been a close friend of painters, playwrights, and musicians, and he played the *qanun*, could perform the Iraqi musical modes (*maqams*), and he drew a number of black ink sketches. He was a personal friend of Haqqi al-Shibli, Abdel Qadir al-Rassam, Mohamed Saleh, and others.

We had a gramophone in our house and records of the most famous classical music, in addition to the Arab and Turkish songs my father listened to regularly. Some of these pieces have remained tied to my memory of him, such as Franz Liszt's "Hungarian Rhapsody." The moment I hear its opening notes, I tear up without knowing why. My father wanted both of us to learn music, and agreed with his friend at Iraqi Radio, the brilliant musician Jamil Bashir, to teach us the violin. Yet circumstances did not allow us to continue.

He also followed theater performances and film screenings and was friends with the well-known cinema owners of the time. My mother often spoke to me of the Arab plays that were performed in cinemas; she'd seen theater performances by George Abyadh, Youssef Wahbi, and Fatima Rushdi, who was dubbed the Sarah Bernhardt of Egypt.[4] We children had our share of cinema-going at the appropriate times and in the company of family, once a week during the school year and during summer vacation. Sometimes we'd see the same film numerous times; I remember we saw Serag Munir's film *Antar and Abla* seventeen times. My brother and I would perform it, having memorized its dialogue.

Most Baghdadi—and indeed most Iraqi—homes were as just as open to those in need, or those offering services for recompense, as they were to friends and guests. There were women from modest families who did the shopping and sometimes helped with housework during special occasions, and usually they became part of the family. Tawfiq was among those who frequently visited us. He was a soldier who'd accompanied my paternal grandfather, and when the war ended he returned to Baghdad. He didn't have a home and discovered his wife had remarried following his extended absence and lack of news of him. He turned to my father for help and was appointed a *muezzin*, the caller to prayer, at the mosque, and continued to visit us often in our home.

Tawfiq was Kurdish Turkmen, and in addition to these two languages, he spoke Arabic with an accent as funny as his personality. He was a source of stories that blended imagination with reality, or reality infused with imagination. We spent splendid evenings listening to his enthralling tales, including the escapades of Mullah Nasreddin (the Turkish equivalent of the Arab Goha). I often imagined him as Mullah Nasreddin, for I noted a perfect resemblance between them. Tawfiq imposed his rules upon us: before telling a story, he stipulated that once he began, no one would be allowed to leave the room. He was a storyteller extraordinaire and acted out the stories he told, including the heroic acts of the Ottoman army in battles he'd witnessed with my grandfather.

One day, our father surprised us by buying a small projection machine with a collection of short films from one of the large Hassou Brothers stores. It was a manual machine that cost five dinars, a large sum at the time. My brother took responsibility for operating it, and we obeyed his stern orders to sit on the ground, the neighbors' children and I, maintaining order and remaining silent.

At the start of each summer vacation, my father would come home from the court, which was located at the entrance of al-Sarray market, accompanied by a man carrying a box filled with books appropriate for our ages, including the weekly periodicals from Egypt in which my brother followed the comics, as well as English-language magazines from the specialized bookshops on al-Rashid Street. Namir was a voracious reader who loved historical stories from a young age. It was from this time that he developed his love of history, especially Islamic history, and later specialized in it.

I grew up in the Alwaziya neighborhood, in a one-story house that architecturally was a development of the traditional Baghdadi courtyard home. Our house was a smaller model of the style prevalent on our street, which included two-story homes on larger properties. Our house had four rooms around a living room with a deep and spacious cellar, part of which was allocated for storage, and part of which housed the family on hot summer days, for it was encased in camel thorn that was doused with water. The large central reception area was connected to a veranda at the back of the house that overlooked a garden centered around a tiled pool with a fountain. At the far end of the garden was an independent building that housed the kitchen, with two attached rooms for living in and a central courtyard. At the entrance to this annex was a clay oven, and every day a baker would pass by all the neighbors twice, once in the morning to prepare the dough, and again around noon to bake it. I loved this baker and would sit to watch her mix the flour with water, sprinkle it with coarse salt, and knead until the dough stuck to her full brown fingers ornamented with tattoos. She'd knead until the dough was consistent in texture, and then split it into loaves called *shuneg*, sprinkle them with flour, and leave them to rise. Decades later, during the 1991 Gulf War and subsequent embargo, we began making dough and baking on a heating stove. I relied on my memory to do this, recalling how Aunt Baker, as I used to call her, would make it.

We children loved modest forms of entertainment. On holidays, swings would be set up in public gardens, and carriages decorated with artificial flowers and bells pulled by two horses would take us from Bab al-Mu'azzam to Sarrafya for fees we paid with our holiday cash gifts. Family visits, in which these gifts were given, were a joy we anticipated in our new clothes starting from eight in the morning. Among other delights we enjoyed in our residential area were the Indians who owned monkeys in embroidered outfits that obeyed their owners' orders, dancing and performing to the beat of a drum. But the greatest delight was the "box of the world," which was a strip of images narrating stories and kept within a box carried on a man's shoulder as he roamed the streets. This box had three peepholes that children would take turns looking through to follow the tales as the man narrated them in his sing-song voice. He had an enthralling way of telling the stories, which included the traditional Antara and Abi Zayd al-Hilali tales, as well as some contemporary ones. I still recall the story about the murder of beautiful Regina, sister of the singer Selima Pasha. She was a rich woman living alone in a palace on the Tigris and was found stabbed to death in her riverboat. The illustrated story went, "This is Regina, who they put on a boat and stabbed with a knife. One cried, 'Oh, mother!' one cried, 'Oh, uncle!' and one cried, 'The unabashed woman is dead!'"

My parents' friends were among the cultured elite who called for education and the creation of a modern life, including respect for women, their going unveiled, and their participation in public life. They were mostly government employees who lived on monthly salaries that allowed for a good standard of life, and the men and women would sometimes meet in homes or attend cultural events together. Regular women's gatherings were held one morning a month, a tiresome tradition upheld by female society at large. The men had their professional clubs, and some joined the British Alwiyah Club after it was opened to Iraqis.[5]

During the summer, the family garden would be spread with carpets, furniture would be brought outside, and colorful lights would be hung. Children were not allowed, however, to appear before guests at social events. The thing I loved most in summer was to spy upon them from the rooftop, eyeing the beautiful attire worn by the women, who usually sat in a circle apart from the men. Early the next morning, I'd sneak out and search the dewy grass for things that had fallen during the evening: an empty metal cigarette case, beads from a woman's bag or dress. . . . I'd collect them, finding a hidden magic in these items that attracted me, and place my bounty in a box I'd take to my favorite corner, or my "house," as I called it. What I loved most were the scents remaining from the previous evening exuding from the grass, earth, and various castoffs.

In the final year of my father's life, his illness grew debilitating. We'd occasionally see him in good health, but most of the time he was restricted to the house, and doctors would come to see him. The last thing he gave us before his death was taking us with him to Istanbul, where we spent three months as he underwent treatment. Our trip began with a four-day journey on the Taurus Express. The first two days were torture, with long hours waiting beneath the harsh sun for meticulous searching of the train's contents on the Syrian border. Then the train took off through mountains, marvelous green landscapes, and tunnels, including the long and dark Taurus Tunnel. The journey was rich with scenery all the way to Haydarpaşa Station.

That was the first time we saw the sea. We sat on its shore fishing and learned the basics of swimming. We stayed in a hotel in al-Su'adya amid a pine forest. It was a traditional Phoenician home with spacious halls and ceilings ornamented with oil paintings framed in gold. Originally, it had been the palace of a wealthy family whose fate had sent it into poverty, and the state subsequently turned their home into a hotel. All the rooms overlooked the Sea of Marmara, and our room also overlooked the summer dance hall where concerts were held by famous Turkish singers every Saturday night. I'd sit on the windowsill and watch the masters of song, including Safiye Ayla and Munir Nurettin, and memorize the songs that were repeated each week. This trip marked the near end for my father, for a few months later he left us, becoming a spirit who would protect us from afar.

School

The bell rang out loudly at the Sa'adoun Exemplary School. I stood in bewilderment as children wielding their small bags rushed here and there down the hall in a joyful clamor. It was my first day at school. My brother had told me, "This is the kindergarten class, come here when you hear the bell." When the bell rang and I saw the boys and girls running down the hall, I went in the opposite direction to where the primary school students were orderly lined up. My brother was in second grade, and I saw him as being very grown up. I stood beside him and held his hand, whispering, "I don't want to stay here, take me to grandmother's house." Her house was nearby, and my brother excused himself with the boldness he was known for despite his young age. Yet, at the school gate he raised his finger in my face and warned, "Your punishment at home will be grave." And so he returned me to the kindergarten classroom. "This is my sister," he told the teacher, and left. Ms. Olivia smiled with her kind face and sat me beside a girl called Khawla, who remains my friend today. Khawla was my companion throughout the primary and secondary stages of school, and, as we got older, her circle of friends kept growing, while mine got smaller. She was the friend of everyone, while I was not close to anyone.

When I was in fourth grade, as we were preparing to enter the mid-year examinations, one of my classmates said to me, "Your father died. They announced it yesterday on the radio." I felt as though she'd insulted me with a foul curse, and screamed "Liar!" running off to search for my brother. I was cut off by the school principal, Martha Assaf, who hugged me and asked what was wrong. I told her what my classmate had said, and she promised, "I'll punish her for what she's done." Then she said firmly and yet tenderly, "Let your brother be, don't disturb him, for he's in his baccalaureate year (the sixth primary grade). Let him finish his examinations in peace. Go wash your face and get back to class."

I could see sorrow in my teachers' eyes and noticed my classmates' reserve as they spoke to me, and whispering could be heard all around. I had a sense that something had disrupted my life. I later would look away when asked, "What does your father do?" and my body would tremble and then my lips as I struggled to come up with an answer. I'd lower my head, feeling as frail as a piece of straw. The word death terrified me, and I was incapable of pronouncing it. As for the principal's advice, she made me face the notion of responsibility at an early age.

When we moved to my grandmother's house our lives changed. Her house in al-Sa'adoun was smaller than ours, although basically of the same design. Her father Wuhayib, a well-known master builder at the time, had built it in 1930. It had four rooms surrounding a large living room, and a cellar used only for storage. The external kitchen was annexed to a large courtyard and a corner called *beit* (home of) *al-hib—al-hib* being a large clay vessel filled with water that was cooled through natural filtration, and which had a clay cup tied to it. This courtyard opened to a 200-square-meter garden. My aunt was not married, and my uncle was seeking a suitable bride.

The house got even more crowded when my mother added to it the furnishings she selected from her home. Our lifestyle changed and we lost our independence; I no longer had a place of my own in which to be alone. It was decided to place my brother's bed with my aunt, and my bed with my mother. My parents had close relations with their friends, and due to the nature of Iraqi society and its customs, they gathered around her, both women and men, in a sense of responsibility toward us, as though they were our uncles and aunts. Every Friday morning, relatives and close friends would visit to check in on us, and they continued doing so until gradual changes in the lives of Iraqis drove us apart.

We grew wary of pronouncing my father's name. Death seemed concealed within our black clothing, and I inhaled it every time I buried my face in my mother's chest. I felt as though we'd become strangers without a roof to protect us. I didn't dare confide in this to my brother, whose liveliness I envied. He poured his energy into sports and studies, and was excelling academically after having transferred to Baghdad College, which only admitted gifted students. He was happy to have enrolled in it and its sports activities. He slept early and rose early, and remained a source of security for me, while his authority was also a source of threat to my introverted nature and reserve. He was grounded and practical in his dealings in life, whereas I was a dreamer and resided in worlds of my own creation.

I can say no more on this period of my life so rich with memories than that I was a worrisome child and a tortured teenager who was extremely shy and introverted. I was never freed of my sense of insecurity.

University Life

Studying literature was an aim I always strove for even before I realized what that meant. I think I felt a strong urge to express myself, and to confide in an extremely small notebook. Whenever asked what I wanted in the future, I would immediately reply to become a writer. And I always got the same response, “Oh, do you want to be May Ziadeh!?” I didn’t know who May Ziadeh was, and when I read about her, I was deeply touched by the story of her life and enchanted by her relationship with Gibran Khalil Gibran. But I was terrified by how her life had transpired in the end, when she spent her final years in a mental institution. That’s how I imagined my fate too, to die alone.

I found in nature a good listener and a friend to keep me company. When I’d return from school in the afternoon I’d spend my spare time in our garden, enjoying the gentle sunlight of Baghdad’s autumn, winter, and spring. I’d observe the pursuits of sparrows and the movements of doves searching the ground for straw for their nests, and follow colorful butterflies, catching one to dry between the pages of my notebook. I’d speak at length with the flowers and listen to their delicate speech. On our summer trips to the resorts of northern Iraq, Salahuddin and Sersink, I’d spend time alone climbing the mountains around the hotel at our vacation spot. I’d lie on the grass and fill my eyes with the sky’s spaciousness, following the clouds in the sky’s blue lined by the peaks of green hills. At the time I wasn’t able to express myself. Something blocked me from grasping the sentiments that stirred within me, and so I’d suffice with filling my eyes in hopes that one day I could say something. At fourteen, my ears began filling with the stirrings of music that quickly developed into words I called poetry. At the time, I’d transferred to the Sisters of the Presentation School in Bab al-Sharqi.

Since I realized that literature was my true desire, I chose to study in the College of Arts in hopes of gaining expressive literary skills. We had English lessons in the Sa‘adoun Exemplary School starting in second grade, and the study of English was much more extensive in the Sisters of the Presentation School than it generally was in government institutions, while we additionally studied French. I chose English literature for my university studies in the belief that it would assist me in getting to know other cultures. This desire was reinforced by a sense of challenge when I learned that very few continued their studies in this department due to its advanced level and its English professors, some dropping out after just the first semester.

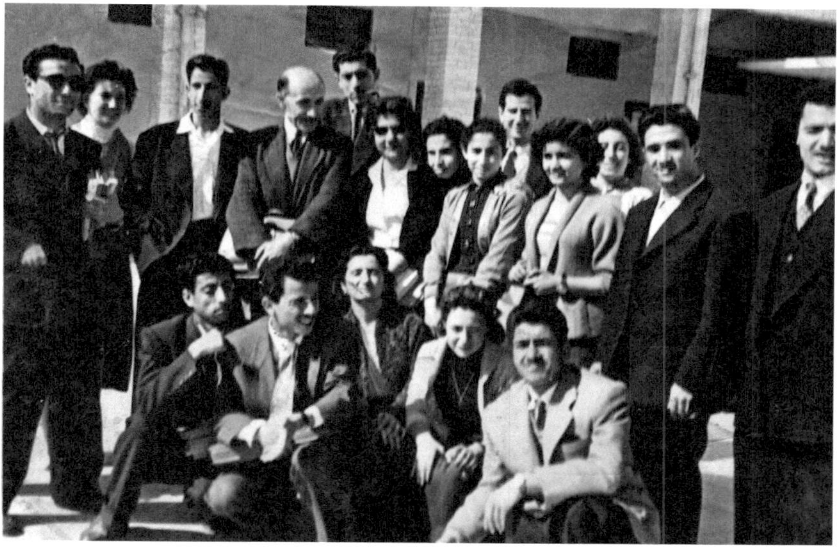

May with other first-year students studying literature at Baghdad University, 1957

Among the conditions for acceptance in the college at the time was passing an examination in general knowledge, and then a personal interview with a committee comprising the college dean, his assistant, and the department head, to assure that the applicant truly wanted to enter the given specialization. I went to the interview with my brother, through whom I'd become acquainted with the poetry included in his English curriculum at Baghdad College. I would listen to him as he recited poems to memorize them. On the way to the interview, he drilled me on what I should say with all confidence before the committee. I was extremely intimidated and shy, and stumbled in Arabic, let alone in English.

I entered the dean's office, as I recall, and stood before three professors sitting at a large table. I knew the professor in the center was Abdel Aziz al-Douri, dean of the College of Arts and Sciences, as it was called before the establishment of the University of Baghdad. Then I learned that the professor sitting to his right was Ali al-Zubaydi, the dean's assistant, and to his left was professor Owen, the head of the English literature department. I stood before them and the three of them smiled, looking at me with some surprise, which often happened due to my small stature and appearing younger than I was. They asked me general questions, and then professor Owen asked me something that departed from everything I'd memorized. "Who taught you English?" he asked, and I said, "Sister Joseph, who is American."

"But your pronunciation is English," he said. Then he asked what had driven me to choose English literature, and I uncharacteristically burst out my response as though I were someone other than myself. I spoke of my passion for literature and writing poetry, my literary ambitions, and the pieces I'd memorized. Then I recited a section of Mark Antony's eulogy of Caesar. I also told them about the recorded poetry readings I listened to at the home of my friend Ilham Ali Raouf. I'd become acquainted with John Keats, Byron, and Shakespeare through these recordings of dramatic readings by leading actors such as Laurence Olivier and John Gielgud. My ears were filled with poetry, most of which I didn't understand and yet which somehow spoke strongly to my senses. My limited experience seemed like a great deal to the committee, and I left the interview with a sense of victory, very different from the state I'd been in beforehand. My brother was astonished and couldn't believe his eyes.

It was the first time there were ten female and ten male students in freshman English literature, although one dropped out following the first semester. When Dr. Owen looked at us in the first lecture in October 1956, he asked in demeaning English sarcasm, "What do I see here? Do I face an endeavor to graduate twenty literary writers?!" We then grasped the scope of the challenge awaiting us. As for his lecture, his English style mixed sarcasm with contempt, including biting comments on what we'd written when asked to explain why we'd chosen English literature. He kept asking, "Is this English?!" In that lecture we also realized what it meant to have graduated from receiving instruction to now having to rely on our own research. "The mission of a university professor is only to point and direct, and it is upon students to research."

University life shocked me at first. I found the free movement of students somewhat chaotic, not to mention the political activity, fiery rhetoric, and protest marches of which the College of Arts was known to be a primary instigator. It was a shock to someone who'd been raised behind high walls, with stern calculations of every move taken. When popular protests and demonstrations broke out, reaching Bab al-Sharqi by the school, we'd hear them chanting and urging us to join as they banged loudly on the iron gates.

Less than two months after we commenced the academic year, the Tripartite Aggression against Egypt, or the Suez Crisis, took place in October 1956. Suddenly, I found myself amid a raging sea of students protesting the attack on Egypt and denouncing the Iraqi government's position and the official media's disregard of the events. The College of Arts at the time was in Bab al-Mu'azzam by the public bus depot. The streets were filled with throngs of students from the Colleges of Medicine, Law, Engineering, Commerce, and Education, all located near the College of Arts, as well as students from Queen Alia Girls' College, which was across the street. I saw male and female students destroying buses, seats, and tables with which to arm themselves, crying out chants expressing their wrath. We did not wait long, I and my friends Mayada al-Madfai and Aida Badran, to rush back to our homes. Study was held up for three months.

When we returned to our classrooms in early January 1957, the College of Arts had moved to a new building in Raghiba Khatcun, in northeastern Baghdad. Despite the general atmosphere of caution, the students were highly energized and enthusiastic to resume academic life.

The building originally housing the College of Arts (established in 1949) was architecturally distinctive for being one of the first built in the 1920s (among other British construction projects), at the start of national rule in Iraq. Dr. Abdel Aziz al-Douri, who was dean of the College of Education, was selected to become dean of the College of Arts and Sciences, as it was called at the time. The building held only the liberal arts lectures, while the science lectures were in a separate building on al-'Adhamya's main street. As enrollment in the College of Arts grew in popularity, additional departments were added, including the Department of English Literature, which was instated during the 1952–53 academic year with English professors.

The new building was more relaxed and welcoming, with open areas and halls filled with light, and we were astonished to find a large courtyard and students' tearoom. The state had directed the provision of opportunities to play sports, including ping pong, badminton, and volleyball. While the comportment of students was generally conservative, especially the women, the female students of the English literature department were bolder and paved the way for other female students to play these male-dominated games, and also to visit the college tearoom, which was essentially restricted to men. And thus, our class was reunited in an air of contradiction. The place felt more relaxed, but there were also whispers among students warning against informers.

The female students of the College of Arts were known for being attractive and well-dressed, in particular those in the English literature department. We were observed with both admiring and critical eyes. Perhaps it's amusing to mention something I was told years later by Dr. Ahmed Matlub, professor of Arabic literature and rhetoric in the College of Arts, who later became a friend and a resource I'd consult, along with his wife Dr. Khadija al-Hadithi, on linguistic matters, and whose generosity I will never forget. He told me, "Did you know the Arabic professors used to fight over who'd teach the English literature students? Sometimes it would reach the point of fist fights!" Yet, we were lucky to have the best teachers throughout our four years, and I remember them with great respect: Ahmed Shallal, Wadi'a Taha al-Nijim, and Ibrahim al-Samara'i. Dr. al-Samara'i taught us in our final year, and with each composition assignment he'd rebuke the students in the Iraqi dialect, saying, "You treat this language like shopkeepers!" and then he'd turn to me and apologize, "But you're different."

Our university life during the first two years was marvelous. We were enthusiastic and active in the college, participating as much as possible in social, cultural, and sports events. We prepared annual parties held at the start of the year, as well as literary competitions at year's end in which both students and professors took part. Our first year laid the curriculum's groundwork, and the most pleasurable course we took, in my opinion, was literary appreciation. Its lecturer, John Kirkpatrick, methodologically selected the most famous pieces of poetry and prose from the nineteenth century. He focused on our clear pronunciation and immersion in poetic imagery, and his recitation was enthralling. But he was also an arrogant Englishman, like the department head, and fortunately unlike the professors of grammar and literary criticism. Students were suspicious of him and accused him of espionage, and I remember one student in our class would glare at him with aggressive looks the professor ignored.

We were all targeted for political mobilization, and for the first time ever I started becoming acquainted with political parties. Yet, my knowledge was limited to the notion that anyone inimical to the royal government was suspected of being a communist.

Every morning, one of the students more senior in our department would wait for me at the college gates. He was incredibly nice and polite, and seemed older than his peers due to his full figure and early balding. He'd tell me news of what was taking place in the college corridors, what he expected to happen, who'd been arrested, and who'd been released. I'd cry or be relieved, even though I didn't know any of the people. He told me, "All the communists are in prison, and everyone you see belongs to other parties." Listening to the organizers trying to sway our convictions, I never fell in line with any of the political orientations and would simply reply with a laugh and make a getaway.

I discovered I felt a repulsion toward political activity when I found it entailed intellectual and logistical limitations I was not willing to engage with. I also didn't feel comfortable with the faces of the politicized or their style of rhetoric often issued in a threatening, commanding manner. That was the manner of our friend who'd always warn me, "That person's a liar, and that one's a spy, so avoid him," and so on. I began getting vexed with this loathsome insistence, and one day, when I was in a foul mood, I exploded in protest, ordering him not to speak to me again. I think it shocked him when he found me transformed from a meek kitten into a fierce woman, and with his regret he left me alone.

July 14, 1958, and Its Implications

During the 1958 summer vacation, I went with my aunt Fadhila to Jordan. Her husband Bahaa al-Din Nuri had completed his mission as ambassador there following the declaration of a Hashemite Federation between Jordan and Iraq and was waiting for a transfer to a new location.

Not a week had passed when the Iraqi chief of staff at the time, staff lieutenant Rafiq Arif, arrived on invitation of the Jordanian government. The ambassador invited him and his delegation for dinner. I sat with my aunt at the edge of the gathering listening to the men's conversation about the situation in Iraq, and the news leaking of a possible military coup against the monarchy in both countries. Arif let out a derisive laugh and declared, "I have the army wrapped around my little finger!"

We didn't know exactly what took place in Baghdad the morning of July 14, 1958. The news transmitted by radio stations was contradictory and jumbled. Upon hearing the news, my uncle Bahaa went to check on the embassy, but quickly returned with a troubled face. He'd found his closest and dearest aide had taken down the state emblem and photograph of the king and trampled on them. He was Kurdish and incredibly well-mannered but had suddenly turned into another person and challenged the ambassador: "The revolution has at last begun, and there's no place for you here starting today!"

This was the cruelest blow my uncle received in his life, as he himself put it. For Bahaa al-Din Nuri had been among those who'd contributed to establishing the modern state in record time, and a national army considered the strongest among the Arab nations. He found it difficult to accept the stature and sanctity of the state being violated. That very evening he received a phone call from Abdel Salaam Arif asking him to send the regiment stationed in Jordan back to Baghdad. The discharged ambassador was firm and decisive: "I do not recognize you or your government!"

His deep sorrow over the replacement of those in rule bore no relation to his experience in political life or awareness of changing circumstances. Rather it was sorrow over a trusted army rebelling, removing the symbol of the state and committing a cruel massacre. Uncle Bahaa al-Din suffered from a hardening of the arteries and passed away a little over a year later, heartsick from the murder of the Hashemites and worried over the future of Iraq, which he saw moving into uncertainty.

The picture of what had happened in Baghdad didn't become clear to us in Amman until days later, when the foreign press reached us and we read the painful reports supplemented with awful images in *Time* and *Newsweek* magazines. Then Amman began receiving victims of the random killings that included Jordanian statesmen attending a meeting in Baghdad. In addition to the dreadful scenes I witnessed, I was in shock that I'd become trapped in Jordan and didn't know how I'd return to my family, whose fate I had no news of. The Jordanian kingdom had cut its relations with Baghdad and closed its borders. Its relations with Syria were also cut off, and Beirut was in a state of civil war, with American fleets stationed on its shores. The Iraqi embassy was closed down and those affiliated with it began returning home by land. My aunt asked the wife of an embassy diplomat, a close friend of hers, to take me with her to Baghdad, and her friend appeared willing to do so, but then quickly departed with her husband, leaving me behind.

Bahaa al-Din Nuri was a modern man, a cultured and encyclopedic writer who was fluent in seven Eastern and Western languages. He decided not to return to Iraq, and his Majesty King Hussein granted him Jordanian citizenship in respect for his stature, experience, and knowledge, appointing him ambassador extraordinary in the Jordanian foreign service. While he waited for the administrative procedures to be completed, he had an extended period of free time, and chose to busy himself with completing unfinished writing projects, including a translation of Omar al-Khayyam's poetry from Persian to Kurdish. Yet he chose to begin by reviewing a book he'd previously published on Genghis Khan, and which he wanted to review and republish. I assisted him by writing down the changes he dictated. During those sessions he told me about historical events that had taken place around the world, including the Bolshevik revolution, which he thought the events in Baghdad resembled. He expected the behavior of Baghdad's rulers to be similar.

He was a sensitive and compassionate man despite his apparent sternness. Following the death of my father, who was his closest friend, he was incredibly concerned with the fate of me, my brother, and my mother, and couldn't help crying every time he hugged me. He possessed deep faith, although he was not committed to religious ritual, and his grief for King Faisal was immense, due to his symbolizing the sanctity of the Hashemite lineage. This was no surprise, for he came from a religious Kurdish family, and his father, Sheikh Nuri Ismail al-Shirwani, and his uncle Sheikh Taha, were Sufis. I recall when I was a small child how my father took me and my brother into Sheikh Nuri's spiritual seclusion room to receive his blessings. I saw a frail old man with a small white beard wearing a traditional white gown. He placed his hand on my head and murmured prayers I did not understand.

Oddly, Bahaa al-Din had three communist brothers, the oldest of whom was the doctor and painter Dr. Qutaiba al-Sheikh Nuri, and they lived in his home during their university studies. After I married Rafa, we'd often visit the home of Dr. Qutaiba and his wife Dr. Samira Babaan in al-Mansour. In the second half of the 1970s, not long before his death in a horrific road accident, we attended one of his many invitations to spend the evening in their home. He greeted us at the door with his charming smile, and whispered in my ear, "May, it seems my forefathers are calling me." Then he told me that he'd begun practicing spiritual reclusion and had immersed himself in Sufi texts, growing close to a belief in God.

One morning, as I sat before uncle Bahaa al-Din, prepared for his dictation, he drew close and said, "You're a grounded, intelligent girl, and I want to tell you something. Jordan is still under threat of a fate similar to what's happened in Baghdad. So, if God forbids this happens, I want to you take responsibility for getting your aunt and our daughter Shirine back to Baghdad; you'll be safe without me." He paused for a moment and then said, "My health won't permit me to bear any violence, so if what I expect indeed happens, I'll end my life with this." He took a small pistol from his briefcase and laid it before me. I didn't fully grasp what was happening and remained silent, but was overwhelmed with a sense of pride that he trusted me, and horror with the idea of a situation and a responsibility I could not imagine.

We continued to wait but heard no news from family in Baghdad until my brother called us from London, where he was studying. He said he'd spoken with my mother and she was well. He was extremely worried about her with both of us so far away, and our uncle reassured him, telling him to not allow his concern to threaten his studies. I could see the anguish and helplessness on the faces of my aunt and uncle as they busied themselves securing safe passage for me. My uncle concealed his suffering, and, so as not to add to their worries, I kept my loneliness and unease to myself. This went on for about two months, until they were able to secure my travel by air to Beirut, with the assistance of the Jordanian embassy there, and then on to Baghdad.

In Beirut I found another surprise awaiting me. I saw a Volkswagen Beetle near the airplane and was met by a man who said he was the *chargé d'affaires*. He quickly led me to the car, got me into the cramped back seat, and asked me to remain with my head lowered throughout the journey. He sat in the front by the driver and told me they'd received communications threatening them wherever they might be. The car sped off, and the young diplomat tried to conceal his concern, and alleviate mine, by warmly welcoming me and apologizing for the difficult, life-threatening circumstances in Beirut at the time. After safely spending the night in Beirut, he accompanied me back to the airport for my flight home. Upon arriving in Baghdad, I found my entire family waiting for me at the airport.

My mother later spoke to me of how she'd suffered without me and my brother, of the difficulties she faced and her horror with the hysteria that afflicted people, including friends. She also held deep sorrow for the injustice inflicted upon the royal family, and this sorrow remained with her until the end of her life. Baghdad's society was small, and everyone knew each other. My uncle Na'el Mahmoud Basri was a brigadier general and commander of the armor school in Abu Ghraib, and he was transferred to retirement because of his high ranking. He and his family lived in a home allocated to him at his workplace, and he had to vacate it immediately, left with no option other than taking refuge in his mother's home. The situation became very difficult for my mother as the house became crowded with four children, and so she moved in with my paternal aunt in al-'Adhamya, where she found peace and calm. When I arrived in Baghdad she'd returned home again after my uncle had rented a house in al-Waziriya.

The start of the academic year was delayed due to administrative changes that took place, and the strange decision taken by Abdul Karim Qassim, known as "the snake charmer," allowing those who'd failed their baccalaureate exams to in fact pass. Dr. al-Douri left us, and professor Mahdi al-Makhzoumi, another distinguished scholar, became college dean. It seemed to me that most of the students were pleased with the political change and the arrival of the age of "freedom," whether in actual belief or out of fear, yet a strange atmosphere blanketed our lives in the college. I was wary, for the violence and cruelty that exploded the morning of July 14 had planted a lasting fear within me.

I kept my silence and continued to distance myself from anything related to political activity, for which my repulsion only grew. I preferred to maintain my independence, and an open outlook on life, especially after literature deepened my sense of affiliation to the spirit of humanity, as represented in love, tolerance, and respect for the other.

We encountered one surprise after the next, starting with the unpredictable behavior of our colleagues, and then a sharp division and animosity between the leftists and nationalists that revealed extremely violent behavior. Abdul Karim Qassim was venerated to an extreme with slogans and chants. One winter morning we found a massive mural, a portrait, of the "Leader" (as Abdul Karim Qassim was dubbed) resting against a wall in the large courtyard. A colleague in our class, communist artist and writer Abdullah Habba,[6] was still working on it, drawing it in charcoal, I believe. It was a beautiful, skilled work, and a first step toward glorification and worship, aside from the chants and songs already dedicated to the one and only.

During my first two years at the university, I formed an impression of the political atmosphere and the urgent calls for regime change made by the majority of people. I witnessed the speed with which some people changed their behavior and rhetoric, or perhaps made public what they'd been concealing. In subsequent years I saw this phenomenon repeated with every change in regime. Such rapid transformation and support for the new political environment—for the strongest and most powerful—would rise in prominence and grow in scope until Iraq became what it is today. But what seemed strange to me were the threats and intimidation people used against each other. As the years went by and the situation in Iraq fluctuated, this intimidation remained a form of blackmail and fearmongering, and in some cases retribution.

The political feuds between parties intensified after reaching their shared goal of overturning the monarchy. But they grew more violent and vicious following the al-Shawaf coup attempt and the horrific massacres in Mosul and Kirkuk, finished off by popular tribunals and the disfiguring of corpses hung from street posts. These scenes brought further pain, anguish, and terror to people's hearts. As for the people's court headed by military judge al-Mahdawi, and which departed from all rules of professionalism and ethics, it was a stain in the history of Iraq's judiciary, which had been one of the highest-standing and fairest institutions of the state. A spirit of revenge and hatred spread widely, increasing after the failed attempt to assassinate Abdul Karim Qassim. This spirit of animosity even extended among brothers.

We never knew what to expect each day at the university. We'd suddenly hear someone in the courtyard call out, "Conspiracy! Shut the gates!" and we'd have to run off to avoid the scenes of violence and chaos that would ensue. In general, our lifestyles did not change, but fear and caution became our constant companions, as we never knew when or from whom accusations would be made. During this period, our main preoccupation was following the latest developments, and our evenings were dedicated to following al-Mahdawi's trials with their black comedy. These took place amid much courtroom ruckus as figures from the monarchy stood accused, followed by those accused with the al-Shawaf conspiracy, and who were executed, and the trial of those involved in the assassination attempt against Abdul Karim Qassim. Another episode was added to our evenings as we followed the fiery verbal sparring between Qassim and Gamal Abdel Nasser. And, thus, politics became present in all the details of our daily life, whether we liked it or not!

With the start of the next year, 1960, our lives became more stable and less violent. The streets quieted down to a large degree when Qassim tightened his fist on the violations threatening the state's prestige, something that a seasoned, nationalist military man could not accept. Such behavior was foreign to society at the time, but quickly became a norm that grew in proportion with the power of subsequent regimes, culminating in the chaos allowed by the American occupation in the name of freedom, with all its grievous violations against humanity. As for intimidation and accusations of treachery, this became a common form of retribution and personal gain, with or without reason.

Literary Experience

I entered the world of poetry through singing and memorizing sung poems or any literary phrasing that touched me, starting in primary school. My Arabic teacher Adiba al-Jarrah chose me to recite the poem "My Brother" by Mikhail Naimy, which I selected myself, before the students at the Thursday flag allegiance ceremony. Flanked by the principal and teachers, I closed my eyes so as not to see anyone, and felt as though I'd entered another realm, only reconnecting when I heard the applause. The teachers hugged me in turn, their eyes filled with tears. "Your recitation made us cry, just as your singing does," the principal said.

At university I twice won the first prize in the English department's poetry recital competition, and the evaluation noted intense emotional energy in my reading.[7] This emotion remained the distinctive force driving my literary journey.

My first experience writing poetry with meter and rhyme was during my intermediate studies in the Sisters of the Presentation School. My head started filling with pressing musical iterations that developed into melodic words. I recited a poem in Arabic class and was surprised by the teacher's mocking. "The poem has mistakes in its meter and language. You must read *The Golden Meter* in order to write poetry," I was told.

Despite my frustration and my ignorance of *The Golden Meter*, I went to al-Sarray market that very day and bought the book, thinking it was a magic key. Yet, I found myself lost in riddles and equations I was completely incapable of fathoming or unraveling, let alone following the lines of thought or terminology. I was bewildered and did not seek the assistance of my teacher again. I continued writing, driven by my force of emotion and the rhythms filling my mind, and did not share that I was doing so.

I began acquiring poetry texts through my own means, and I had two sources. The first was sung poetry, especially the poems of Ahmed Shawqi sung by Umm Kulthum and Mohamed Abdel Wahhab, as well as the beautiful poems performed by reciters on a weekly evening radio program. The second was books I found in a small book shack in Bab al-Sharqi on my way home from school, where I'd purchase what my modest weekly pocket money would allow. The bookseller would advise me on his newest arrivals, and I'd purchase what I could afford. At the time books cost on average 100 to 250 fils.

The loveliest of my purchases was a book called *The Beauty of Women Among the Arabs* that included a selection of pre-Islamic poetry illustrated with black-and-white drawings. Among the most remarkable was a poem called "The Nude One" by al-Nabigha al-Thubiyani, and I was astonished by its bold description and flowing expression. I hid it amid my piles of books.

Then I started to regularly purchase *The Book of Songs*, which was published in parts, without editing or annotation, in Beirut. One day I came across Bishara al-Khoury's 1953 poetry volume *Love and Youth*, in a beautiful and stylish print wrapped in cellophane. I gazed at it wistfully, for it cost 550 fils! Then it so happened that I fell extremely ill, and my mother wanted to do something to please me, and I asked her to buy me the poetry volume, which she would not have expected. I kept it beside my pillow and memorized many of its poems. Some of these books remained until recently in the considerable library that Rafa and I compiled, and which we left in the safekeeping of a friend in Baghdad.[8]

The Sisters of the Presentation School didn't have programs or activities outside of its strict curriculum, as opposed to the public schools, including al-Markaziya, al-Hariri, and al-Sharqiya. Even our sports class was usually turned into additional lessons for subjects such as mathematics. Yet, in my final year of high school, we had an

Arabic teacher called Ma'areb Ali, who was a writer and spoke formal Arabic. She had a commanding presence and was resolute, speaking to us in official Arabic and asking us to reply in it, which caused much confusion and embarrassment. She departed from the textbook curriculum and was the first to introduce us to modern poetry, a bold step at the time. She selected for us Nazik al-Malaika's moving poem about Baghdad's massive flood in 1954, "The River Lover," and Nizar Qabbani's poem "Letter to a Spiteful Woman," which is the poem that introduced me to the world of Nizar Qabbani.

One time Ms. Ma'areb held a story-writing competition on a topic of our choice, and announced my story as the best, due to its intense and moving emotion. The story recreated a painful memory from my early childhood, when I saw a woman at the entrance to the royal hospital's emergency room, crying over her child who had been crushed to death. It was a memory that never left me. Ms. Ma'areb later wrote a beautiful text in my diary, complimenting my talent and wishing me a successful literary future:

> My dear May,
>
> A tender melody floating on the whispering breeze of the convent's garden, its echo ringing in ears and stirring the hearts of friends, as hands reach out to applaud.
>
> This is an image I will remember of May, the shy girl who greets me in a soft voice that is both bashful and well-mannered, and then runs off with her little friends.
>
> There's another image of her that remains in my mind: my admiration when I'd read what she'd written in her essay book. What delighted me most was finding throngs of ideas and images, one after the next, in your essays, showing me that their author has brilliant talent and quick wit.
>
> May God always be in your aid and widen the path to success before you.
>
> Ma'areb Ali
> March 27, 1956

My dear old friend Na'ous al-Rawi had congenital vision impairment that affected her mobility, although it did not prevent her from continuing her studies and excelling in them. She chose Arabic literature and made serious inroads toward expressing herself, and she found herself in the right place. She got to know a number of students in the Arabic literature department, including poets Kamal Abdullah al-Hadithi, Khalid Ali Mostafa, and Amaal al-Zahawi, and one evening we attended with them a meeting with the leading poet Badr Shaker al-Siyab in the Solidarity Club (Al Tadhamun Club), which he frequented. He seemed pleased by our presence, but remained awkward until he began reading his poetry.

My main concern after completing my university studies was my intention to develop my potential in Arabic language and literature, and to revisit the fundaments of Arabic poetry. Ideally, I needed a job in a cultural or media institution. A year before graduating, I was obliged to work during the summer vacation in a company run by one of my father's friends, and then I decided to continue part-time. After graduating, my opportunities for work were limited, and I had to accept my first offer. On the recommendation of a close friend of my uncle, I applied to the newly established Iraqi Reinsurance Company.[9]

The company needed someone to write and edit their English correspondence, given the nature of their relations with foreign companies around the world. I was uncertain about it, but had no other option, and it seems that fate had prepared for me this place I'd never considered. The work I did there for eighteen years helped me develop other skills, including the fundaments of research and translation, and I gained an economic language that enriched my literary language. My work there also allowed me to meet distinguished figures who contributed to the development of my literary experience.

My first few years in the company passed in a pleasant atmosphere and amid kind relations, and I gained good experience, since I liked my professional work and immersed myself in it. In the evenings, I lived another life in the worlds of literature and music, yet I lacked guidance. My distracted reading included random examples from Arabic literature across the ages, and I found myself lost in it. I didn't have anyone with which to discuss what I was reading, and my isolation from literary circles compounded my sense of being lost. And yet I consistently wrote on the basis of strong emotion, although I was always filled with doubt over what I wrote.

Baghdad's political events with all their surprises remained a constant source of anxiety. For after life relatively settled down, and the intense pressures on people lightened, the February 1963 coup took place,[10] with the Baathists in control at first. We fell into another spiral of violence, arrest campaigns, and retribution. While most employees in the company, including the general directors, were professionals and removed from political activity, a few of our colleagues were arrested by the youth in the national guard—some returned, but others disappeared. The situation was terrifying, and also embarrassing for management when armed forces invaded the company offices and led employees away to an uncertain fate. I was angered and pained when I witnessed colleagues we'd spent time with and grown attached to being led away before our eyes to God only knows what or where.

We worried that the political change would affect the company management, but that didn't happen, thank God. Circumstances quickly changed again, and the nationalists overpowered the Baathists following a few months of struggle between them. Yet they were soon targeted, and their rule also wrested away, as the army intervened to maintain security in the cities and prevent chaos from breaking out, allowing life to stabilize. With time we grew accustomed to coups, with their manifestos and curfews, and adjusted to them. I took advantage of these periods of change, in which there were generally curfews, to focus on reading important novels I'd put off, and to fully immersing myself in the sublimity of their worlds as an escape from everything.

Nizar Qabbani

In 1962, the renowned Syrian poet Nizar Qabbani came to Baghdad on a trip both official and private. He was a close friend of Ms. Adiba Khidr, a friend of my mother, and she asked Nizar to spare an hour of his time with me in her home. I went nervously to the meeting carrying a notebook filled with poetry. He read them out loud, and then asked me to read them, which I did in a soft and flustered voice. It was clear I was influenced by him, although he did not comment on this, and simply said, "You're certainly a promising poet and you possess beautiful imagery, which is an important asset. But you need to develop your tools in order to properly take on poetry." He suggested I mail him my texts so he could provide his comments and corrections.

At that time, Nizar had moved to Madrid on a diplomatic mission, and I'd periodically send him letters, receiving in turn detailed comments. The most important of these was alerting me to the

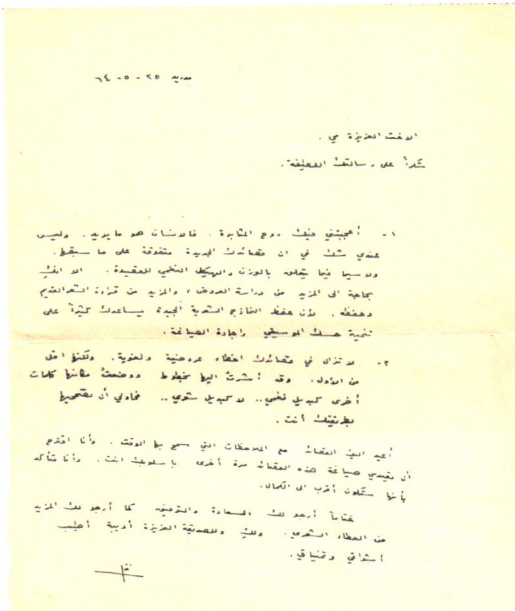

مدريد ٢٥-٥-٦٤

الأخت العزيزة مي .

شكراً على رسالتك اللطيفة.

١- أعجبني فيك روح المثابرة . فالإنسان هو ما يريد . وليس عندي شك في أن قصائدك الجديدة متفوقة على ما سبقها. ولا سيما فيما يتعلق بالوزن والهيكل الفني للقصيدة . إلا أنك بحاجة الى المزيد من دراسة العروض ، والمزيد من قراءة الشعر القديم وحفظه . لأن حفظ النماذج الشعرية الجيدة يساعدك كثيراً على تنمية حسك الموسيقي وإجادة الصياغة .

٢- لا تزال في قصائدك أخطاء عروضية ولغوية . ولكنها أقل من الأولى . وقد أشرت اليها بخطوط ووضعت مكانها كلمات أخرى كبديل فني.. لا كبديل شعري.. فحاولي أن تصححيها بطريقتك أنت .

أعيد اليك القصائد مع الملاحظات التي سمح بها الوقت . وأنا أقترح أن تعيدي صياغة هذه القصائد مرة أخرى بأسلوبك أنت . وأنا متأكد بأنها ستكون أقرب الى الكمال.

ختاماً أرجو لك السعادة والتوفيق كما أرجو لك المزيد من العطاء الشعري . ولك وللصديقة العزيزة أديبة أطيب أشواقي وتمنياتي.

نزار

Letter from Nizar Qabbani to May Muzaffar, 1964

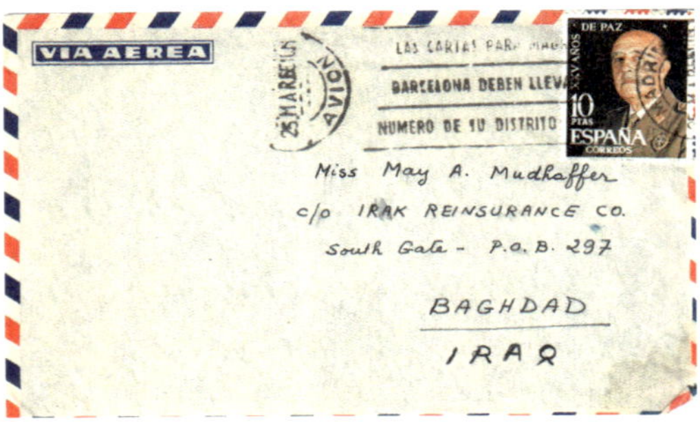

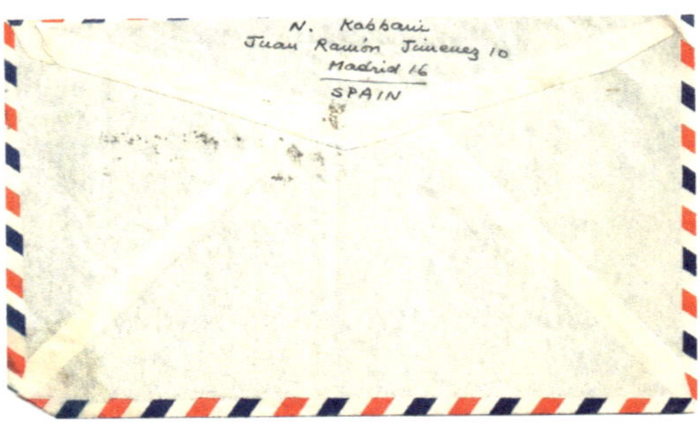

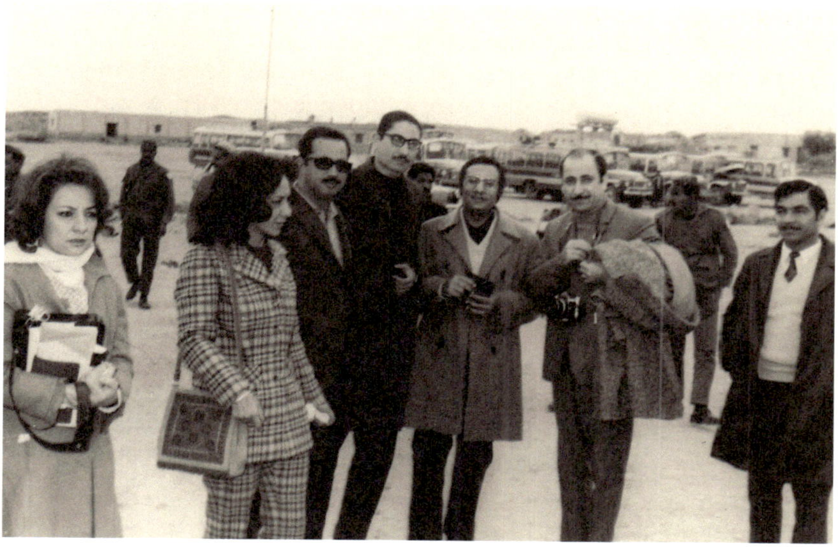

May on a trip to Mosul, in the context of Abu Tammam Festival, 1970. With writers Assia al-Turaihi, Sabry Hafez, Fouad Takarli, Musa Kuraydi

necessity of imagery comprising intellectual meaning. "I noticed you don't pay attention to semantics, and that you pose images haphazardly," he wrote (May 25, 1964), offering an example with a phrase from a poem I'd sent. In another letter, he alerted me to the dominant tone of sorrow in the poems: "Sorrow is essential to our lives, but we shouldn't allow it to consume us. . . . Failure does not mean death, but rather, to the artist, it is transparency and depth" (June 25, 1964). Another thing he told me was, "If you want to enter the world of literature with its doors thrown wide open, you must tear up many things before showing the results of your efforts to people, for they are cruel and deal incredible injustice" (Madrid, January 12, 1965). This was all advice I held dear throughout my life.

The engagement and sincerity I found in his replies encouraged me to remain in contact, and our correspondence increased. Nizar possessed refined and cultured taste in art, and he admired Rafa both artistically and as a person, ever since they met in Beirut when Rafa had his first exhibition in Gallery One. His 1962 visit to Baghdad was primarily to meet Balqis al-Rawi and to ask for her hand in marriage. He'd heard of Balqis through family ties; she was a childhood friend of mine, and her mother was a close friend of my mother. The news of his proposal quickly spread throughout Baghdad's social circles.

When Balqis's father refused Nizar's proposal that year, they held on to their dream and finally married in Baghdad in 1969. Our relationship grew stronger, and I began meeting them every time I visited Beirut, where they lived, or during their family visits to Baghdad. In addition to her attractive looks, Balqis had a strong personality; she was strong-willed and knew what she wanted. She was also kind-hearted and sensitive, and able to create a family life filled with love. She opened her heart to all with no exception. And, thus, the Baghdadi lived with the Damascene in a shared life that brought both cultures together.

Najib al-Mani'

The year 1965 was a turning point in my literary life, for I met famous Arab writers who passed through Baghdad, including Abdul Rahman al-Sharqawi, Ahmed Rami, Mohamed Mandour, Nasser al-Din al-Assad, Ihsan Abbas, and Mahmoud Hassan Ismaiel. A few of them I maintained a friendship with, including Khalil Hawi and the Sudanese poet Mohamed Mahdy al-Magzoub, whom I remained in touch with

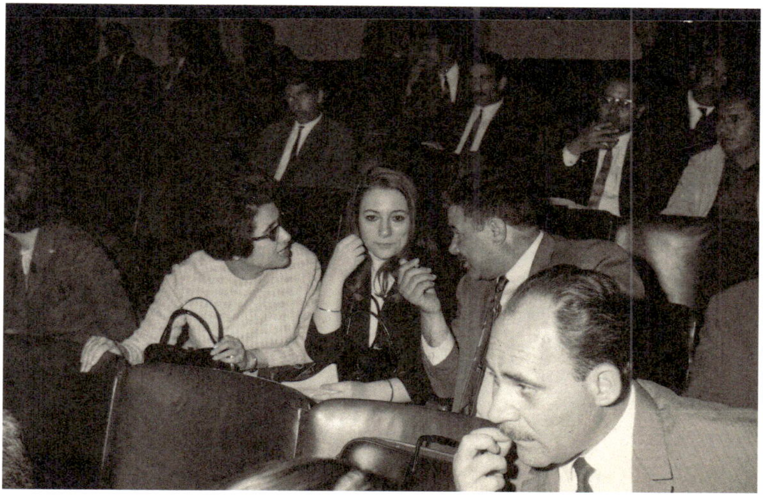

May at the opening of the Writers' Conference and Arab Poetry Festival, Al Khuld Hall, Baghdad, 1965

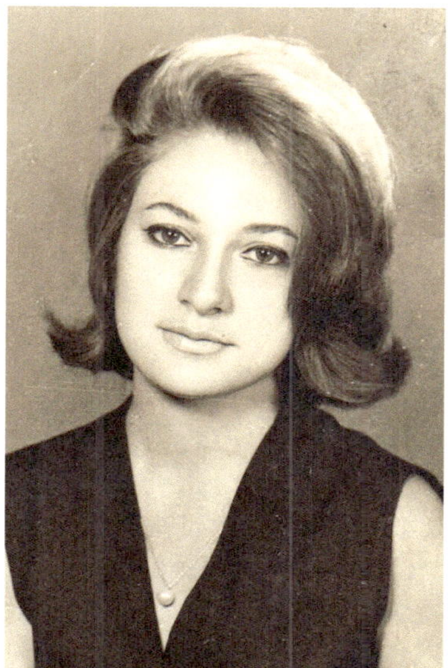

May Muzaffar, Baghdad, 1965

for nearly the rest of his life.[11] I received letters from him that were literary gems in themselves, resembling the Arabic genre *maqamat*, but, unfortunately, they have been lost. I'd sent them to Dr. Salma Khadra Jayyusi when she was preparing a book on him, and I don't know what happened to them afterward. At a later time, I developed a close friendship with Dr. Ihsan Abbas, when Rafa and I moved to Jordan. Likewise with Dr. Nasser al-Din al-Assad, whom I worked with for five years in the Royal Academy for Islamic Civilization Research in Amman, and who years later recommended me to write a book on his literary journey. I also wrote of my experience with him, and it was published in a commemorative volume about him.

In 1965, I also met Najib al-Mani‘ when he was appointed to the Iraqi Reinsurance Company. A few years earlier he'd been removed from the Ministry of Foreign Affairs, due to his refusal to sign approval for the execution of officers charged with conspiring against Abdul Karim Qassim in 1959. He was in principle against the concept of execution. We developed a deep intellectual and personal friendship during the years he worked there and maintained it until he passed away.

Najib played a primary role in the development of my literary character, and it was he who drew a methodological road map for me to master culture in its widest sense, and to develop my language skills in both Arabic and English. He guided me to the finest musical, literary, and artistic heritage in both East and West. I started with him from scratch and followed the program he set for me, supporting me with selections from his Arabic and English library rich in literature, theory, and art.

Najib Al-Mani‘ (1926–1992) had a great mind. His existential questions were without limit, as was his great generosity. His passion for culture was awe-inspiring in its scope, and contagious when in contact with it. When he spoke of an eloquent poem, prose text, or piece of music, he'd get flustered and wipe tears from his eyes, before mumbling shyly, "I'm sorry, I'm sorry." You'd feel that this man of striking presence had melted into nothing but a bundle of feelings. He might cackle with laughter, "Human weakness is not a fault," and I'd say to him, "Rather, it's the jewel of humanity." He'd be put at ease with my response and carry on revealing his personal suffering. He rebelled remorselessly against banality and the unchecked spread of ugliness in daily life. He believed the collapse of the nation was the result of the downfall of its Arabic prose, and this notion would reduce him to tears.

Each day I felt that my awareness was expanding and I was seeing what I'd previously not perceived. That same year, the poet Shathel Taqa (1929–1974) joined us at work. He was a sensitive poet and a marvelous person, an Iraqi full of all the contradictions that entails. Together, we created an oasis shading the desert of our dry and serious work at the company. Najib's and Shathel's offices became a destination for both leading and emerging writers, poets, and intellectuals. Najib was a liberated leftist and visited by intellectuals specializing in various fields, as well as by young writers and artists. Shathel was an older generation Baathist, easy-going and generously accepting of criticism. Two friends of his, Shafiq al-Kamali and Youssef al-Sayegh, would often seek refuge with him. And, thus, I started getting acquainted with the cultural world and its figures.

I now committed to a strict daily schedule following my return home from work, from 5 p.m. until midnight. I found Najib's frankness to be sometimes harsh, at times to the extent of mocking me and others. This frankness often led to fierce battles with writers, and animosities that lasted a lifetime. In the beginning, his demands seemed impossible, for his standards were those of leading writers of poetry and prose, whether Arab or Western. He told me no more than what he'd told others, but our proximity allowed me to speak with him directly and discuss what I'd written and read. With his harshness and mocking humor he'd call my attention to the negative aspects, and I'd become all the more determined. When he expressed satisfaction with what I'd written, I'd fly with joy.

During the first year, I'd listen to what he said without discussion or objection. As he saw my responsiveness to his comments, he'd demand more and more effort from me. I was prepared to face any challenge he placed before me, until our dialogue transformed into one of give and take, and later into fierce arguments, for example when he'd throw my texts in my face, exclaiming, "You'll never become a writer!" I'd reply forcefully that I would indeed become a writer, and that he'd see.

He found within me something of everything, and a readiness to absorb all forms of art. And thus I began following supposedly disparate threads of diversity, locating points of correspondence between arts and discovering the relationship between them, and my writing became the outcome of this. At first, music propelled me toward poetry, and poetry drove me to stories, while modern poetry led me to seek the history of visual arts and the development of relations between the arts, until I grasped the threads intertwining and connecting them all. During that early period, I wrote two articles, the first a comparison between a short story by Alain Robbe-Grillet and abstract compositions by Mondrian, which was published in *al-Aqlam* (Pens) journal in 1972. The second was an attempt to study pre-Islamic poetry through a visual reading, starting with al-Shanfara's "lamia," the rich natural scenes of which I examined in an article subsequently published in *al-Aqlam* (Pens) journal in 1983.

Despite this, I continued to feel there was something lacking in my Arab culture, both linguistically and artistically. I learned that the respected scholar Sheikh Jalal al-Hanafi gave lessons at the Institute of Melodic Studies in Koranic *tajwid* recitation, prosody, and Arabic phonetics, and that he was an open-minded and accommodating man. I wanted to try this traditional style of learning. Rafa knew him from China, where he'd taught Arabic.

He was the imam of al-Khulafa' Mosque, and we went there to meet him. He was surprised by my request when he learned that I had a degree in English literature and asked why I wanted to study prosody and Koranic *tajwid*. I didn't tell him I wrote modern poetry because he was a fierce opponent of modernity, so I told him I wanted to study the arts of poetry and language to complement my study of English literature. He allocated an hour each week for me, and I met him at the mosque, where we'd sit in the open courtyard or in his office crowded with papers and books, an oud hung on the wall beside his cloak and cane.

All that remains of the historic site is its famous minaret, one of the few remaining elements of Islamic architecture found in Baghdad. The renowned architect Mohamed Makiya undertook the mosque's reconstruction in keeping with its historic specifications. The mosque is located beside al-Ghazel market, which specializes in birds and pets, across from the Latin Church in the al-Shorja neighborhood. There were many bird breeders who gathered on the rooftops overlooking the mosque courtyard, a destination for men and women, Arabs and foreigners, to whom Sheikh Jalal al-Hanafi explained its history, relying on his rich knowledge of Baghdad's heritage. The mosque's many visitors made the open-minded Sheikh Jalal subject to mockery by the youth in al-Ghazel market, but he'd return it twofold with his quick wit and calm nerves, and his deep knowledge of local society with all its flaws.

Sheikh Jalal would begin his lessons by reviewing the poetic texts he'd asked me to arrange in various meters. He'd then explain elements of Koranic *tajwid* recitation and would focus on phonetics, including the lengthening, shortening, or assimilation of consonants or vowels. Sometimes our discussion would lead us to other matters, such as his complaints of harassment from his extremist colleagues. Often, he'd ask me to wait until he'd finished reading the newspaper, without thought for the specific time frame in which I was to be absent from work. The sheikh had no concrete relation to time, which he saw as elastic and fluid, always amenable to delay. At times, he'd cover his mouth and laugh as he read the complex meters I'd used, such as the *mujtath*. Surprised, I'd ask why he was laughing, and he'd say, "By God, I didn't imagine you'd be able to compose with this complicated meter." He chose Taha Hussein's book *The Days* to train me in pronunciation, and our discussion would turn to the beauty and eloquence of Taha Hussein's prose. He'd fall silent for a moment and then say, "You are a master." He always addressed me thus.

I spent a year studying with Sheikh Jalal, during which I heard him state many wonderful things. I also witnessed his firm positions and bold decisions concerning Islamic legal opinions when he did not find them humane. Sheikh Jalal wrote a Chinese-Arabic dictionary; his love for China led him to give his children Chinese names, and he spoke to them in Chinese.

My Relationship with the Visual Arts

Although I do not excel practically in any form of visual arts, I am deeply affected by artistic works. When it was decided that we'd move from our home in Alwaziya to my grandmother's home in al-Sa'adoun, my mother had to get rid of some of our furniture and other possessions, first of all my father's library, which a bookseller in al-Sarray market purchased. He had two large and beautiful bookcases fashioned from teak with inlaid glass doors.

My mother kept one for us and got rid of the other. Before the bookseller came to see it, I snuck in and opened them, a little girl with no experience and at a loss as to what to choose. I stood before massive volumes with yellowing pages and books in foreign languages, many of which used Arabic script. Without any specific direction, I felt drawn to old books and their smell, and so selected a few randomly. But the books I chose based on their content were art books whose prints I was taken by. My father loved the arts, and our house was filled with his own pencil drawings, as well as paintings, some of which were European and others by Iraqi artists, and which we took with us. My father loved painting as much as he did music and playing the canun, and he made beautiful ink sketches, only one of which has survived, a sketch of the Carmelite church where the priest held his regular meetings. I still have it. My father wrote on it in French, "Eglise De la Commission des Piers Caramels" and signed it in 1926.

During my first trip to Europe in 1968, Issam El-Said accompanied me to the museums in London, and I visited other museums when I traveled by bus from London to Paris. I stood in admiration before great works, facing the dramatic sensibility in the paintings of Caravaggio, the sensuality of Rubens, and the perfection of David's paintings celebrating Napoleon, or his imagery in the *Death of Marat*. My blood rushed as I encountered Delacroix, and I was enchanted by the school of Impressionism.

As for my understanding of art, it deepened through my varied and interconnected readings when I realized there's a deep and shared relation between all the arts. Early on, I did not possess great knowledge of the modern art movement in Iraq; my knowledge was originally limited to the leading foundational names, due to their relation to the modern poetry movement. My serious contact with artistic culture came only through my intense readings later on.

Perhaps my first entrance into Iraq's modern art movement, one that entranced me, was the exhibition of Shaker Hassan Al Said titled *Routes of Ascent* held at the National Museum of Modern Art in 1969. I was taken by the abstract compositions exhibited, without asking why or what they were. In them I encountered an astonishing spiritual experience of ink drawings and watercolors, mainly in white, blue, and black. Shaker approached me there and introduced himself, and I was astonished when he called me by name, for I had not published much and did not make many public appearances. He accompanied me through the exhibition, answering all my questions, which somehow made it all the more mysterious. It was a marvelous experience, like falling into the threads of a poem without knowing how. I left the exhibition exhilarated, fulfilled, and with many questions.

As for my serious immersion in the world of art, it began in 1970, when I was in Beirut and Adonis asked me to get to know the New Vision group, and to visit their exhibition to be held at the start of the following year. I questioned how I could do that when my knowledge of art didn't permit me to undertake such an endeavor. He raised his hands and said, "I don't know. I believe you're capable and that it will enrich your poetic experience. I'll wait to read what you write." This was another time I faced a challenge that I had to overcome. When I returned to Baghdad, I spoke with Najib Al-Mani' about it, and he said, "That's the perfect decision. You have my library available to you to prepare yourself for this beautiful project. You're capable of it."

I spent a few months intensely reading about visual arts and the development of their movements across the world, which was not an unusual thing for me to do. It helped me to also follow the critical articles published weekly in the cultural supplement of the British *Times* and *Guardian* newspapers; they were my guide in how to look at and treat the material. As for the articles published in Iraqi newspapers on art exhibitions, I found them mere standard essays in typically vague language, with the exception of the writings of Jabra Ibrahim Jabra and Sa'adoun Fadhel, which were close to what I read in English in terms of language and approach.

In early 1971, the New Vision group held its first exhibition at the National Museum of Modern Art (Gulbenkian), and I held an interview with Dia al-Azzawi and sent it to *Mawaqif* (Positions) journal on the request of Adonis, and it was published immediately. Decades later Dia surprised me by including it in his book *Color Seeking Vision*, published by Touch Art Publications in London. It was then republished as a document from the early 1970s in the comprehensive 2016 book published by Mathaf: Arab Museum of Modern Art on Dia's vast experience over sixty years, and which accompanied his select retrospective exhibition in Qatar.

As my marriage with Rafa settled down and I continued to publish art articles of my choice, my following of art ran parallel to my literary production of poetry, stories, and translation, becoming studies that I contributed to conferences or were published as chapters in art books. Perhaps the most prominent of these was a chapter included in *Iraq: Its History, People, and Politics* (2002) edited by Shams Inati. My chapter is an introduction to the history of the visual arts movement in Iraq, including its roots and development. The book's cover was Jewad Selim's painting *The Musicians*.

I continued to write regularly in these fields, perhaps reaching a peak in the last few years after Rafa entrusted me with his artistic and literary legacy, and the scope and responsibility of my writing grew exponentially. But as I recall the past and all the efforts I made, I get a lump in my throat, for I can see that time slipped away without my grasping hold of it, and that I gave to others much more than I gave to myself.

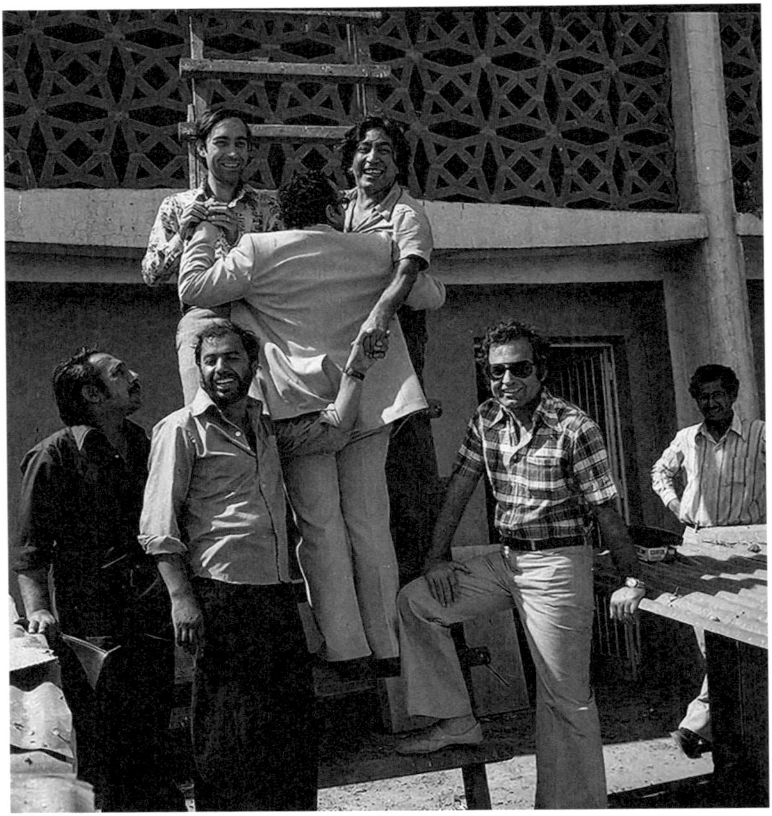

Mohammed Muhreddin,
Jassim Al Zubaidi,
Ali Taleb, Nizar Selim,
Ismail Fatah Al Turk,
and Rafa Nasiri,
Museum of Modern Art
(Gulbenkian), Baghdad,
1973

1 Mahmoud Said al-Basri, an Ottoman cavalry officer, joined the Arab revolution upon the establishment of the Iraqi state. He died at the age of forty during a 1924 military cavalry show in which a horse struck him in the head. He had defected from the Ottoman army and joined his family in a perilous journey from Turkey to Iraq, and due to his great enthusiasm for the revolution suffixed his name with "al-Basri," meaning "of Basra."

2 Bahaa al-Din al-Sheikh Nuri (1901–1960), staff brigadier (lieutenant general), was a cofounder of the military academy in Iraq and then followed a civilian route, being appointed governor of al-Suleimania, then a minister, and finally an ambassador.

3 The al-Khalidi family is descended from Mawlana Khalid, the founder of a Naqshbandi Sufi order. They migrated from the Arabian peninsula and settled in northern Iraq, integrating with the Kurds and speaking Arabic, Kurdish, and Turkmen, yet taking pride in their Arab identity. From Abdel 'Aun al-Rawdan, *Mawsu'at 'asha'ir al-'iraq* (Encylopedia of Iraq's familial clans), vol. 1 (Amman: al-Maktaba al-Ahaliya, 2003), p. 244.

4 New films were announced with a sign carried through the streets of Baghdad and bearing the name of the film and cinema. To the beat of drums, it was announced over loudspeaker, "Today, we are opening the film . . ."

5 In the second half of the 1920s, the English opened a social club in the Alwiyah neighborhood of Baghdad called the Alwiyah Club. It was mixed-gender, and exclusive to English families, while membership was also permitted for foreign communities affiliated with embassies, as well as Iraqi government employees with high salaries. Later membership was further opened to those who had been vouched for by two club members. The club remained conservative with regard to its traditions and bylaws, even after the English departed and Iraqis took over its management. It was the first mixed-gender club, preceding the al-Mansour Club in 1951. According to *The New Babylon* by Desmond Stewart and John Haylock, there was a bar on al-Rashid Street that was exclusively for the English and had Christian staff. Baghdad mainly had male-only social clubs, while there were some mixed-gender Christian clubs such as the Mashriq Club. In Basra, the English opened the Oil Company Club, al-Fayha' Club, and the Port Club. There were also clubs in Kirkuk that belonged to the oil company.

6 After graduating, Abdullah Habba moved to Moscow and completed his studies in literature. He did not return to Iraq as far as I know. He has closely followed the developments of the art movements and is among the few Iraqi academics who excel in art criticism, combining academic method with an artistic reading.

7 In my second year of university study, I selected a text from Shakespeare's *Romeo and Juliet*, and the following year I selected a poem by Elizabeth Barrett Browning.

8 The library was ultimately lost when our friend unfortunately passed away.

9 He was Dr. Mustafa Rajab, who earned a PhD in international law in Switzerland. He was renowned worldwide in the field of insurance, and within a few years made the company a model institution comparable to any in Europe. It was well organized, and the employees, whom he carefully selected and whose capacities he always strove to build, were highly proficient.

10 Also known as the Ramadan Revolution.

11 Al-Magzoub's letters were clever pieces of literature resembling the Arabic genre *maqamat*. He would carry on most freely, cursing whom he pleased and praising whom he pleased, in a beautiful and unusual handwriting of African style. It's incredibly sad that they were lost with many other papers I wasn't able to retrieve from our Baghdad home. I had photocopied the letters and sent them to Dr. Salma Khadra Jayyusi, who had requested them as she prepared a book about him, but I did not hear news of them again.

The First Ten Years

My life changed drastically after Rafa and I settled down together; it was turned head over heels. Prior to living with Rafa, my day followed a largely organized schedule, starting at 8 a.m. when I arrived at my office in the reinsurance company. I'd work with focus until 2 p.m., a continuous span regularly interspersed with chats with Anan. She'd been moved to the desk beside mine after an official order barred women from occupying the office adjacent to the general director. She maintained her position nonetheless due to the director's dependence on her organizational skills and trustworthiness. In contrast, my new life included a nightly program that did not end before 2 a.m., if it didn't extend until dawn.

Rafa's day at the Institute of Fine Arts began at 11 a.m., and my work schedule started at 8 a.m. We needed at least twenty minutes to traverse the distance from al-Qadissya to al-Karkh to al-Sa'adoun Street in al-Rasafa. I no longer suffered merely from daily tardiness, which I was held accountable for, but also lack of sleep and exhaustion. Even if we didn't have visitors or accept an invitation out, Rafa would spend the evening hours painting until late at night. When I'd wake him in the morning, he'd linger a bit and then get up calmly, obediently, and with a smiling face, always with a smiling face. I never saw him frown or get up in arms, unless an event in Iraq upset him, or an incident with a friend or relative irritated or hurt him. After preparing to leave, he'd have a cigarette and a large cup of concentrated black coffee. He'd take a quick but contemplative look at the work he'd completed the night before and might ask for my opinion or remain silent if he wasn't satisfied with the result. He'd drive without speaking, then casually state as we reached the bridge, "I'm still asleep and a radar is guiding me along the way." In the second year of our marriage, his work hours changed to match mine, and his lectures began at nine or sometimes eight. In later years, he began rising early and came to love doing so in order to enjoy the morning light he adored.

At exactly two in the afternoon, I'd leave work and find him waiting for me. He was never late. We'd go to my mother's house, which was nearby, to have lunch, and then he'd leave us to take a siesta in my room, which remained just as I'd left it. Throughout our life together, Rafa never forfeited his siesta except on very rare occasions. This arrangement saved me from preparing food, which I was not at all good at at the time, and also allowed me to visit my mother, who I needed to check in on every day.

We were extremely happy and comfortable living in our cottage, until winter arrived and we experienced problems with the roof of the

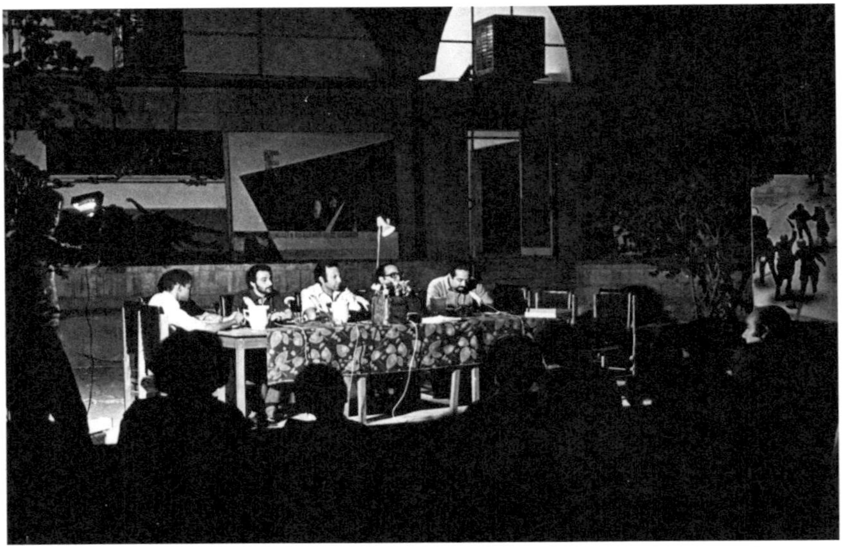

At the Arab Artists Union Conference, Baghdad, 1974. Left to right: Yahya Alsheikh, Rafa Nasiri, Nizar Selim, Mohamed Chebaa

annexed area. When it rained, it became apparent the roof had gaps allowing water to flow into the center of our home. We'd rush to place containers to catch it, feeling cold, but not able to do anything other than monitor it and laugh at our situation. We again turned to our friend Mekki Hussein to fix the roof, and with his experience he soon set it right.

Despite the small space, our life in the cottage was comfortable and intimate. We'd welcome friends in limited numbers appropriate for its size and number of chairs. Each evening would linger on with the rich and intimate conversations held. My hosting was limited to light foods my mother prepared, and which I'd heat up in the small electric oven, or we'd all go out to eat delicious kebab.

It so happened that in 1974, the First Biennale of Arab Art was held and attended by a large number of leading Arab artists and art critics, and critical symposia were held on its sidelines. Following one symposium, a number of friends suggested coming to see Rafa's latest work, and their number was appropriate for the space in the cottage. Then we were taken by surprise when Ismail Fattah also came, accompanied by a number of other guests. The cottage was filled beyond capacity and they made do wherever they found space, some sitting on the floor. Rafa offered drinks, and I prepared what I could of traditional mezze, but the night went on and the conversations lingered. I wasn't prepared for such a gathering in our home, and at a loss, I found no option other than preparing plates of sausages and eggs, which they devoured.

Salzburg: The First Test

Three months after we settled into our cottage in 1974, Rafa told me, with some indifference, about an invitation that had come to the institute for graphic artists to join the printmaking course at the Summer Academy of Salzburg. He seemed reluctant as he had no knowledge of this institution, and the costs of travel and accommodation were the responsibility of participants. I screamed in delight when I heard the name Salzburg: "This is a dream I never imagined would be within reach!" In astonishment, Rafa asked if I knew it, and I replied, "It's the city of Mozart and his annual festivals performed by the top musicians, ask Dr. Ghanem about it, it has so enriched my imagination with its enchanting atmosphere."

My cousins Ghanem and Hani had one of the largest classical music and opera libraries in Baghdad. Together with a group of doctors and intellectuals, they organized regular sessions for listening to classical music and to foster musical appreciation. As part of each listening session, a lecture would be given on the selected piece by one of the knowledgeable participants. It was a continuation of an initiative started by a group of medical school students who loved to play and listen to music.[1] Salzburg, to Dr. Ghanem, was the site of a pilgrimage he made sure to include in his annual holiday, in order to attend concerts he'd reserve tickets for months in advance.

Rafa was filled with excitement, and we discussed the trip's costs to see how to make it possible and take advantage of this lovely opportunity. He immediately obtained the required forms and sent them off to reserve a workplace and arrange appropriate housing. We suggested to Dia al-Azzawi and Saleh al-Jumaie that they participate, and they were enthusiastic about joining us. At the time, Dia was an employee in the department of antiquities, and worked at the Mosul museum. He wasn't able to obtain vacation time that July, but Saleh al-Jumaie did join us.

En route to Austria, we first stopped in Beirut at the invitation of my maternal aunt, who'd been living in Amman since 1958. She hosted us with her for two days in the Riviera Hotel and was eager to meet the man I'd chosen as my husband. She was a society lady who was committed in her lifestyle to custom and tradition. She'd been incredibly concerned with her appearance and behavior since her youth and became all the more attached to it following her marriage. Before departing from Baghdad's al-Muthana airport, Rafa met a relative who asked him to look after two young female relatives on the same flight, and to ensure their accommodation for a night in our hotel. The two girls became Rafa's responsibility and sole concern. In the hotel lobby I saw my aunt and mother getting up to greet us, but as Rafa was focused on his "big mission," he completely disregarded them. I brought them to his attention, and he greeted them coldly and walked on to the reception desk. I could see the shock on my aunt's face and embarrassment on my mother's and tried to lighten the situation while Rafa busied himself with the reception staff to arrange a room during the crowded summer season. He only took a breath once he'd guaranteed a place for the girls to stay.

Rafa was wearing his favorite outfit, a white short-sleeve shirt, tight white pants fitted over his slim figure, and white canvas shoes with no socks. His appearance was odd and unfamiliar to my aunt, not to mention his cold greeting. She looked at him from afar and said,

"So this is who May chose!" My mother defended him with all she held in her heart of admiration, respect, and love from the few months she'd known him. But Rafa always realized his mistakes and made up for them afterward, and during the lunch outing my aunt arranged for us at Yildizlar restaurant in Raouché, he turned the situation around. He spoke with her sweetly, smiling and conversing about the mutual places they'd visited and their trips in Europe to Rome, Paris, and various museums, until he'd gained my aunt's heart and made her forget his earlier behavior.

After getting to know her better in subsequent years, Rafa grew to greatly admire her strong personality, her polite yet open-minded sociability, and her orderly and elegant lifestyle. In 1978, when she hosted us in her very small rented apartment in the Shmesani area of Amman, Rafa said to me, "Everything in this house speaks of beauty and tradition." At the time we were on our way to the Scandinavian countries, and stayed in her apartment consisting of one bedroom and a living room, in which she displayed what had been salvaged of the treasures she'd owned, including an old china set and a painting by Faiq Hassan from the early 1950s (which was later sold to the Jordan National Gallery of Fine Arts after my aunt passed away).

Our journey began in Vienna, and it was a wonderful beginning. I marveled at the city with its eminent, stately buildings, and we spent two comfortable nights in a small and extremely elegant pension. Our mutual satisfaction in our choice of accommodation was a source of delight for us, as was our mutual love of what we saw, and our shared astonishment in the beauty surrounding us in this enchanting corner of the world. Everything was elegant in Vienna, both in general appearances and their smallest details.

Our previous trip to Mosul had been a lesson in how to look at things, and my visual intelligence sharpened. Rafa's eyes caught beauty far and near; he observed the world with a loving eye and was halted by the smallest and grandest of scenes, whether natural or architectural. We'd walk long distances and get tired, and then find even greater pleasure in sitting on a public bench as we observed people coming and going: a beautiful woman, an enchanting child, bountiful almond and pine trees, fields of flowers, the harmony of the streets and elegant shopfronts. And soon his mouth would dry, and he'd whisper, "I need coffee."

On our second morning in Vienna, we took a short group tour to Grinzing, a wine town. By chance there was a group of young Chinese men and women on our bus, in the seat in front of us. Rafa's face lit up, and with a touch of self-consciousness he whispered to me happily, "I'll try speaking with them in Chinese." After a moment of hesitation, he greeted them with, "Ni hao." In surprise, they turned around to return the greeting, and check that they'd indeed heard someone speak their language.

Like him, they spoke Mandarin, and they chatted until we arrived at our destination. I could see his delight as he drew out the conversation, their amazement growing. I didn't know what they were saying, but there were many exclamations of astonishment and admiration, and they turned to me smiling. His face brimming with joy, he told me, "The language is slowly coming back to me."

On the train to Salzburg our eyes were bathed with stunning scenes of forests and mountains, all the way to the small and enchanting city. We went to a motel at the city's edge, put down our bags, and rushed right off to the bus taking us into the city center. In ten minutes, we were in the heart of Salzburg, which advised tourists to leave their cars behind and tour on foot. Standing there in the old city's main square lined with Baroque buildings had a magic of its own.

Rafa was eager to see the academy and register his attendance, so we walked to the cable car station shaded by trees. Its cars departed regularly every fifteen minutes, transporting people to the old mountaintop fortress dating to the eleventh century. Now the Hohensalzburg Fortress was prepared to welcome students of the Summer Academy established by Austrian artist Oskar Kokoschka. The academy offered training in painting, sculpture, graphic art, architecture, photography, and jewelry making during the month that coincided with the Mozart music festival, held annually since 1920. Rafa's face was filled with delight when he found himself in the printmaking studio.

We were greeted by the German professor supervising the course, Otto Eglau, one of the most renowned printmakers in Berlin. He was in his mid-sixties, had a plump figure and incredible energy, and was cheery. His face was framed by a small white beard. He welcomed us happily, saying this was the first time an Iraqi artist had attended the school. He was surprised to learn that Rafa had studied printmaking in China, and later in Portugal. We also met his assistant Wolfgang, also from Berlin, and they both became our close friends.

We walked around the fortress and by now it was lunchtime, and some of the students and teachers were having lunch in the restaurant. In the outer courtyard young men and women relaxed on the grass, enjoying the sunshine shot through with drafts of cold. Rafa turned to me in delight, proclaiming, "Oh, and now I've guaranteed my siesta too!" He was energetic and fidgety, eager to start work immediately now that he'd found an opportunity to return to printmaking, and in such a splendid professional setting, following a five-year hiatus. He made his favorite statement, one he repeated throughout his life to express a strong urge to work: "I want to attack." Yet, his schedule was to begin the following day.

We spent the rest of the day walking around the city and exploring its beautiful sites. I was provoked by the many signs everywhere for the Mozart Festival starting in a few days. All along the streets I saw pictures of the famous conductors and opera stars I'd known for years from the humble collection of records I owned. I'd gasp with each name that appeared before me: Herbert von Karajan, Rita Streich, Riccardo Mutti, Claudio Abbado, and others. Would I really be able to see them in person, given the expensive price of tickets and the seats being long reserved in advance? Rafa squeezed my hand to reassure me.

During our walk we came across a small, incredibly beautiful theater, and discovered it was the marionette theater, which performed Mozart operas to the finest Deutsch Gramophone recordings daily. We were charmed by the space with its comfortable chairs, beautiful décor, and reasonable prices, and decided to attend *The Magic Flute* that night.

Rafa rose early the next morning, a bit nervous about making a new start, and made his way to the fortress to start work at 9 a.m., continuing until seven in the evening. I thus found myself facing a long stretch of hours to spend alone in the small city, with time crawling by incredibly slowly. We agreed I'd visit him in the studio whenever I felt discontented or lonely, but I held myself back from doing so until he asked me to have lunch and see what he'd accomplished. I found that everything in Salzburg was in German: bookshops, film screenings, plays, and newspapers. Music was the only common language.

In Vienna, I'd purchased two books by the English novelist Margaret Drabble, who I hadn't heard of before,[2] intrigued after I read in her short biography that she was of my generation. I was taken by her smooth literary style and sincere revelations. In this novel she wrote of a contemporary experience: how the liberalization of conservative English society amid the late 1960s economic and social changes affected a woman caught up in the West's transformations. I felt close ties connecting us, from our age to a heightened sense of dignity. I pleasurably spent my free hours absorbed in her work as I sat beside the Salzach, my ears filled with the murmuring of its flowing waters.

Sunday was a holiday and I'd spend it with Rafa. I'd take him back to the places I'd been, showing him what I'd discovered and experienced. We'd pass by the ticket centers to no avail, drink coffee in the open air, and have lunch in one of the many traditional German-style taverns consisting of old cupolas serving fine wine and draft beer alongside simple meals served on long shared tables. Whenever Rafa found a young man and woman sitting beside us, he'd whisper, "I'll draw a portrait of this pretty woman." He'd search around him for paper, sometimes requesting it from the tavern owner, or drawing on the napkin if nothing was available. The woman would be surprised by her portrait and express her delight with it, and we'd get to know them and exchange toasts. But at the end of the third week, Rafa told me he needed extra time to complete his work, thus depriving me of my weekly pleasure.

I began spending part of my days waiting in long lines in hopes of obtaining returned tickets for the concerts. There was very little chance of doing so, but it was not unheard of, and in this way I met students and lovers of music who'd come from around the world with their backpacks for an opportunity to attend a concert, and we'd talk about their experiences and studies. Many of them managed to get a ticket, and sometimes I, too, would get one, but only one, so I'd give it up to someone else.

The first ten days passed with great difficulty. Rafa would leave at nine in the morning and not finish until seven at night, exhausted from the effort he'd exerted, but to a large degree pleased. I'd meet him at the cable car station in the large square and he'd briefly tell me what he'd produced, insisting I go see it and have lunch with him. Then his face would light up as he spotted the frankfurter vendor, and he'd rush over for its delicious meal with biting mustard. He'd drape his arm around my shoulder and we'd walk through the streets, whose details and shopfronts I'd memorized like the back of my hand. He'd ask about my day and I'd tell him every little detail, whom I'd met, where I'd gone, and whom I'd spoken with. I don't know if he really listened, as soon enough he'd stop in his tracks when something caught his attention, capturing it with his trusty camera.

Two weeks after our arrival, Dr. Ghanem al-Saffar arrived, for he'd reserved tickets for two concerts in Salzburg. I awoke cheerfully that morning knowing I'd have a companion. The age difference between us was great, and I treated him with respect and reserve that I only shed years later. I picked him up at his hotel and we went together to the fortress. This was my third visit to the studio; the first had been when Rafa completed his first work, and the second had been a week later when he invited me to lunch. Rafa welcomed us, pleased to meet

Ghanem, and showed us what he'd accomplished. He introduced Ghanem to his supervisors as one of the top specialists of internal medicine and cardiology in Iraq. We spent about an hour there and walked around together, and then we left Rafa to continue his work and returned to the city, with plans to have dinner with him at nine. I spent two full days with Ghanem, who shared his vast knowledge of music and entertaining accounts of the city, the festival, and Mozart's work with me. Ghanem al-Saffar, as a doctor and as a person, was rich in knowledge and culture. Our two days together inspired me to write articles on the city, fortress, and festival that I sent to the culture page of *Gumhuriya* (Republic) newspaper, and which were published as a series.

The outcomes of Rafa's artistic practice that summer were outstanding and gained the admiration of the supervisors and other students, whether with regard to the composition and colors of his prints, or his very approach to the art of printmaking. He'd studied in 1968 in the Paris studio of Stanley William Hayter and adopted a method using a roller. Eglau asked him to demonstrate his method to the trainees, and called him master, "Maître." His output for the season was six prints of extreme beauty and precision.

From the very start Rafa had become friends with Eglau and Wolfgang, and we'd all meet after the end of their day in the Tomaselli café, which was Eglau's favorite café in the square just beneath the mountain in the heart of the city, at the crossroad leading to the opera. They'd exchange both serious and light-hearted commentary on what Rafa had accomplished, and there was always discussion of his technique and brilliant use of color. Eglau would typically choose names for Rafa's finished works in accordance with their color, and once suggested the name Tomaselli for a print in which brown was dominant.

It was from this café that we witnessed the opening of the Mozart Festival a few days after our arrival. At sunset, before the city's electric lights turned on, candles were lit outside the windows of the buildings around us and alongside the flower beds in all the alleys and streets, the candlelight dancing to the famous tune of *Eine kleine Nachtmusik*. The people of Salzburg and its visitors all came out, gathering in the streets and squares to celebrate the opening of the city's largest tourist season. It's ironic that Mozart, a son of this city, died penniless at a young age while his city has continued to profit from the glory of the works his genius produced.

It was also from this café that we watched people on their way to the opera in their formal suits and splendid dresses. Exuberantly Eglau exclaimed, “This right here is the true opera performance!” He hated constricting himself in official attire, but his wife insisted he accompany her to all the performances. It remained nearly impossible to obtain tickets, and I practically lost my mind at the idea of leaving Salzburg without ever getting a seat. Then the opportunity came that I did not expect. On one of my visits to the studio, Wolfgang whispered to me, asking to keep it our secret, “I’ll give you my opera ticket.” The studio supervisors were given tickets each season, and Wolfgang told me that, like Eglau, he didn’t like wearing full official attire or feeling restricted in a formal atmosphere. Unfortunately, it was only one ticket, but thus my dream came true, and I attended *The Marriage of Figaro* conducted by Herbert von Karajan.

That day, Rafa accompanied me to the opera house, pleased with my delight. He regretted he hadn’t been able to obtain a ticket for himself but was intoxicated with the success of his artistic work and the admiration of the other students, and especially their supervisors. I sat beside a young man who rushed to become acquainted with me, thinking I was on the teaching staff since the seats were allocated for academy instructors. Embarrassed, I sufficed with a vague response. He was an architect supervising the architecture department at the Summer Academy.

I’d been to a few opera houses before, the most memorable of which were the Royal Opera House in London’s Covent Garden and the Palais Garnier in Paris and was impressed with Salzburg’s recently constructed opera house. Yet, the architect beside me gestured toward it in objection, saying, “I’m shocked. How could they build an opera house today in this worn-out classic style?” I was taken aback and asked him, “Don’t you think it’s attractive?” to which he replied, “It’s backward.” He went on to explain his opinion with a quick relay of comments, while I insinuated that I understood and agreed. I recognized his intent as similar to modern Iraqi artists’ harsh critique of works they found lacking in innovation and modernity.

The performance commenced with the entrance of Herbert von Karajan, who, with his slender figure, black attire, and silver hair, crossed the stage proudly to the thunderous applause of the audience. With a commanding presence, he stood before the musicians and raised his baton, and the musicians readied themselves to fill the hall with music. I shuddered deep within and teared up at this opening; that’s how I am when I attend an awe-inspiring event. When the performance ended, I found Rafa at the door and gleefully embraced him, enthusiastically telling him all about the opera hall, performance, and Karajan's stage entrance, as well as my embarrassment and ignorance before the young Dutch architect.

One of the most delightful coincidences that summer was a concert we attended on the festival sidelines in which renowned Iraqi oud player Munir Bashir and his Baghdad group performed a segment of Iraqi *maqams* accompanied by Sha'oubi Ibrahim, the famed *joza* (spike fiddle) player, and Hashim al-Rajab, the *santur* (hammered dulcimer) player. At the start of the concert, Munir Bashir played an oud duet with the German pianist Friedrich Gulda. Saleh al-Jumaie attended with us, and it was a lovely surprise for the Iraqi musicians when Rafa called out, "Sha'oubi!" who looked around before happily realizing who'd called out his name.

Rafa returned from this trip elated, and indeed victorious, carrying beneath his arm a protective portfolio we'd bought to hold the prints he'd produced that month. He was eager to participate in the 1975 session and was later extended a personal invitation. This time, I preferred not to repeat the experience, especially as he'd be in the company of Dia and Saleh. I suggested we travel to Istanbul with my mother and spend a few days together, after which he could take the train alone to Salzburg. It was our first extended separation, and we exchanged nearly daily letters as the best way to share our experiences.

I missed his company in my many walks around Istanbul and visits to its Islamic heritage sites and art venues, and we made up for it decades later. All the same, it was lighter on my heart than the cruelty of spending long hours alone in Salzburg.

Life and Work

For over two years, I was at a loss as to how to schedule my time and adjust to my new living situation. The change of place and the transformation of my life, and perhaps the excessive exhilaration I felt, all unsettled me. Everything was different, and I felt I'd lost touch with myself and no longer knew what I wanted to do or say. My morning job required great effort, and my work responsibilities took up a lot of my mental and emotional energy. I had to keep on top of administrative work that demanded an alert mind, careful review, and the use of special terminology. I was editing an insurance periodical under the supervision of the general director and the periodical's chief editor, and it required me to collect a great amount of information and many translations.

There was a sharp division between the atmosphere of my morning work, which I was in dire need of, and my evening literary activities, which led me to live a split life. After transitioning to married life this gap grew even larger as new responsibilities surfaced, and with my new lifestyle, creative work became the first victim to fall by the wayside. This alarmed me and drove me to focus on intense readings. I scheduled my life in a manner assuring that my home duties would be fulfilled, and these were not many thanks to my mother. Otherwise, I dedicated my time to filling gaps in my knowledge and taking advantage of the hours in which Rafa was fully immersed in painting. I set aside at least five hours for continuous reading, distributed between literature and visual arts, with an hour each morning in my office devoted to classical Arabic poetry, as a continuation of my usual practice. I remember once a high-ranking Swiss visitor came into my office with the general director, who was introducing him to the different departments, and noticed a book with a decorative cover on my desk. With curiosity he asked what I was reading, and when I told him classical Arabic poetry, he turned in astonishment to the general director, who seemed embarrassed and cried in objection, "Poetry!"

When our financial circumstances improved somewhat, I decided to leave my job. I'd completed the years of service qualifying me for early retirement and guaranteeing a monthly pension. It wasn't easy to do at the time, but I succeeded in retiring during the fall of 1979, and thus gained ownership of extended hours of freedom that I had to firmly take control of. I'm indebted to the institution that taught me organizational skills and the respect of time.

With a horrifying sense that my abilities to express myself had been fully paralyzed, I began reviewing what I'd written in the previous years and was shocked. "Was it truly me who wrote this?" I asked myself. "Is it true what's said about marriage killing the creative abilities of women?" I was sitting alone one evening, surrounded by my papers, when I took my head in my hands and hit it against the wall in hopes that I'd again brim with creative energy. I went over what I'd written and published, and the creative projects my reading had prepared me for, such as finding parallels between literature and art, an endeavor I don't believe anyone before me had embarked on in Iraq in the early 1970s. How could I move past this period of disorientation, and how could I justify it to Rafa, who had great faith in my abilities? Every time I grasped a pen I felt utter hollowness, and fearing the waste of time without productivity, I'd resort to reading.

In the evening Rafa would paint with a voracious appetite for work, and my frustration would compound as I saw him bent over a canvas using a brush, his hand, a rag, a knife, anything that would allow him to catch up with the visions overflowing his imagination, output that might be intentional or coincidental. He worked quickly, as required by fast-drying acrylic paint, and did not speak, or allow speaking or moving around, let alone stolen glances. Yet we'd share the space, brought together by the sound of music selected from my library. He'd spread his work on the available floor space between the writing table and the printing press. I'd sit a few feet away on the sofa between the two bookcases/barriers. He wouldn't allow me to look or comment until he gave permission, or I heard him take a deep breath announcing the completion of the work, or a stage of it, at which point he'd grant me a green light. His anxiety persisted until his vision had materialized and he signed the work, finally freed of his tension.

In silence and satisfaction, I observed his gradual transition from the firm lines that had dominated his compositions following the New Vision group's first exhibition, to a liberation from these lines, as he moved toward endless spaces grounded by a base filled with symbols. I remained thrilled with the beautiful works he produced and grew all the more convinced that Rafa was a major talent, if I don't say exceptional. His talent complemented his solid academic establishment at Baghdad's Institute of Arts and then at the Central Academy of Fine Arts in Peking, followed by his training in Lisbon, thus bringing together East and West. Art, for Rafa, was a way of life in terms of practice and creativity, and he set nonnegotiable conditions for it.

One day, noticing sorrow and distraction in my eyes, he asked, "What's wrong?" I complained to him of my inability to write. He anxiously rushed to counter, "Am I the reason?" and I told him, "Perhaps the beautiful life I've found myself in has unsettled me." Rafa replied calmly, "You'll no doubt return to it. Don't be alarmed, all of us go through this stage." But at the end of every such discussion he'd blame me for hesitating to publish and withholding what I'd written. Our quarrels would sometimes develop into full-blown battles.

We were friends with the director of the French Cultural Center, Mr. Du Buvet, and his assistant Gerard, due to the center's prolific cultural activity and their great admiration for the sophisticated output of Iraqi artists. In the fall of 1975, they informed us that a leading art history professor would visit Baghdad upon his retirement, as part of a tour of Arab countries held in recognition of his academic efforts. As part of this tour, he would visit the studios of prominent

Iraqi artists, including Shaker Hassan Al Said, Dia al-Azzawi, Rafa Nasiri, and Mohamed Muhereddin. Due to his limited time, it was decided that he'd visit us to see the works of both Rafa and Dia.

Dia came over early that winter morning, carrying his works all wrapped up, and we sat waiting for the arrival of Mr. Du Buvet and professor Bernard Du Rival. We found an impressive-looking man with white hair walking tall into our modest cottage via the large garden leading to our private entrance, a look of pleasure and astonishment on his face. He commenced by praising the beauty of the place with its unique location amid the apple, apricot, mulberry, and palm trees.

Dia sat on the ground and laid out his works, one after the other. Rather than viewing them from a standing position, the professor knelt upon his knees to gaze closely at the attractive compositions in vivacious Eastern colors, shifting his focus between the beauty of their design and their elements drawn from ancient Iraq, Iraqi popular heritage, and handwritten Arabic texts. He expressed intense appreciation of their fiery colors and charming expressiveness. He looked at the works as though he were praying, leaning close to inspect a work and unabashedly commenting to himself, "Astonishing, brilliant . . ." After viewing the collection of works on canvas and paper, he leaned toward Dia and most respectfully grasped his hand in admiration.

It was with the same admiration and astonishment that he viewed Rafa's abstract compositions painted in acrylic on canvas, wood, or paper, and then moved on to Rafa's prints, contemplating their strong lines and poetic compositions, and expressing his admiration to Du Buvet. I stood nearby, following every expression on the serious, stern face of the experienced professor who'd spent thirty years in the lecture halls of Paris. He turned to me and said, "Votre mari a beaucoup de talent" (Your husband has great talent).

The professor only spoke French. With my limited proficiency, I took advantage of the opportunity to ask him questions on matters preoccupying me, sometimes assisted by Du Buvet. "I want to write professionally on visual arts, but I cannot paint," I told him. Smiling, he replied, "Neither can I, my dear. But grasping the applied aspects in all their details, as much as possible, is necessary for you to understand the artistic process." Then he gestured to Rafa and Dia and said, "Here you are, at the heart of the experience." Professor Du Rival's visit granted me my first professional lesson in art appreciation and exposed me to the modest behavior of a knowledgeable expert.

Another motivation to write emerged during that period when our friend Nadhim Ramzi suggested I work with him in preparing a series of art books about the pioneers of the modern art movement. Nadhim Ramzi was an artist and designer, and a pioneer of modern graphic design, which caused a shift in public taste and helped to elevate it. He was an important part of the modern art movement, a friend and professional colleague who'd offered his press to young artists starting in the 1960s. He'd collaborated with the younger generation and contributed his abstract paintings to one of the New Vision group's exhibitions in the 1970s.

At the time, it was not possible in Iraq to specialize academically in graphic design. Rafa and Mohamed Muhereddin had had training in it as part of their graphic arts studies in China and Poland, and had worked on poster art and design alongside printmaking. In the mid-1970s, artist Ali Taleb earned a master's degree in graphic design from Cairo. As for Dia, he included design as part of his artistic practice, and, starting in the 1960s, created beautiful book covers for poets such as Muzaffar al-Nawab, and also contributed to the design of invitations to art exhibitions. We began seeing attractive guides, posters, and invitations for art exhibitions designed by Dia, Rafa, and Ramzi. In addition to his captivating photography, Ramzi designed and printed the first book documenting the modern art movement in Iraq, published by the information ministry with a foreword by Jabra Ibrahim Jabra (1971). This was followed in 1974 with another book written by Jabra, *Jewad Selim and the Freedom Monument*.

Ramzi told me he'd commence the project with a yet-incomplete study on Faiq Hassan and aspired for the second book to be on Shaker Hassan Al Said. Upon consulting the artist on who should write this volume, Shaker chose me. I was overwhelmed with joy, but also daunted by the huge responsibility, for Shaker was not just any artist. I later told Rafa, "This project is too big for me," and he scoffed at my fears. His faith in me was the greatest responsibility I faced. It was 1975, and I was still working at my job.

I began reading all that Shaker had written, and reread what I'd previously read. The more I attempted to unravel mysterious statements scattered throughout his studies and articles, the more I was confused and questioned what he truly wanted to say. Upon close reading I noticed a somewhat nonlinear use of language, or rather that certain sentences did not seem to have been accurately delivered. Things that were unclear to me subsequently were made apparent when our relationship developed years later in Amman.

At the same time, I was also reading English sources, both theoretical studies and artistic analyses of artworks that bore similarities to

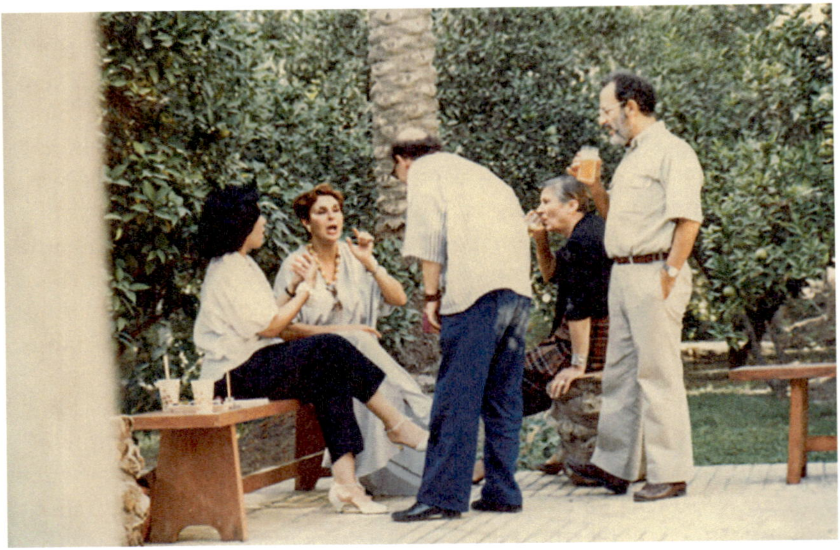

Nidal Al Achkar, Wijdan Maher, Helen Khal, Amin El Bacha, and Samir Sayegh, at Nuha al-Radi's house, Baghdad, 1986

those of Shaker, who at the time had begun a project tracing the effects of time on the environment as apparent on the walls of buildings. I didn't encounter the same obscurity here that I did in Shaker's own language, or that of those writing about him at the time. I requested an interview to learn directly about his experience, and benefited greatly from it, for it allowed me to follow his journey from his artistic beginnings and through the stages of his practice's developments and major transformations. A few months later I began writing the study and sent a draft to Shaker for his opinion and comments. He was pleased with it and said he'd always wished to be written about in such clear language. He always praised what I wrote, and asked in wonder, "How do you write so clearly?"

Unfortunately, new circumstances took place that unsettled Nadhim Ramzi and drove him to relocate his family to London and reestablish himself there. Although he was determined to complete the project in the future, as he told me, he postponed it to work on another of wider scope, which was publishing an Arab art journal. As for my study of Shaker, I left it behind in Baghdad with other papers and manuscripts, and it's remained only a draft until this day. But my involvement in this methodological work paved the way for me to make a new start.

Throughout our life together, Rafa loved the prose and poetry I wrote, and was always my first reader and critic. He selected verses from a poem I'd written to include in two beautiful drawings (ink on paper, 1972) that he gave to me after we married. It seems that during the "on-and-off" phase of our relationship, he produced another collection inspired by my poetry, for decades later I saw two similar pieces (watercolor on paper) in the Beirut home of our close friend, artist Nidal Al Achkar. She proudly said she'd purchased them at Rafa's Beirut exhibition, which I'd declined to attend.

In the first year of our marriage, I showed Rafa a long prose poem I'd written in 1972 titled "Is There a Space between Movement and Stillness?" He read it lovingly, and two days later surprised me with a small handmade art book (eighteen by thirty-two centimeters). This art book, with the poetry in his handwriting, was left behind in Baghdad, and I was sad to only receive it again after Rafa's passing away.

Every morning on my way to work, we'd make the trip from our house in al-Qadissya in al-Karkh to Bab al-Sharqi in al-Rasafa, passing over Tahrir Bridge. We began encountering a beautiful young woman crossing the bridge, walking in the opposite direction just before 8 a.m. each day. Her beautiful features and tasteful style caught my attention, and I asked Rafa if he'd noticed her, certain that an attractive woman would not escape his eye. He laughed loudly and cried, "How could such beauty escape me!" We began wondering where she went, what she worked in, and how she'd look that day. One day, Rafa turned to me and said, "I challenge you to write a story about her."

When placed before a challenge, I seek refuge in silence and avoid accepting or rejecting it, and yet it somehow remains within me until it's met in spite of myself. I didn't know anything about this girl other than what her appearance suggested to me, so what could I possibly say about her? Sometime later, I noticed that we no longer saw her, and both of us were perplexed. It preoccupied me, and I started wondering what had happened to her whenever we crossed the bridge. Then one evening, like a passing breeze, she appeared before me in her green dress and loose, flowing hair, as birds soared over the Tigris. I rushed to my notebook and wrote a story, recalling incidents from previous experiences as dictated by my imagination. I called it "The Bridge Friend," and when I showed it to Rafa his face filled with delight I'll never forget as he cried, "We'll publish it immediately!" He took it to *Afaq Arabiya* (Arab Horizons) journal, and it remained with the editor a long time before he apologized to Rafa, saying that May writes better stories.

Rafa came home disappointed and doubting himself, but I was confident in the story's literary value and knew this particular editor lacked good artistic judgment. So, I took it to the writers' union journal, and found it published in the next issue alongside many positive reviews. And thus, I returned to regularly writing stories and poetry.

Rafa's style of critique was gentle. When he didn't care for what he read, he'd remain silent. I'd ask him about it, and he'd say, "I'll reread it later, as it seems my mood's cloudy." Then I'd realize that something in the text, or perhaps the entire text, didn't appeal to him. I'd insist on hearing his opinion and he'd say, always questioning his statement, "I expected a stronger ending" or that he found my treatment of one scene or another longwinded, or overly direct. Or he might say, "You write stronger texts than this." He had a general tendency toward brevity, and abstract expression was an indivisible part of his nature, whether in speech or artistic work. And typically his opinion of what he read was related to his mood. When he showed me commentary or articles he'd written, I'd find that he skipped over details that needed to be included to complete the picture, whether with regard to artistic matters or general topics. He always assumed the reader, like himself, had full knowledge of the topic. When he began writing his memoir of China, I'd ask him where such-and-such incident happened, and he'd

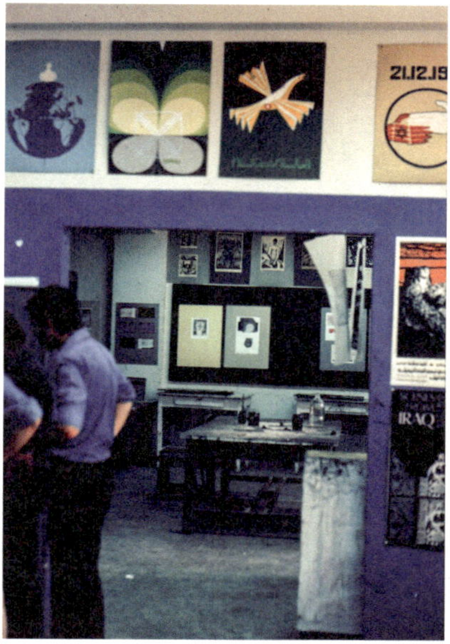

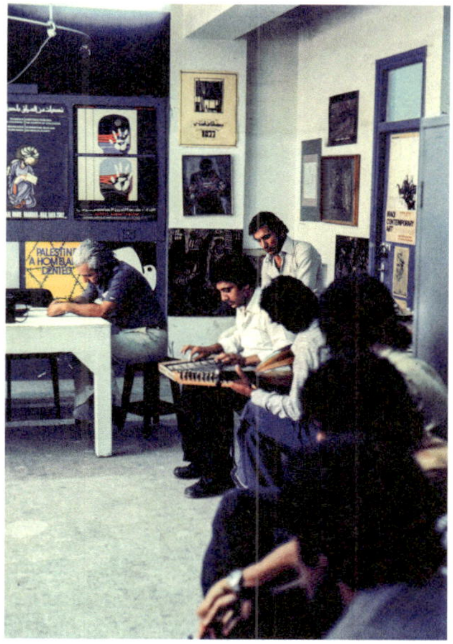

Institute of Fine Arts,
Baghdad, 1977

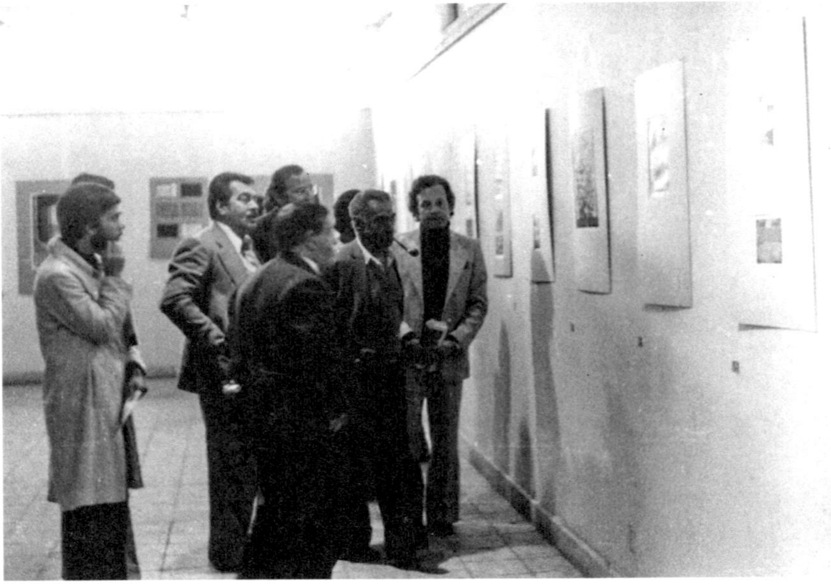

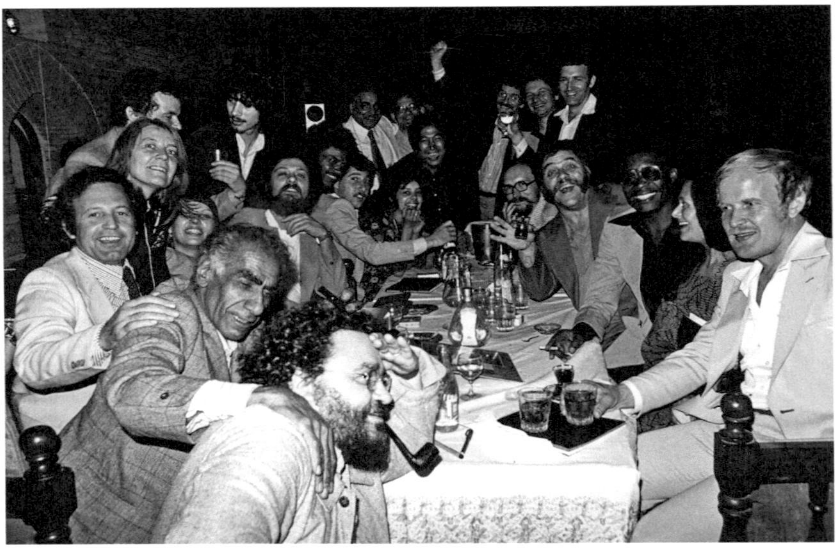

Top: Faeq Hassan inaugurates the first Graphic Arts Exhibition, Fine Arts Institute, Baghdad, 1978

Bottom: Event at Khan Murjan on the occasion of a conference by the International Association of Art (AIAP), Baghdad, 1979

ask if what he'd written wasn't sufficient. Then he'd return to the text and find that, as he worked, further details emerged from his memory, and he'd excitedly write with great enjoyment.

This early period of our life together was one of intense production for Rafa in painting and graphic art. He held a number of solo exhibitions in Kuwait, Baghdad, Casablanca, Amman, and Paris, and participated in many group exhibitions in Baghdad, Beirut, Paris, and London. He also organized Iraqi exhibitions and participated in artistic committees, which required him to travel often, sometimes for up to a month. During these trips he'd often write to me on a daily basis, until we arrived at another form of communication, which was keeping diaries of our days and activities as though discussing them together and exchanging them when we met in person. His diaries were supplemented with sketches and images that were alive with movement, as well as vital descriptions of scenes. They were artist's books par excellence.

I always believed that marital life needs occasional distance in order to kill routine and reinvigorate the relationship. I'd feel an emptiness when Rafa traveled, or in fact a sense of being lost. I'd move to my mother's house to be close to my workplace and my friends. Following every separation, Rafa would return brimming with talk and stories, his face overflowing with joy, and bearing the most unique and beautiful gifts.

Of course, our life together was not completely devoid of problems, or difficult situations each of us faced for the first time. News of our marriage was welcomed in cultural circles, and many of the people we knew, and also those we didn't, saw it as a perfect pairing, considering Rafa lucky in his choice and feeling I would be his best support. A few others had doubts, and perhaps even bet that our marriage would not last. Over the years, I faced positive situations, and as well as negative ones that bore no real value. As the years went by, our friendship grew, as did our need for each other, and we grew closer and more attached. Our compatibility and mutual tolerance became ever clearer. And thus, we came together and carried on together, differing only over small matters that might quickly lead to battles that in turn soon dissipated as though it they'd never taken place.

1 Dr. Ghanem al-Saffar was among Baghdad's most prominent specialists of internal medicine, a 1948 graduate of Baghdad's College of Medicine, and my paternal aunt's oldest son. Among others, these musical gatherings were spoken of by Dr. Khalid al-Qassab in his book *Dhikriyat fanniya* (Memories of art), published by Dar al-Hikma in London, and the economist and writer Mahmoud Ahmed Uthman in his book *Masabih wa dhalamat* (Lights and darkness), published by the Arab Institute for Research and Publishing in Beirut.

2 *The Needle's Eye* and *Jerusalem the Golden*.

3 Pages from some of these diaries were published in *Rafa Nasiri: Artist Books* (Milan: Skira Editore, 2017).

Travels 1977–1990

Planned Trips

With the establishment of Nerine Transportation in the late 1920s, and later Angurli Iraqi Transportation, well-off Iraqi families began traveling to summer resorts in Syria and Lebanon, where they'd rent accommodation for periods of up to three months. With further development of the economy, Iraqis' passion for travel became a real phenomenon in the 1970s, especially after the Iraqi Airways began offering incentives, including a 33 percent discount for government employees and the possibility of paying for tickets in installments. Travel agencies multiplied and began competing in their European packages covering travel to several countries, accommodation, and visits to important sites. Even the travel agency affiliated with the Soviet airline Aeroflot began organizing all-inclusive two-week trips to Moscow, Leningrad (Saint Petersburg), and Kyiv for the cost of eighty dinars, and their popularity raised the price to 120 dinars the following year. Yet Iraqis' infatuation with London surpassed that of all other destinations.

Baghdad's al-Muthana airport was small at the time and crowded with chaotic droves of passengers milling about its terminal. They carried large suitcases, sometimes on their heads, as they pulled their children behind them and rushed to reach passport control before the others. The funny thing is they all complained of this chaos and criticized it as though they weren't a part of it themselves. As for the return from London, the same can be said. Iraqis spent all they had, huge sums, to return with purchases and gifts. At the time the Iraqi dinar was worth about two pounds sterling, and each adult could carry 1,000 dinars. We'd often see women in a fix, not having had taken into account the cost of overweight luggage, removing items to place in bags they'd carry by hand, or wearing heavy coats they'd bought despite the hot weather. And thus, the chaos would be continued in Heathrow Airport just as it had begun in Baghdad.

Rafa and I decided to take advantage of annual vacation time to plan visits to places we love and explore the world together. Our trip to Salzburg, which I spoke of in the previous chapter, was our first experience traveling together for weeks outside of Iraq, and it was an unplanned trip provided for by pure and good coincidence.

London: The Print Center

We spent our summer vacation of 1976 in London, where Rafa found another opportunity to practice printmaking. He spent every day in the printmaking studio run by Hugh Stoneman, after meeting him through our friend, the Iraqi artist and architect Issam El-Said,[1] who'd lived in London since the mid-1950s. Issam had been my friend and classmate since childhood. We lost contact for some years, and then in 1965 met by chance in Beirut when he held a solo exhibition at Gallery One upon the invitation of Youssef al-Khal.[2] During my first visit to London in 1968, he'd helped me find appropriate accommodation in South Kensington, close to his mother's residence. This time he chose for us a stylish place on Portobello Road, the home of an English friend who was traveling on vacation and left him the key in order to rent it out. Portobello Road was among London's boisterous, working-class quarters, largely inhabited by people of color. A Sunday market was held on this street, with vendors displaying clothing, houseware, used books, and treasures of all kinds. It was a veritable festival: bursting with activity, festooned in color, and brimming with visitors.

This was the first time Rafa and Issam met, and they soon formed a strong rapport. I'd paved the way for this meeting through the image I'd conveyed of Issam, an architect, academic, and artist with a big heart, brimming with energy and generosity, extremely tolerant and respectful. Issam had suffered greatly from the cruelty of Iraqis following 1958 due to his being the grandson of former prime minister Nouri al-Said, may he rest in peace. The cruelest action taken against him was the new Iraqi embassy refusing to renew his passport, and yet none of this affected his love and devotion to his homeland. Issam found Rafa to be a comfortable, open, and caring person, and they hit it off as though they'd known each other for a long time. Issam was aware of Rafa's skills in printmaking, and the two artists grew to become incredibly close friends, especially after Rafa discovered Issam's own talent in printmaking. Issam had been one of the first Arab artists to enter this field. His sudden and shocking death in 1988 meant the loss of a friend and brother and affected us deeply. We were asked to contribute to a book on him, and I wrote of my experience with him since childhood, while Rafa wrote of him as a person, artist, and printmaker. The two texts were drastically abbreviated by the editors for reasons we do not know.[3]

That trip to London was marvelous. We structured our time so that Rafa went to the studio at nine in the morning and we met again at six in the evening. It wasn't Rafa's first visit, for he'd been to London before and knew its museums. I'd prepared a schedule for important new exhibitions to visit and concerts we'd agreed to try to attend. From time to time, Rafa would free up and we'd go to museums and bookstores together. I adore London, and I'd spend time in the places I love to visit and attend plays or films that Rafa wasn't interested in during the afternoon. That summer Dia al-Azzawi joined us and stayed with us the first week before moving elsewhere. It was his first time in the city, and when he arrived, work opportunities opened up before him, and he chose to reside there for the remainder of his life.

Morocco, Portugal, and Spain

On the invitation of our friends Mohamed Benaissa and Mohamed Melehi, we traveled to Morocco and stayed in Asilah during the summer of 1977. We'd become friends with these Moroccan artists when they came to Baghdad in 1974 seeking out Dia and Rafa, and then again with the Moroccan delegation attending the First Biennale of Arab Art held in Baghdad that same year. Rafa suggested we take advantage of this trip to visit Portugal and trace some of his memories there, and then travel on to Madrid and southern Spain.

Our trip started in July from Cairo, where we spent a few uncomfortable days. I'd previously visited Cairo, the first time in 1965: I'd been eager to attend an Umm Kulthum concert and longed to see the city that had so long charmed our senses and imagination. That year at the Arab Poetry Festival in Baghdad, I'd been introduced to the poet Mahmoud Hassan Ismail by Dr. Nasser al-Din al-Assad, who'd advised me to bear with his odd personality due to the importance of his work. And although my encounter with him in Baghdad had not been encouraging, I sought him out in Cairo. He arranged for us to meet at a café he frequented, on the outskirts of Cairo via a dark and desolate desert road. I found the place as disturbing and uncomfortable as the odd poet himself. Yet, he was as nice as he could possibly be, for despite his rough manner he had a kind heart, and was simply awkward and extremely shy. He praised some of my texts but harshly ridiculed others, and in both cases I found it difficult to interact with him.

During that first visit, I was also introduced to the critic Dr. Abdel Qader al-Qutt, by the novelist Yusuf Idris. I was overjoyed when he selected a text of mine to publish in the journal *Shi'ir* (Poetry), of which he was chief editor at the time. We then remained in touch after he became chief editor of the journal *Ibdaa'* (Creativity). I gained great confidence from him, especially after he published a poem that had been rejected by *al-Aqlam* (Pens) journal. During our last meeting in Baghdad in the 1980s, he commissioned me to write about Rafa for *Ibdaa'*, and this was published but after he left, replaced by the poet Ahmed Abdel Moati Hegazi, who also published the poetry that I sent him.

This second visit to Cairo, in Rafa's company, was ten years later, and I found the city and its people exhausting. The density, chaos, intense heat, and overall misery, not to mention the transit crisis, made any movement within the city a tortuous journey. Yet we took advantage of the five days we spent at the Shepheard Hotel to visit the Egyptian Museum and a few historical sites and were delighted to meet the artist and critic Hassan Suleiman, a close friend of Rafa's. In the evenings, we'd go in search of art galleries, the very few of which were not particularly active. A few years earlier, Rafa had sent prints to be exhibited at Safarkhan Art Gallery, but they'd been impounded at the Cairo Airport and no one had ever been able to free them, not even the gallery owner.

In 1996, I traveled alone to Cairo at the personal invitation of Dr. Gaber Asfour to attend the Poetic Creativity Festival, which was a large event attended by leading Arab poets, and I was happy to meet many Arab poet and writer friends there. My fourth visit to Cairo was with Rafa, when he was honored at the 2000 Misr International Print Triennale, and a special pavilion was dedicated to his print works. As for our final trip, it was in 2006 at the invitation of the American University in Cairo, when Dr. Ferial Ghazoul hosted a symposium titled "Gender and Empire" about the position of women under the American occupation. I participated with a paper on female Iraqi artists who were in one way or another victims of American aggression. I was on a panel with Haifa Zangana, Bothaina al-Nasiri, and filmmaker Maysoon al-Pachachi. During these last two visits, we enjoyed Cairo and its museums, especially the Mahmoud Khalil Museum, among other sites. The city has an intimate character that clings to you.

After that short stay in Cairo, we began our planned trip, first to Casablanca and then on to Asilah by train. The ride took eight hours along the beautiful coast with its stunning scenery and fresh air. Mohammed Benaïssa's home was in the old city, which Moroccans call the Casbah, with narrow alleys and homes painted blue and white in harmony with the roaring Atlantic Ocean.

Asilah was not yet equipped to host visitors except in very modest hotels, and in this beautiful home so gracious with its hosting we met other guests of Benaïssa, friends of different nationalities. We met the

Moroccan poet and novelist Taher Ben Jelloun, who came from Paris with a beautiful Lebanese artist called Dima. There was also a Japanese professor and his wife, and two artists, one Spanish and the other Italian. Everyday Mohamed Melehi would join us with his wife at the time, the Italian author and critic Toni Maraini, and Farid Belkahia; both of them were from Asilah and had homes there. Typically, Moroccans who worked in other cities, including those who lived abroad, would spend their summers in their hometowns, maintaining and renovating their homes and contributing to the upkeep of their communities. We had a marvelous time, traveling between Tangier and nearby coastal cities, swimming in the ocean, and sitting in fishermen's cafés eating fresh shrimp.

At the time of our visit, Morocco was holding its parliamentary elections, and both Melehi and Benaissa had nominated themselves to represent Asilah. They both dreamed of hosting an international cultural festival during the summer, such as those held in French coastal cities. Everywhere we went in the city, we saw their photos on walls and poles, in distinctive affiliate colors meant to aid voters who were illiterate.

During that visit, Benaïssa discussed with Rafa the idea of setting up a graphic art studio in the Andalusian-style Raissouni Palace still belonging to Spain, which had occupied northern Morocco. The mostly deserted palace remained the home of one elderly woman, who Benaïssa ensured kept her home when he won the elections. Then, when she passed away the following year, his dream of the Asilah festival came true, and the first season was held in 1978. Unfortunately, we didn't attend as we traveled that summer to the Scandinavian countries, as I'll recount shortly, but we accepted the invitation the following year, in 1979, and it was one of the loveliest festivals we attended. I spoke of it in the introduction.

We continued our journey by plane from Tangier to Lisbon. Rafa was extremely excited about visiting the city in which he'd developed his printmaking skills, and where his creative expression had shifted from the figurative to abstraction. He had memories of places and people of whom he'd often spoken to the point that I could picture them in my mind. During our four days there, we covered large areas on foot so as to see as much of the city as possible, and usually the distances would grow because we got lost. On our first day we went to Gravura Studio to seek out Rafa's friends and teachers but found that most were away enjoying their summer holidays. Then we visited the Gulbenkian Museum, which is the largest art and culture site there and formed an oasis of light in the capital. Portugal was still under the rule of António de Oliveira Salazar and suffered from economic austerity measures and political pressure. Despite the richness of Portugal's natural environment, I found Lisbon impoverished in comparison to other European cities. In fact, I found it somewhat like Istanbul and Beirut, lacking of course the rich sites of Istanbul and the elegance and vitality of Beirut. When we returned thirty years later, the signs of economic invigoration and development were quite clear to see, as Portugal had joined the European Union and opened its doors to foreign investments, including from prestigious Iraqi families such as the Al Baqir and Al Khudairy families. Yet, fortunately it had preserved the density of its forests stretching along its populated coasts, thanks to a law enacted by Salazar that prohibited encroachments. I later got to know Portugal better through the novels of José Saramago and the poetry of Fernando Pessoa.

On our way to Lisbon, Rafa spoke of his Portuguese artist friend, whom he described as "a brilliant artist, but crazy." They'd been in an intimate relationship while he was undergoing his training, but lost contact when she traveled to France and he returned to Iraq. He took me to the café they'd frequented in hopes of meeting her there, saying excitedly, "She'll certainly come and you'll see how crazy she is!" We ordered coffees and sat near the entrance, Rafa's eyes pinned on the street. Suddenly, he jumped up as he saw her passing by with her large portfolio case. He called out to her, and she greeted him joyfully with an embrace. She was dark-skinned with a pleasant face free of makeup, and her portfolio appeared massive in comparison to her small frame. They came into the café and I stood up to greet her as Rafa introduced me in English, "This is May, my wife." She extended her hand coldly and gave me a quick, cold glance, then turned away to resume her conversation with Rafa in Portuguese and a few English phrases.

Her tone kept rising and the discussion grew heated. I sat quietly finishing my coffee and watched the live performance unfold before me, culminating in shouting and her angrily storming out of the café. Rafa sat back down, trying to remain calm. He took a sip of his coffee, a forced and tense smile on his face. "I told you she's crazy," he said. "Bravo, my love. Did you expect anything else?" Rafa had been attached to her, as his brief diaries indicate, but they lost contact upon his return to Iraq, when he grew consumed with another life and other relationships. I tried making light of things by joking about the situation he'd created, and we spent the rest of the day traveling in a worn-out train to the coast.

On our last evening in Portugal, Rafa fulfilled his promise to take me to hear Fado, a style of singing based on musical modes similar to our own *maqams*, and which amazed me. I was no stranger to this style of singing, for in Baghdad I had recordings of the renowned Amália Rodrigues, who'd died in a plane accident, and another marvelous singer called Nati Mistral, who sang and recited the poetry of Lorca. I very much enjoyed this live performance of sorrowful singing.

From Lisbon we flew to Madrid and spent two nights there. First, we visited Museo Nacional del Prado, and then Toledo, the Imperial City, as it was called, and the meeting point of Eastern and Western cultures. I was eager to see the city of El Greco, and to visit El Escorial. We laughed as we viewed the Crusades murals depicting the heroic acts of its soldiers. Although it was very hot, we spent hours on the streets of the ancient city walking and enjoying our connection to history, our feet following the same paths of those hundreds of years before us. This was a feeling I always sensed in my visits to historic cities, especially those I took with my family to Jerusalem, Ramallah, and Hebron prior to 1967, when we'd pass by ancient churches, markets, and homes. It's an incomparable feeling.

I had one unpleasant experience during the two days we spent in Madrid. Rafa told me he had an appointment with a former student of his who'd asked him to view his work for an hour, and then he'd accompany us to tour the city and have dinner. In his small and dark Madrid home, this artist immediately began showing his works one after the other, with endless and repeated commentary on repetitive abstract compositions dominated by black. It was a gloomy and boring experience. As the hours went by and his works never ended, there was no glimmer of light. The atmosphere enveloping us was so heavy that I felt my breath would be cut off. Rafa seemed embarrassed and incapable of putting an end to this torture, so I found no option other than excusing myself and leaving them to continue the evening without me. Outside I was disoriented, unsure of which direction to take or where our hotel was. I knew I wasn't far, as we'd walked there from the hotel via a side street. Adding to my confusion, the street was virtually empty, until a man rushing by saved me by pointing in the right direction. I hurried off tensely, as the distance seemed lengthy and unknown to me.

When Rafa returned to the hotel after midnight, I'd had sufficient time to calm down. Rafa was a public figure and subject to being approached by admirers and other artists, and especially his students, whom he'd selected with care for the Institute of Fine Arts' new graphic arts department. Rafa took interest in his students and was proud of them, and from time to time he'd ask me to visit the department so he could show me their creative work. Typically, he'd select a distinctive piece to hang in his office. I met his students as they were first starting out and followed their journeys, and they were proud when I wrote on the first graduates' exhibition in 1977, opened by the artist Faiq Hassan. This connection between teacher and students was maintained, and in some cases developed into solid friendships. Rafa remained committed to them and helped them to take part in international exhibitions. On that depressing evening in Madrid, I was hurt by the situation with Rafa, who'd allowed me to leave alone, but I felt it wise to make peace with what might happen again, to condition myself before anything else. Rafa apologized profusely when he returned, saying, "I was incredibly worried about you, and I too was irritated and bored. The artist was selfish in his insistence, and that aggravated me, but I couldn't let him down, and I'd promised to have dinner with him."

At the main transport hub in Madrid, we had two choices, either to travel by train or scheduled bus. We chose to travel by a train marked "rapido," but ironically, a few hours into our trip, we found the "fast" train as slow as can be, so we tossed our tickets and continued on scheduled buses that stopped in all the historic cities we planned to visit.

We were completely lost tourists. Rafa saw no need for a guide or tourist agency, and we therefore had great difficulty finding appropriate accommodation in cities teeming with tourists. And yet we bore our hardships gracefully and enjoyed exploring the beautiful cities, visiting awe-inspiring sites such as the grand mosque of Córdoba, whose Islamic character was maintained despite its transformation into a church, and likewise with Alcázar in Seville. Aimlessly walking the alleyways and passing the Levantine-style homes with tiled fountains in their front courtyards, not to mention the jasmine hanging from their balconies, was exhausting, but a delight. Alhambra Palace inspired in us both awe and sorrow. We spent a long time slowly walking about its rich halls and gardens, Rafa capturing images and focusing on the façades ornamented with Koranic verses pulsing with the magic of calligraphy.

At the time, we had to climb a mountain peak to reach Alhambra, and midway up heard a guitar being played wistfully in a small grotto. We drew close and found a little shop in which an old man tenderly embraced his instrument, captivatingly playing with immense sensitivity. He made guitars for a living, and I asked how much the instrument he was playing cost. He stated what for us was a modest amount, but added, "This is a flamenco guitar I made for myself, and it's not for sale." He invited us to sit and continued playing. I sat on the ground and listened reverently with Rafa by my side. When he finished, I repeated my request with an entreating look, and he said, "I'll concede it in respect to you, for I've never met someone who listened with such passion." With great generosity he gifted me a case in which to keep it. I embraced the instrument like a newborn and returned with it to Baghdad, taking it with me from place to place even until today. In Baghdad, I took lessons with the talented musician and oud maker Saad al-Tayyar, a young man at the time and incomparable artist, but I did not keep up with my practice.

We returned to Morocco by sea from our last stop in Spain, Algeciras, after spending the night on café chairs.

On our first trip to Asilah we'd met the artist Malika Agueznay, who was from Marrakesh but traveled every summer to Asilah and the northern coast with her husband, the surgeon Mostafa Agueznay; they were among the closest friends of Melehi and Benaïssa. Malika invited us to spend some time with them on our return in Casablanca, where they lived in a beautiful villa overlooking the coast in Anfa, the most sophisticated of the city's quarters. From there Malika accompanied us to Marrakesh, where we stayed in a beautiful Andalusian hotel and spent two days walking around the enchanting city. On the long desert road from Casablanca to Marrakesh, Malika spoke to us of the palm oases, and said that the climate and topography of Marrakesh resembled that of Baghdad. As we passed each palm oasis and I saw the skinny trunks of Moroccan palms with their sparse branches, I recalled the richness of our groves and the beauty of Iraqi palm trees with their fruit hanging like beads of amber.

It was Ramaḍan, and we took part in their beautiful Islamic holiday rituals. Tables were set up across Elfna Square when it was time to break the fast, as if the entire city were attending a collective feast. Behind these tables, restaurant owners offered the most delicious grilled meats to customers, alongside *harira* soup, essential to the fast-breaking meal. Ramadan fasting was expected of everyone, and restaurants were barred from serving food before fast-breaking time. It was assumed that all Arabs were Muslims and required to fast, so only non-Arab foreigners could freely eat meals in hotels. In the home of Malika and Mostafa, who were not fasting, they ate behind closed doors in respect for the servants in their home, which deeply impressed me.

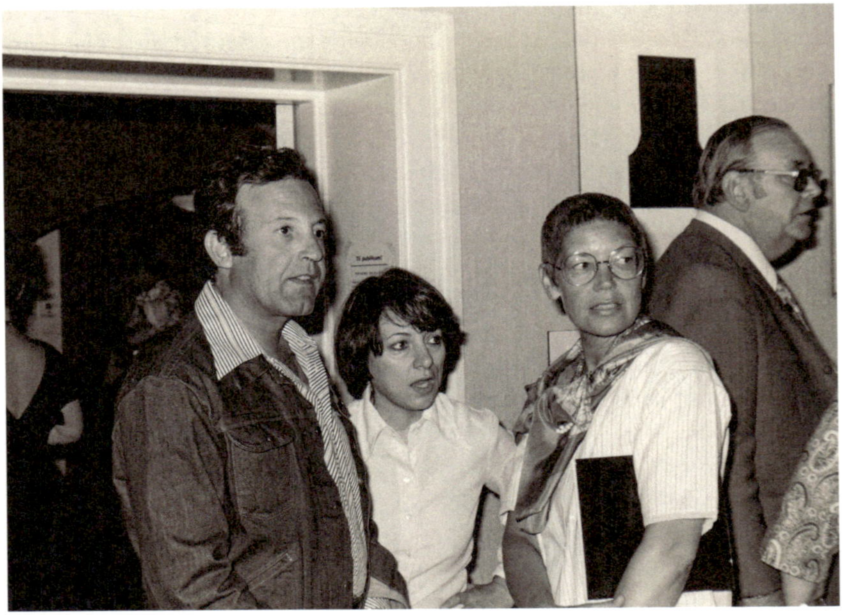

Rafa and May
at the IV Norwegian
International Print
Biennale, with the wife
of the organizer Herman
Hebler, Fredrikstad, 1978

Every Friday, Elfna Square in Marrakesh hosts a huge popular market filled with Bedouins who arrive from the desert's edge. They kneel their camels and spread blankets on the ground to display food, medicinal herbs, and traditional handicrafts, including pottery, silver jewelry, and stones. They sell their wares, sing, practice magic and tricks, and read fortunes, wearing colorful garb and handwoven cloaks in a carnival that's rich in beautiful tradition and diversity.

After that, we returned to Asilah whenever we had the opportunity, and each time we visited what we hadn't before of Morocco's mountain and coastal cities. We'd meet Moroccans and foreigners active in the arts, and return with beautiful memories, unique experiences, and a deepened understanding of Morocco's people. I never found anyone to honor the Iraqi people as did the Moroccans, for they burned the French flag, as we were told, when France participated in the Gulf War and bombed Iraq in 1991, which was an unprecedented event. When we visited Asilah for the last time in 2010, we found it had changed a great deal. A new port monopolized the seafront, and its vast open spaces had been exploited to build imposing residential complexes. Yet, the heart of the old city, the Casbah, still maintained its beautiful spirit, with its alleys and homes painted in blue and white and covered with hanging plants. This last trip was noteworthy for the companionship of Rafa's younger brother, Sabah Nasiri, and we met old friends there, foremost the stupendous Sudanese artist Mohammad Omar Khalil. This was the first and last time that Rafa entered their printmaking studio as a visiting cofounder and not as a working artist.

The Scandinavian Countries

The following summer, in 1978, we decided to travel to the Scandinavian countries when Rafa was invited to participate in the Norwegian International Print Biennale in Fredrikstad, Norway. It was Rafa's third time to participate in the international exhibition, but his first time to actually attend. We flew on Royal Jordanian Airlines from Amman, and this was a good opportunity to visit my aunt. This time I insisted we plan the trip in advance. Our flight was to Denmark, and in Copenhagen we had Thomas Cook organize round-trip train travel, guaranteeing arrival in Oslo and Stockholm, and reserving accommodation in the two capitals.

The day following our arrival in Oslo we left in the afternoon for Fredrikstad, ninety kilometers away, to attend the opening of the fourth biennial. Rafa was participating with a few new prints he'd produced in London. We arrived a little late to the ceremony hall and found a jury member taking to the stage to announce the winners. Then we heard Rafa's name, followed by applause, but didn't understand what was happening until we found the wife of the biennial's organizer, artist Herman Hebler, congratulating Rafa on winning the jury prize. Hebler promptly followed her when he also saw us, and it was a most marvelous moment. We spent a lovely evening there and got to know a community we hadn't met before, but were surprised when it ended at 11 p.m. We later learned it was required by law to stop serving alcohol at eleven, a measure taken to limit excessive drinking.

The following morning, we went to the waterfalls, where the sound of rushing water was deafening. Although their fierce flow was frightening, their beauty was breathtaking. That day the city was mourning four rock climbers who'd met their fate climbing the opposite peak. At the time the population of Norway was only four million, and the loss of these four priceless individuals was no doubt an utter tragedy.

To travel to Stockholm, we had to change trains in Trondheim, the last point on the border. The train arrived at midnight, and the connecting train left early in the morning. In Baghdad, Saleh al-Jumaie had told us he'd stay with a friend of his, an artist from Trondheim, before continuing his trip to America, and invited us to spend the night with them. We made our way from the station to her address, which was very close by, and she generously welcomed us in her home. She suggested that on our return we again stay in her house, which would be empty, saying she'd leave us the key near the door, and that we could later secure it for her at the station. When we left at dawn, we didn't find the key, and it wouldn't have been appropriate to wake her.

On the clean Swedish train, as we were having coffee with the traditional breakfast (waffles with jam or honey), a man in uniform approached us and asked, "Are you Rafa Nasiri?" We were surprised and somewhat alarmed, and then he handed us a sealed envelope saying, "This is the key to the house, and the madame apologizes for forgetting to give it to you before you left." It seemed stranger than one could imagine; what a country and what people!

It was the middle of August and yet I found Stockholm chilly. We stayed in a beautiful and comfortable pension owned and run by a strongly built sixty-year-old woman, who welcomed us warmly. Iraq was not familiar to most Swedes at the time, yet there were immigrants in the city, most of them Kurds, both Iraqi and not. We didn't know anyone in Sweden other than Rafa's friend and former classmate, Pierre Olo (Peter). They'd been very close and had spent four years together in the Central Academy of Fine Arts in Beijing.

Our Stockholm trip was incredibly organized, with time allocated for getting to know the city's heritage, as well as some boat rides, including a trip to Finland that took an entire day, with us sleeping on the boat. Still dreaming, we arrived at the Finnish coast in the morning and took a bus tour of the city, quickly passing by the sites, the most important of which was the Helsinki cathedral with its unique architecture. In these Scandinavian travels I found it remarkable that the borders were open without restriction and wished for a stamp in my passport just for the sake of the souvenir.

We spent most of our time in Stockholm visiting museums and immersing ourselves in the works of the influential Scandinavian artist Edvard Munch. Rafa enjoyed frequenting the city's many Chinese restaurants and was pleased I'd become more accepting of the cuisine I'd not liked the first time I'd tried it in London. Toward the end of our visit to the Östasiatiska Museet (Museum of Far Eastern Antiquities), Rafa looked around and said he felt certain it was Peter who'd established it and still ran it. I said, "Why don't you ask?" and without waiting for a reply continued, "Of course you won't ask!" Rafa laughed.

We were in a corridor leading to the main entrance on our way out when we noticed the museum's cafeteria. Rafa peered in, with the intention of having coffee, and shouted in delight, "Peter's sitting in the café!" The happy reunion of these two friends was filled with emotion. After exchanging personal news at lightning speed, Peter suggested he host us that weekend in his home on one of the islands. At the appointed time he picked us up and took us to his small and beautiful home, where we met his wife and had dinner, Peter and Rafa speaking unabatedly of China and their teachers. After earning his bachelor's degree, Peter had returned to China to complete his graduate studies. He'd appear in our lives again in an intimate meeting twenty-five years later in Paris, which I'll speak of later.

Despite the beauty of the Scandinavian countries, there's something forlorn about them that takes possession of your heart. The days were incredibly long, lasting over twenty hours. We'd go out in the morning to various places and return at noon for Rafa's siesta, and then go out again in the evening, choosing a restaurant or a cinema, or walking around downtown. We'd avoid staying there late, however, as we'd been warned that it was not safe after dark. Usually, we'd return at 9 p.m., stopping at a café near our pension that offered American coffee and tea with milk, always served with a cookie, until 11 p.m. I'd gaze at the small, separate tables where men and women sat alone, their eyes pinned to the television screen, living in closed-off worlds, their despondent faces awash with sorrow.

Among the regulars was a large-bodied man who occupied a table at the far end of the café, facing the television. One night I saw him laughing incessantly and it caught my curiosity. He was roaring with laughter, his body shaking vigorously. Our eyes met and we connected, and perhaps he imagined that I shared in his humor with him. A few minutes later I'd caught his laughter, and placed my hand over my mouth, turning away from him to suppress it. The state I fell into irritated Rafa, but I couldn't stop, and my eyes filled with tears from laughing so hard. I tried hiding my face, but nothing helped, and Rafa got embarrassed and scolded me a few times. I swore to him, gasping with laughter, that I couldn't control myself, so he dragged me out by the arm. The man followed me with his eyes, raising his brows in surprise and his body still trembling with laughter. I kept laughing all the way home, and even after we arrived, and in fact I still laugh whenever I recall the incident. It's no surprise that although the Swedes enjoy a high standard of living, the suicide rate there is high.

I have another story in Stockholm, with the woman who ran the pension we stayed in. I noticed that she did absolutely everything, from cleaning to washing to carrying the breakfast trays to her guests in the morning, all with vigorous strength and a smiling countenance. She was curious to know who we were and where Iraq was, and she'd linger speaking with us when she brought us our breakfast. One day I asked if anyone helped her with the work, and she said that sometimes her daughter came on Sundays to help her for a wage. How foreign this was to our close relations in Iraq that we sometimes complained of! Another day Rafa was wearing a cotton shirt printed with colored squares that he'd recently bought there. She patted his back and said, "Oh, what a beautiful shirt!" As our departure day approached, I wanted to gift this kind woman something she'd like as a token of appreciation for the thoughtful care she'd given us. I was accustomed to traveling with things that I'd gift as needed, and this time I had with me a handbag I'd crocheted with prominent bright flowers. Two days before we traveled, I asked her to choose between a shirt resembling Rafa's or the bag. She gasped when she saw it in my hand and accepted it with great joy, turning it about in her hand and holding it up to her face. She hugged me fiercely and said, "Oh, what a kind heart you have! This bag is truly marvelous." I teared up despite myself.

The day we departed she insisted on carrying our two heavy bags down the stairs, as the elevator was too small, and she stood at the entrance bidding us farewell in the heavy rain. We left on the Swedish train and stopped in Trondheim, resting in the artist's home and leaving again at 8 p.m., securing her key at the station as agreed. The train returning to Copenhagen was German, and left at 10 p.m. We were its first passengers, and stood in the passageway beside our assigned carriage, watching the other travelers arrive.

As we did so, a beautiful little three-year-old girl ran through the train corridor toward us, and we warmly welcomed this golden butterfly. She was followed by a young woman calmly searching for her compartment, and we immediately recognized her as the child's mother and source of her inherited beauty. As the train departed, the child had already facilitated our conversing with one another. We remained in the passageway, getting to know each other, and she was eager to speak with us when she learned that we were an artist and writer from Iraq, for it turned out she worked for an art institution. Rafa gave her one of his catalogues with which he often introduced himself, bearing samples of his work and including a text I'd written in English.

The passageway was cramped with us all standing there, blocking the path of other passengers, and I was tired of standing. Rafa suggested we continue our conversation in the buffet car, but the little girl had fallen asleep and her mother needed to remain by her side. I went to rest, leaving them to continue their conversation, sitting on two wooden seats in the passageway and toasting glasses of beer Rafa retrieved from the buffet. As it was difficult to sleep in the train, I immersed myself in recording observations about our trip, while Rafa spent the hours of the journey with his lovely new company. The woman was an elegant type that appealed to Rafa. He was selective about people, and held special respect for women, with a heightened appreciation of their behavior, culture, and intellect. Since he had great charisma and was well-mannered without being formal about it, women generally felt comfortable with him. I expected him to be strongly attracted to this woman and was not surprised that they continued talking until dawn.

We reached Copenhagen at seven in the morning, each of us exhausted and remaining silent. In the car taking us to the airport, Rafa rested his head on the seatback as I gazed at the sights of the magical city, filled with happiness and a satisfaction that we were returning to Baghdad. We had breakfast at the airport and exchanged no words more than necessary. Once seated on the plane, Rafa put his head on my shoulder, closed his eyes, and fell into a peaceful sleep.

London, 1981 and 1982

In the summer of 1979, a few months before leaving my job, I requested an extension to my annual vacation in order to enjoy one of our loveliest trips. To start with we attended the second Moussem culturel d'Asilah in Morocco and stayed there for three weeks, during which Rafa produced a number of prints and continued setting up the graphic art studio with Mohammad Omar Khalil. We then traveled from Tangier to Nice, where we rented a small Renault 5 and drove the rural roads to Paris. I spoke of this trip in the introduction.

Rafa tended to quench his thirst for printmaking whenever we traveled to Asilah, London, or any other city that allowed him to work. Typically, we'd return with a beautiful collection of prints that satiated his need to experiment and create as he sought an intersection between painting and printing, a practice that reached its climax in later years. Rafa used a roller in his printing, a method he learned while training in the French studio of Stanley William Hayter during the summer of 1968. And so, he carried this metal tool, despite its heavy weight, to anywhere he thought he might not find one.

Following his wonderful experience at Hugh Stoneman's Print Centre in the summer of 1976, we decided to return to London in 1981 so Rafa could produce more prints. We'd planned to visit Paris, Rome, or anywhere the plane stopped en route to London, but when it came time to travel Rafa changed his mind, coveting use of the entire month to work.

I knew London well and was happily distracted by its rich cultural life. I knew the summer programs in advance by following the weekly literary supplements in the *Sunday Times* and *The Guardian*, which I got from friends after the import of non-Arab newspapers was banned in the mid-1970s. I also listened to the BBC's English broadcast every morning and followed its culture programs. As for films and concerts, we'd go to most of them together. Rafa would go to the studio in Islington, in east London, every morning at 9 a.m. and until 6 p.m., except on Sundays. I'd wait for him at the subway tunnel in Oxford Circus near his workplace, and we'd spend the rest of the day together, at times following a program and at others not.

Rafa would leave work cheerful and chatty, describing details of the work he'd accomplished and pleased with his new discoveries, especially when in the company of Issam El-Said. Then he'd ask me what I'd done and whom I'd met, and I'd speak in a gushing flow as though my tongue had been released from captivity. During this trip in 1981, Rafa produced five prints (zinc etchings) of different sizes depicting a dome and horizon, expressively intertwined with Arabic letters.

That summer, we took a trip to the historic coast of Cornwall in southwest England with our friends the architect Amin Mohieddin Youssef and his wife Ghida al-Askari, who was specialized in a number of European languages. They were recently married, and we arranged to travel in their car. Ghida planned the trip and made reservations, and we spent a wonderful time in the embrace of nature where the green hills meet the Atlantic Ocean.

Rafa was pleased with our experience of London and wanted to repeat it the following year in 1982. Before traveling, he'd been selected by the Swedish company constructing the Al Rasheed Hotel in Baghdad to produce various sized prints of his abstract compositions. These were to be placed in guest rooms, and others were to be used in the Babylon Hotel. Both hotels were in their final stages of construction, yet the company was still to gain the necessary permits from the designated authorities and follow up with us. During the first month in which he worked in London, Rafa produced six medium-sized prints (zinc etchings) of outstanding beauty. Their theme was the horizon, and Rafa compiled them in portfolios titled *Beyond the Horizon*. As our stay neared an end, we'd still not yet heard any official news about the commission from Baghdad.

Rafa would immerse himself in his work to the extent that he'd lose his sense of time and everything around him. He preferred to work in spaces that allowed him solitude, and thus chose to isolate himself on the second floor of the Print Centre. One Saturday night he was unusually late as I waited for him as usual in Oxford Circus. Then a cab stopped at the curb and Issam got out. "What a lovely coincidence!" I cried. Issam laughed his boisterous laugh and said, "Come along, Miss Coincidence, let's go see Rafa, as he's trapped in the studio!" Everyone in the studio had left at the end of the day, not realizing Rafa was still on the second floor. Once he took note of the time, he found the studio empty and the door locked. He looked out the window, hoping to seek someone's aid, but the street was empty, so he worriedly searched Hugh's desk in hopes that he'd find the phone number of someone he knew. He found Issam's, and by coincidence Issam had a copy of the center's key and was just about to go out when Rafa called, seeking his aid and asking him to bring me with him. On our way there, and just as joyfully, Issam told me that Rafa was more worried about me than he was about himself. Without his rescue Rafa would have remained locked in the center until Monday morning.

During this trip, we attended a number of social events and accepted private invitations from friends who'd settled in London. George Za'ani, who was Lebanese, held a dinner party in his restaurant attended by a number of Iraqi and Arab intellectuals and artists, including the poet Buland al-Haidari and Lebanese artist Arif al-Rayyis, among others. We also attended an exhibition at Graffiti Gallery of works on paper and prints by Arab artists specialized in printmaking, including Dia, Rafa, and Issam. It was a lovely occasion to meet artists and intellectuals, and a truly important and eye-opening exhibition. The gallery owner invited us to dinner at her home after the opening, and it was a pleasant gathering that began quite late. I got tired after midnight, but Rafa was excited to be there, surrounded by so many people you could barely distinguish him. By nice coincidence, the gallery owner's husband was a reader of poetry, and although he surprisingly didn't care for English poetry, told me he loved French poetry. Luckily, I'd read a great deal of French poetry in English and had recordings of famous French poems, some of which I'd memorized. And here was the galley owner's husband, reciting French poems he knew by heart!

Christie's auction house made regular visits to the Print Centre and followed the artists who printed their works in Hugh Stoneman's studio, including Issam, who had a contract with them. When they saw Rafa's works they offered to publish them in their annual catalogue, sent to art collectors around the world, if he conceded the rights of sale. Issam advised him to grasp this opportunity and Rafa nearly accepted the offer, which would have guaranteed him wide distribution. However, a telegram arrived from Baghdad the next day, asking him to produce the works in accordance with the agreement the two parties had reached. And thus we extended our stay another month.

During this period, Rafa found an opportunity to carry out other experiments in printmaking. He'd been guided to a studio with a press that accommodated large-sized prints, which he'd often dreamed of making. Its rent was expensive in relation to the money we had remaining, but we agreed to make it work out. Over two consecutive days he produced two large monotype works and was proud of the remarkable results he accomplished. He gave them to his dear friend

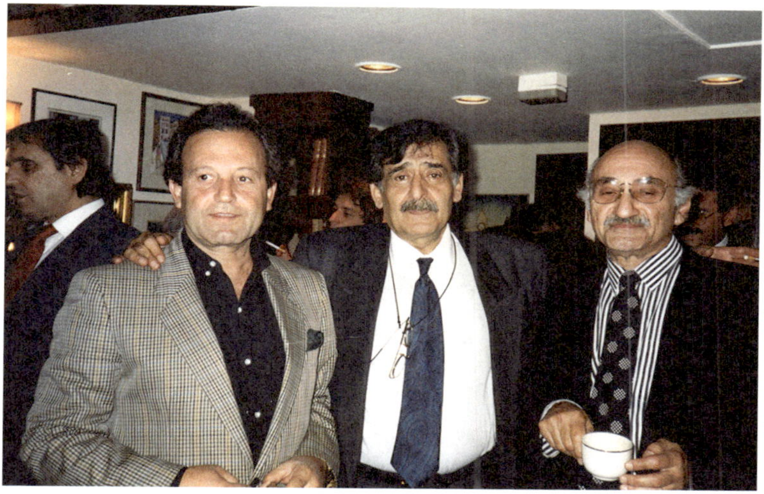

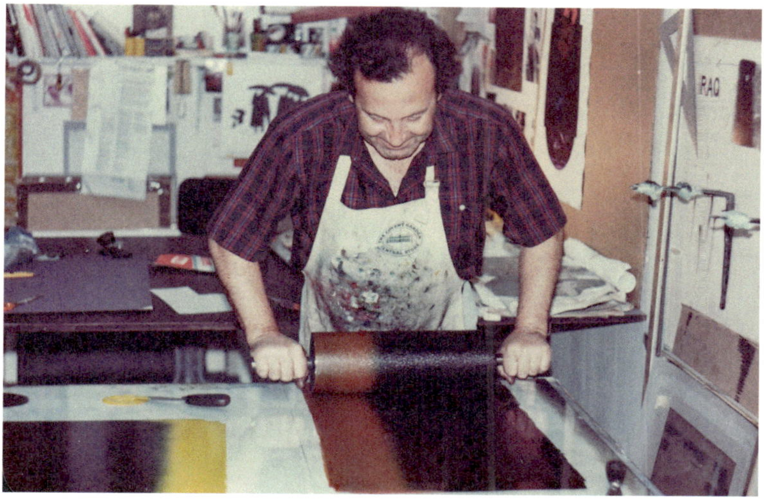

Top: Rafa with poet Buland al-Haidari and artist Aref El Rayess, London, 1982

Bottom: Rafa at his graphic workshop, Baghdad, 1988

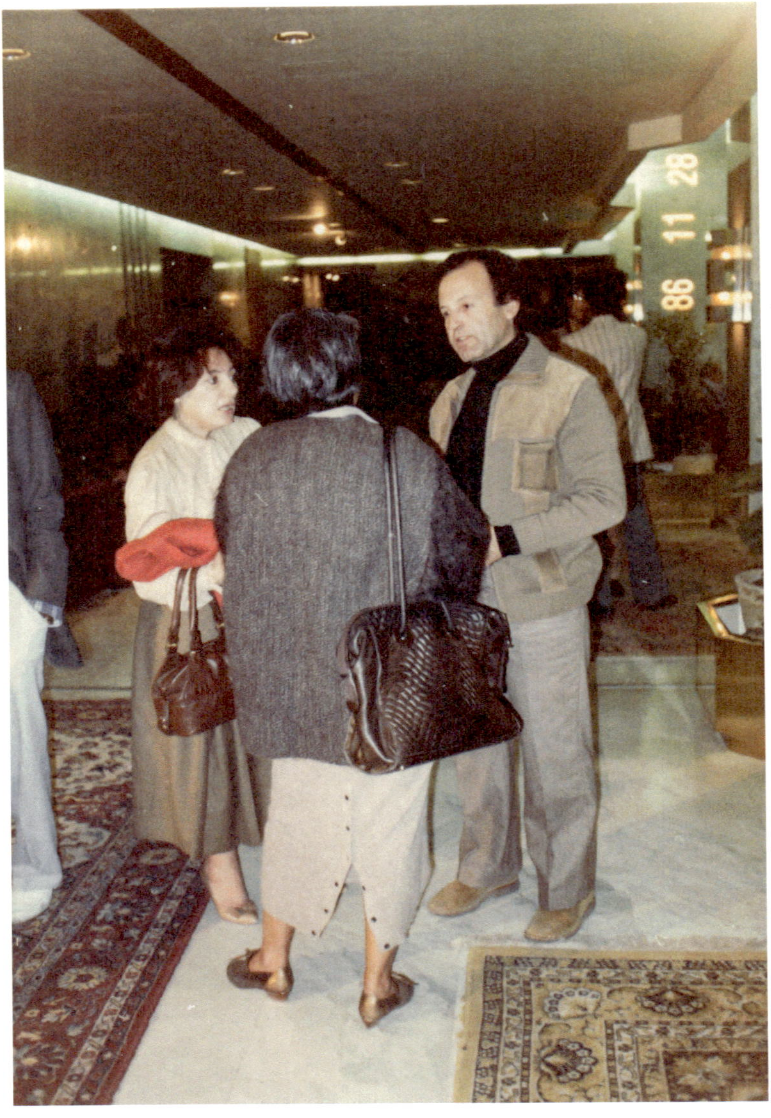

Al Marbid Literary
Festival, Baghdad, 1986

Wadah Faris, who'd always admired Rafa's graphic art prints. At that time, Wadah had left London and moved to Paris, where he opened Faris Gallery in Saint Germain and exhibited the works of Arab artists selected with great expertise. The following year, in 1983, he invited Rafa to hold a solo exhibition in his gallery that included thirty of his works, including paintings and graphic art prints. This was Rafa's first solo exhibition in a western European city.

Starting in 1983, Iraqis were prohibited from traveling for tourism due to the Iran–Iraq War; travel was limited to severe cases of illness and official invitations from established entities or official delegations, although spouses were prohibited from also traveling in such cases, even to take part in cultural or academic symposia. This happened to me in 1985 when we received an invitation from Mohammed Benaïssa, who was the Moroccan minister of culture at the time, to attend the Moussem culturel d'Asilah. Since he was aware of our circumstances, he sent a personal letter to the Iraqi Minister of Information requesting permission for both of us to travel, and for me to take part in a roundtable discussion on the relation between poetry and painting. Rafa received permission to travel, while the status of my permit remained uncertain until after the festival ended, when I received an official reply from the ministry stating, "Approval not granted." Later, when we attended the 1990 festival, Benaïssa told me he'd realized the aim of this policy was to hold wives hostage, thereby guaranteeing the return of their husbands to Iraq.

1989–90

The prohibition of international travel for tourism continued even after the Iran–Iraq War ended, although permission was now given to spouses for travel on official invitation. During these years, our professional and social lives continued amid ongoing Arab cultural events for poetry and theater, and even international art events held in Baghdad and other cities. The annual Marbid Poetry Festival continued to take place and was attended by leading poets, writers, and Arabists. The Babylon Festival for Arts, with its diverse range of activities, held evening performances by international, Arab, and Iraqi groups in Babylon's ancient stadium. Perhaps the most important events of the 1980s were the first and second International Baghdad Biennale in 1986 and 1988, held under the slogan "Art for Humanity," and which welcomed an impressive attendance by renowned Arab and international artists. In 1988, we held a party in our new and spacious house to honor our attending friends.

The year 1989 was filled with social activities and constant events in Baghdad and beyond, especially after Rafa completed his service in the Institute of Fine Arts and was free to work on his own art full-time. He'd accomplished much of what he'd aimed for in building his artistic future and providing a satisfactory life for us. We owned a house with a large art studio, and in 1987 he opened a graphic art studio in al-Mansour. Rafa split his time between working at home in the morning and then working on printmaking in the afternoon. During this period, he underwent personal transformations that were embodied in his artistic experiments, and his intense production of prints reflected a deep engagement with the mixing of techniques.

It was also during this period that we received an invitation from Princess Wijdan al-Hashemi, head of the Royal Society of Fine Arts in Jordan, to attend the opening of the contemporary Islamic art exhibition held by the Jordan National Gallery of Fine Arts in London's Barbican Centre in 1989. Rafa took part with two works, and I participated with a chapter on the history and development of Iraq's modern art movement for a book published in conjunction with the exhibition. The war had ended and travel restrictions had lightened, even though the general prohibitions had not yet been lifted, and we easily gained permission to travel. Rafa thus found himself in London again, fully immersed in his printing experiments. During the three weeks we spent there he produced a portfolio of five large-sized prints (zinc etchings) using multiple techniques that he titled *An Oriental Quintet*. Before arriving in London, he took part in an international graphic arts workshop at the Museo Español de Arte Contemporáneo (Spanish Museum of Contemporary Art), and during the month there produced two marvelous, limited-edition prints (copper etchings), and the Madrid museum acquired an edition of each.

Invitation to China

In the autumn of 1988, on Rafa's recommendation a Chinese delegation attended the second International Baghdad Biennale, "Art for Humanity." This was following China's general opening up and subsequent acceptance of abstract arts, which had previously been prohibited as bourgeois and lacking direct rhetoric. When the Chinese

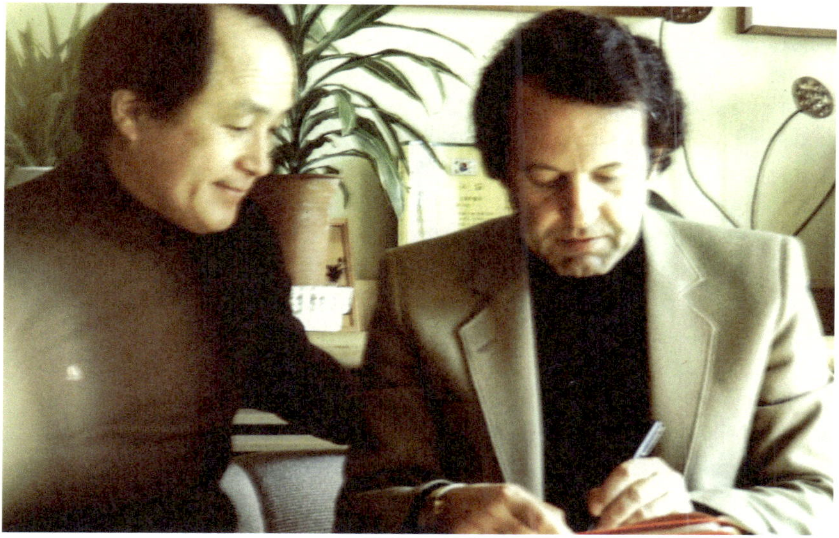

Rafa in Beijing, 1989

delegation saw how Rafa's diverse artistic practice had developed, they extended a formal invitation to visit Beijing and hold a retrospective exhibition covering a quarter century of his experience in printmaking (1964–89). They scheduled the visit for late October 1989, so as soon as he completed his work in London, he left for Beijing. It was a marvelous and exciting experience he described in his book *Rihlati ila al-sin* (My journey to China), in which he expressed his joy in visiting the academy again and daring to give a speech in Chinese at the exhibition opening, in allegiance to the original support that had allowed him such a unique artistic career.

When the internet entered our lives Rafa was able to communicate with one of his most prominent Chinese teachers, and the one closest to his heart, Huang Yongyu, who was now ninety years old and one of China's most eminent modern artists. His teacher replied with a warm welcome, inviting us to stay in his opulent Shanghai home. That was in the summer of 2013, when disease was mercilessly spreading through Rafa's bones although he resisted with hope and a desire to live and work. In cheer and confidence, he told me, "We'll go in the new year, as that's the best time there."

In the spring of 1990, I received an invitation from activist and writer Khadija Tanana and critic Rashida bin Masoud to attend a women's creativity symposium in Fes and take part in a poetry reading with well-known Iraqi poet Amaal al-Zahawi, alongside other female Arab poets. During our 1979 stay in Asilah, I'd visited Fes in the company of writer Shadia Sunbur, for Rafa had preferred to use to the time to work. And so he wanted to accompany me this time, to see the city he hadn't visited before and photograph its age-old sites. I was pleased by the warm welcome Rafa received from the festival organizers, and especially Khadija Tanana.

It was a wonderful trip in every detail and all its activities, which included creative readings of stories and poetry, alongside critical studies. There I met for the first time the brilliant professor Ferial Ghazoul,[4] the great novelist Assia Djebar, and Latifa al-Zayyat and Ahlam Mosteghanemi, and was delighted to see my friend the great critic Khalida Said, and my friend Mohamed Barrada.

I was pleased to discover I had readers who followed me in the Lebanese journals published in London and Paris. That day I read poems that reflected the humanitarian crisis in Iraq, and my performance stirred the emotions of the audience, who were generous in expressing their engaging responses. My turn came directly after Souad al-Sabah had fired up the hall with her direct, feminine poetry.

Perhaps the challenge of following her encouraged me to effectively deliver my short and dense poems to the audience.

Time had gotten away from Rafa in the bookshops, and he arrived late. It was his first time to do so, and he was caught unaware by the positive responses and congratulations rained upon him, as well as the regrets for his tardiness. He said he'd never forgive himself for not being there. Rafa's presence at events like this usually granted me a sense of comfort. But during this period, in which he was at his greatest freedom and ease, he also seemed more distracted and self-absorbed. I often noticed an absence in his presence, as well as a great joy in what he'd accomplished.

Despite his letters and diaries (in which he always wrote, "I wish you were here") that I mentioned in a previous chapter, Rafa returned from all of his solo trips with additional details to tell, and gorgeous gifts acquired with his limited budget. He always amazed me, for he never made a mistake in the size of clothing, his choices of things for the house, or jewelry. But the most beautiful gifts he so happily brought home were from India in 1986. This was one of Rafa's rare, one-off trips, when he participated in the Sixth Triennale-India in New Delhi, in the company of two polar opposites, Khalid al-Rahhal and Shaker Hassan Al Said. He had to perfect a balance between the two of them and spoke jokingly of their fights, quarrels, and moods over those two tumultuous weeks.

Rafa returned with a suitcase full of gifts, for India is the land of wonders. And although he got home at 2 a.m., he insisted on opening it, spreading its contents across all the chairs and tables, his face bursting with joy. I was amazed and felt as though I'd entered Ali Baba's cave. My eyes flitted back and forth between the colorful fabrics, cashmere shawls, jewelry with semiprecious stones such as carnelian, amber, and coral, pieces of naive art, and tablecloths and bedspreads sufficient for the entire family.

1 Issam El-Said (1938–1988) was a distinguished Iraqi painter, printmaker, designer, etcher, architect, philosopher, and author who designed several major public buildings in Baghdad and London.

2 Youssef al-Khal was a renowned Lebanese poet and married to the American artist Helen al-Khal, and they were the owners of the gallery.

3 Samir Chorbachi, *Issam El-Said: Artist and Scholar* (London: Issam El-Said Foundation, 1989).

4 Ferial Ghazoul is an Iraqi-American professor of English and comparative literature at the American University in Cairo.

Travels 1991–2008

After the Iraqi prohibition on travel was lifted and we took up residency in Amman and Rafa returned to teaching, other countries only permitted our entry with visas procured through private or official invitation, with very few exceptions. In 1992, I received an invitation to participate in a poetry festival in southern Italy dedicated to Arab female poets including Fadwa Tuqan, who also resided in Amman at the time. Fadwa held great importance to me. Her volume *Alone with the Days* inspired my ambition to write poetry and was my exemplar of how to approach doing so. I'd found the volume in the library of judge Sabiha al-Sheikh Daoud, when I visited her with my mother at the age of twelve, and I remember shaking, so affected I was by what I read.

During our second year in Amman, Inaam Orfali opened a gallery in her home to show the works of Iraqi artists. One day, she contacted me to say she was hosting a poetry evening with Fadwa Tuqan and asked me to introduce her. And thus I met Fadwa in person and told her how important her poetry had been to my literary formation. When the event had concluded she asked me to read something from my own work, and expressed being deeply touched, although she also did not conceal her surprise at the nature of the poems I read. Through this evening we established a connection, and we would meet from time to time.

When she received her invitation to the festival in Italy, Fadwa requested traveling with me, as she found it difficult to travel alone. Due to my circumstances as an Iraqi, I asked the festival hosts to procure my visa on their end, and they were shocked by the harsh refusal given by Amman's Italian embassy, which warned that I should not even approach their locale. The festival organizer called me from Italy to ask, "Why this refusal? Are you a terrorist?" I told her, "No, but I'm Iraqi!" and that the embargo of Iraq included cultural sanctions. She couldn't believe it. I was later told by Fadwa Tuqan, and again by the Moroccan poet Wafaa Lamrani when she came to the Jerash Festival of Culture and Arts, that my poems had been translated into Italian and read by a theater actress in protest of the measures preventing my personal attendance.

In 1994, Rafa received an invitation to serve on the jury of the Norwegian International Print Biennale in Fredrikstad, Norway. He traveled alone and met there his beloved students Modhir Ahmed and Ammar Daoud, as well as his friend Herman Hebler, the man behind the great event. The trip lasted over ten days and was an opportunity for Rafa to enjoy himself and regain his faith in life, after having lost it in the aftermath of the war and upon leaving Iraq.

I also had the opportunity to participate in Cairo's 1996 Poetic Creativity Festival, and, unfortunately, I did so alone due to Rafa's commitments at the university. There, I met many poet friends from the East and West, some of whom we were accustomed to meeting in Baghdad. It was a wonderful and well-attended festival, and I was pleased that my poems were well received by a large audience of Arab poets and poetry lovers.

Germany, the Netherlands, France

In our first few months of residing in Bahrain (1997–2003), we received a call from Katrina Eglau, the daughter of Otto Eglau, who'd been the supervisor of the two graphic art workshops Rafa attended in Salzburg in 1974 and 1975. Rafa and Otto had remained in touch until Otto's death. When we'd seen them in Salzburg, Katrina and her younger brother Johann had been children, lucky to be raised and loved by marvelous parents. At times we'd go swimming with them in a nearby lake with icy cold water. The boldness of these youngsters would put us to shame as we hesitated to immerse ourselves, but when we did finally rush into the lake, we realized how warm one's body feels when meeting extremely cold water.

Katrina reminded me of herself and our relationship, for fear I might have forgotten her a quarter of a century later. She told me she was visiting Amman and had seen Rafa's works exhibited at Darat al Funun. She'd requested our phone number from them, and said she'd like to meet us with her husband Martin, so we agreed to meet during the imminent holiday. When her father passed away, Katrina held on to her father's inheritance, which included a house and studio in seaside Kampen, Sylt, which is one of four large islands and an attractive holiday community in northern Germany. Katrina wanted to keep her father's memory alive by bringing his studio back to life and holding personal exhibitions of his friends' work there, and she knew her father had had a close relationship with Rafa.

Our meeting with Martin and Katrina in Amman was not one of strangers. We found Katrina still the same child we'd known, with the same mannerisms, enthusiasm, and openness. As for Martin, despite his reserve and serious-mindedness, he was loveable and the perfect companion for Katrina after suffering the great loss of her parents while so young. A close relationship quickly developed between us, especially given their great sympathy for Iraqis following the 1991 Gulf

War. Martin Ghelen was a high-minded intellectual and prominent journalist working for *Der Tagesspiegel*, Berlin's second-biggest newspaper, and Katrina was a photographer. We agreed to hold a graphic art exhibition in Eglau's studio in August 1999.

We spent our first week in Berlin, hosted by the marvelous couple. It was my first time visiting the city, and Rafa was my certified guide, as he'd last visited in 1987, before its reunification, when he served on the Intergraphic Biennale's jury. First, we visited the Berlinische Galerie, and allocated another day for the Pergamon Museum and its wing dedicated to Mesopotamian civilization. We began with the Babylonian Ishtar Gate and walked along the Processional Way, passing by the winged bulls and complex, mythical creatures the Mesopotamian sculptors had made life-sized. This is not to mention the many symbolic carvings, cylinder seals, and other artifacts on display. I trembled before their greatness and was moved to tears. I'd previously visited the Louvre and the British Museum, and had been duly impressed by all I'd seen, but never before felt the awe and amazement I felt in the Pergamon Museum.

On one of our outings, we walked along the river to the Bauhaus Archive in its distinctive modern building. We found that all of the items designed and invented in the late 1920s as household appliances, furniture, or architecture were still used in our everyday lives. Among what I'd read about the Bauhaus school was the idea of employing art in everyday life, which reminded me of our Islamic arts and their vision of beauty as a characteristic of divine perfection that artists were inspired to achieve, craft and creative art being inseparable features of produced objects. Beauty thus came to be found in the details of everyday life: in opulent attire, household appliances, and the splendor of gorgeous miniatures and Arabic calligraphy, all elevating life to a horizon of perfection.

From Berlin we went to the island, Martin driving four hours on a scenic road as Beethoven's fourth piano concerto accompanied us under a soft spray of rain all the way to Sylt. We stopped twice, once to have lunch in a charming village, and the second time to visit the Nolde Museum, which was set in a garden that Nolde had landscaped himself. The museum was the house that Expressionist painter and printmaker Emil Nolde had lived in after being exiled by the Nazis, and it showcased the works he'd produced during that period, as well as the burned works saved from his apartment and studio in Berlin.

In Eglau's small two-story house, Rafa and I were given a room on the second floor overlooking the garden and adjacent to the graphic art studio. The house was typical of the cottages on the island, which was absolutely heaven on earth. The days were long, which allowed us to roam the delightful island and see its distinctive houses with their tiled roofs covered in coastal vegetation. On the way to the city center there were cafés and shops displaying clothes, innovative jewelry, and very expensive watches, alongside one or two art galleries exhibiting the works of leading German and international artists. This was no surprise, as the island was a holiday resort for the wealthy German elite.

Many of the island's residents and visitors attended Rafa's festive exhibition opening, and he made a brief statement in English to the crowd listening attentively amid his stunning print works. Rafa received many comments and queries that suggested knowledge and respect for this art form as much as they did awe for the prints' techniques, subjects, and captivating Eastern colors.

Upon Martin's request, Rafa exhibited his second war artist's book, titled *No . . . It's a Dirty War*, and which he'd created as part of his daily diary documentation during the 1991 American bombardment. It was one of the most important artist's books he created about the war; it documented the brutal bombing of Iraqi cities and was shocking and confounding to those attending the exhibition. It was a handmade Chinese book, folded like an accordion, its pages stretching three meters by thirty centimeters. The pages bore the prints of Rafa's palm dipped in shades of brown acrylic paint and followed by ink brush strokes in a Chinese style, expressing the intensity of his anger. This was the first time any of his artist's books had been exhibited publicly.

The festive opening went on well into the evening, and the guests spread out around the garden, enjoying the spread of Eastern dishes I'd prepared, including Lebanese salads and sweets I'd brought from Amman. I'll leave the description to Rafa:

Kampen, July 17, 1999

In the morning, we went with Katrina to the Saturday market to buy some things we needed for the opening, and some flowers. After a stroll in Westerland, we returned home.

The opening was at 6 p.m. Guests started arriving at the gallery, and within half an hour it was filled with people of utmost style and respectability. They had different professions and came from different places, for here was a poet and there an engineer, and here an architect, not to mention the mayor. Shortly, the pianist began performing, and after a few lovely jazz pieces, the opening officially began. The mayor gave a speech in which he spoke of the role Otto Eglau had played in creating an artistic environment on the island, followed by his wife, Johanna, who'd drawn international artists, and followed in turn by their daughter, Katrina, who'd built upon their efforts, and whose most significant endeavor to date was this exhibition. Then Katrina gave a speech, in which she narrated how she'd met me and how we'd agreed to hold this exhibition in the memory of her father, who'd considered me one of his most important students, and the closest to him. When it was my turn, I spoke in English and Martin interpreted in German. I spoke of my long-time dream to visit the island after Otto sent me a picture of the place fifteen years ago, and how this impossibly beautiful dream came true. And I invited them to meet me again in my next dream.

The opening went on for a long time, with a buffet of Eastern foods that May prepared, Lebanese sweets, and red Lebanese wine. Many of them bought copies of the exhibition poster and catalogue and asked me to sign them.

Some of them purchased works with great love, and others reserved pieces, some of them promising to come back to buy them. Everyone admired the works, which they found astonishing, and many asked about the techniques I used. The war diary notebook was admired, and sparked their curiosity to learn about the circumstances in which I'd created it. Everyone was sympathetic with Iraq and the Arabs, and understanding of our cause in the German manner, meaning rationally and from a humanitarian perspective at the same time.

After the opening we went to an Austrian restaurant on the seafront to celebrate this great success.

When the exhibition ended, we returned to Berlin, and with some time to spare before returning to Amman and then Bahrain, we traveled to Paris on the invitation of our artist friend Ziad Dalloul.
We both loved traveling by train and enjoyed the rich natural scenery along the route between these two age-old countries. We reserved Berlin–Amsterdam–Paris tickets on the Thalys fast train, which traveled at 280 kilometers per hour; it was our first time experiencing it. En route we spent two days in Amsterdam, where we visited the Rijksmuseum and enjoyed taking our time contemplating the masterpieces

of Rembrandt, Rafa's role model for his brilliant use of light and shadow. As for Vermeer, it was my desire to see many of his masterpieces, especially his painting *View of Delft*, which lived on in my imagination after reading Marcel Proust's novel *In Search of Lost Time,* in which Proust described a yellow stroke that enlivened the painting. Despite the difficulty in doing so, Proust went every morning to the Jeu de Paume in Paris to reverently stand before Vermeer's representation of women at a window, contemplating the effect of light and the magic it imparted to the scene. As for the Van Gogh Museum, I'd previously devoured Vincent van Gogh's life story, correspondences, and works, and yet the museum illuminated much of what had remained unclear to me. The pleasure of wandering the streets of Amsterdam, filled with canals lined with old buildings, flowers, riverboats, and museums, was made all the more enjoyable in the company of Rafa, even in moments of silence.

From the Netherlands, passing through Brussels but not stopping, we arrived in Paris, where our stay was warmed by the generosity and kindness of Ziad Dalloul and Laila Muraywid, a distinguished artist and fine human being, and their wonderful children Bady and Jad. During our four days in Paris, and despite August being the month of holidays and rest for the French, we visited all the art museums and galleries we could, as well as the places Ziad recommended with his good taste and experience. Then we visited his large studio in an old building in east Paris, in an area in which the revolutionaries had advanced in an attack on the Bastille prison. Two centuries later it was turned into the most beautiful modern opera house, which we didn't yet know we'd visit many times in the future.

Sanaa, Damascus, and Aleppo

Sanaa

We'd often dreamed of visiting ancient Arab cities such as Muscat, Sanaa, and Aleppo, and some of these dreams came true while others remained unfulfilled. In 2006, we received an invitation to attend an Arab art symposium and poetry reading sessions organized by the Omani Ministry of Culture. Although it was an official invitation, we did not receive the visa and lost the opportunity we had so long awaited. Two years later, in 2008, we received an invitation from Sanaa to participate in the annual Arab Visual Artists' Convention. At first, we received a rejection from the Yemeni embassy, and so Rafa contacted the Yemeni artist and convention organizer Hakim Al Akel to notify him. He, in turn, told the leading poet and writer Abdel Aziz al-Maqalih, who at the time was the cultural advisor to the president of the republic. And just like that we obtained special approval. It was a marvelous trip and a perfect opportunity to visit Yemen, which we'd always wanted to do. I was especially pleased to be invited to a morning poetry event with leading Yemeni poets including Hoda Ablan.

In one of the sessions, Rafa spoke on his rich artistic experience and made a presentation of works by leading Iraqi artists. In another session I presented a paper on talented young Iraqi artists of the 1980s generation who took refuge in different parts of the world. The study focused on the artists' personal efforts and ordeals during their stay in Amman, Jordan, in the aftermath of the 1991 Gulf War and before resettling in the diaspora.

Beyond the chaos of Sanaa's main streets and its modern areas, the old city, called Bab al-Yemen, took you into a world of wonder. Classified as a UNESCO world heritage site, it immediately transported you to another, distant time, where life continued as it used to, embodied in the city's layout, alleyways, shops, and even the faces of its people. At the entrance to Bab al-Yemen there were also some modern buildings here and there, in which Yemeni artists such as Hakim Al Akil and Nadira Mahmoud had studios, and we were hosted by them there.

All Yemeni women wore veils, but those who revealed their faces were in fact called "unveiled," and it was only those who also covered their faces, appearing in black from head to foot, who were called "veiled." I did not feel a need to cover my hair, however, once I saw how civilized the Yemenis were, and how accepting of tourists, with friendliness and great generosity. While walking with Rafa, we'd be constantly addressed with greetings of welcome, along with the question, "Where are you from?" The moment we pronounced "Iraq," it would be followed with friendly phrases and praise. We'd walk through the city's narrow alleys, past its ancient buildings, shops, and mosques going back to the first Islamic century, and the path would take us past fresh fruit and vegetable markets, including dried fruits such as raisins, and mounds of nuts, especially almonds, of all kinds and sizes. If one carried on to the silver and precious stone market, one would feel as though they'd entered a world only recounted in stories. As for the khat market, it took up an entire section of the area and was always crowded.

The conference organizers scheduled a program for us to visit some of the few Yemeni cities safe to go to at the time, allowing one to truly grasp Yemen with its heritage sites, lush environment, and unique topography. Despite the bitter reality of poverty and chaos so apparent in Sanaa and the few cities we were able to visit, the country's rich traditional architecture, astonishingly unique and lush natural environment, and its people's generosity and warm welcoming of Iraqis, all made us glad to visit Yemen.

Rafa returned from this trip with a collection of photographs of the city we so loved. Upon his return he edited them into a portfolio of three collagraph prints and a mixed-media acrylic painting, titling it *Bab al-Yemen*, and gave two editions to the Yemeni Ministry of Culture. He later repeated this experience with Bab al-Bahrain in Manama, documenting the ancient market with a collection of photographs of other places that he later reproduced in a fascinating portfolio of ten editions.

Damascus and Aleppo

When touristic travel to Syria became possible for Iraqis, we grasped the opportunity while in Jordan and traveled to attend Rafa's solo exhibition in Mona Atassi's gallery in Damascus in 2004. Rafa had previously visited Damascus and held a group exhibition there with Dia al-Azzawi and Saleh al-Jumaie, and I'd visited with my family in the mid-1960s on our way back from Amman, but it was a short trip and I didn't see much. In that short stay, however, I felt the city had stolen my heart, and I longed to visit again. We subsequently made many visits to Syria from Jordan by road, passing through the beautiful countryside adjacent to Damascus.

Visiting Aleppo and its sites remained an aspiration of ours until we were able to plan a special trip to it. Aleppo is the twin city of Mosul, and each were most sorrowfully destroyed by the same barbarity, so I'm grateful that we made this visit in 2009. Whenever we entered any site, the locals would ask, "Are you from Mosul?" We visited the Umayyad Mosque and explored the entire Aleppo fortress complex, climbing its stairs to the roof where we sat and gazed at the panoramic view of the historic city. Then we dedicated an entire day to its bazaar so rich with diverse goods and local products, especially silk and other fabrics the city was renowned for, alongside wood, copper, and glass handicrafts. Spatially it's the longest-stretching Arab market.

From there we entered the maze of the city's ancient alleyways, where some of the houses had been turned into restaurants offering Aleppo kibbeh dishes. Every Syrian city was proud of its kibbeh and other delicious foods.

We spent three days in Aleppo and had traveled lightly. On our last night there we went to a newly constructed neighborhood filled with residential buildings standing side by side with ancient homes, or what remained of them. On the main street Rafa stopped before a humble shop in whose front window he'd noticed a number of good quality inks and paints. His appetite to shop was suddenly whet when he found it carried acrylic paints in a spectrum of hues he usually obtained in Paris. Rafa started picking out colors, and the shopkeeper filled a box with various supplies until it was so heavy that Rafa couldn't carry it. We had to end our walk and return directly to the hotel with his purchases, Rafa indescribably happy.

Paris – Cité internationale des arts

During our sixth year in Bahrain, we began looking into returning to Amman, and took a final decision to resettle there following the 2003 occupation of Iraq. That year Rafa received an invitation from the Al-Mansouria Foundation to host him in its studio at the Cité internationale des arts in Paris for three months starting in November. This invitation came at a nearly perfect time, for we were standing at a crossroads and transitioning into a life free of all restrictions and fully dedicated to creativity. Residency in the studio did not come with any stipulations, but rather hosted artists were free to produce work and exhibit it in their gallery or keep it themselves. The studio belonged to the foundation owned by Princess Jawaher Al Saud, and it was larger than the studios owned by other nations and foundations from around the world.

The Cité internationale des arts was established in Paris in 1965 to host artists from around the world, providing an opportunity for cultural establishments and nations to own private studios, and creating a dialogue of sorts between the world's different cultures. It's located in two historic areas: Le Marais, which hosts 248 studios of between twenty and sixty square meters each, and Montmartre, which has forty studios. We lived in Le Marais, an area with very old buildings, some of which were constructed in the fourteenth century.

The Al-Mansouria Atelier was in a building constructed in the seventeenth century, and we'd see architecture students coming to see it and other historic buildings in the area, which they'd photograph. The studio was on the second floor, and we'd climb the stairs gingerly as there were cracks in a number of the steps. The space consisted of a bathroom beside the entrance, next to a kitchen and dining area with a small table and two chairs, and a large arched window looking onto the building's inner courtyard. This space led to a bedroom with two beds and a small wardrobe, and a similar window also looking onto the courtyard. The kitchen also opened onto a spacious studio with a large worktable, two comfortable sofas, and a large window overlooking the building entrance that filled the space with daylight.

We were indescribably happy to find ourselves in a place pulsing with history and art. In one direction we were close to the Bastille, whose horrific prison had been turned into a modern opera house, and in the other direction only a small bridge separated us from Île Saint-Louis, where the Gauls first settled in Paris, and which stretched along the left bank across from Notre-Dame. When we arrived in Paris it was early in the morning, and we were surprised at how cold it was (one degree Celsius). Once Rafa completed registration of our arrival with the Cité administration, including review of the regulations and conditions for our residency, we received the studio key and found it very warm inside. We immediately contacted our friend Ziad Dalloul, who was in his studio not far from us. He came over straight away to take us on a tour of the vicinity's vital areas, subway and bus stops, the places nearby on rue de Rivoli, and the alleys that led to the Centre Pompidou and shopping areas. He spent the entire day with us.

We were in Paris in the middle of autumn, and my head was filled with a poem by Jacques Prévert, "Les Feuilles mortes," as sung by Yves Montand in his deep voice. The trees were shedding their leaves and the ground was ornamented in yellow and red shot through with orange, arranged in beautiful formations by stormy winds or gentle gusts of breeze. Paris was decorated lavishly, and the shopfronts, large and small, competed in their creative ornamentation welcoming in Christmas and the new year.

We settled into our space and began contacting other close friends, starting with Himat Mohamed Ali, who rarely left our side and was a wonderful companion on this trip. We got in touch with Etel Adnan, who welcomed our arrival with great joy and immediately made plans for us to meet. We also contacted our friends the musicologist Sheherazade Qassem Hassan and the novelist Inaam Kachachi, whom I became very close to on this trip. Along with a number of other Arab friends, we had a nice social life in Paris that complemented the cultural life we found so full that season. Rafa was also eager to be reunited with his beloved brother Sabah Nasiri, who'd resided in France since the 1970s, after decades of being apart. Sabah still had commitments at the University of Limoges, where he was a professor of Arabic literature, but he'd visit us from Limoges on the weekends and we spent a wonderful time together filled with rich and interesting conversation, shared memories, and strong emotion.

We arrived in Paris on the first day of Ramadan, and I chose to commit to fasting. Rafa loved fasting in Ramadan and had grown accustomed to it during our years in Jordan and Bahrain, and he enjoyed sharing with me the breaking of the fast. Even when he wasn't fasting, he'd arrange his eating schedule so that his main meal would be at fast-breaking time, for which he always had suggestions and requests. When Ramadan ended, he'd ask me why we didn't follow this system year-round. In Paris, however, he excused himself from fasting, for he was extremely eager to put his full energy into his work and make the best of his time.

One of our first outings was a walk with Himat to cross over to the left bank and visit the long-established art supply store Magasin Sennelier. Usually, we'd have to return home right away due to the weight of supplies, paints, inks, brushes, canvases, and handmade paper we'd buy. We scheduled our time around Rafa's work hours, and he decided to spend the mornings painting, for he loved to paint in the daylight and only did so in the evening when he had to. He began working a few days after our arrival and remained consistent except for on cloudy days when the daylight coming through our large window was not satisfying to him. He'd finish work before noon, and then we'd go to an art museum or an important seasonal exhibition or roam the main streets and enjoy the city's Christmas decorations. In between we'd walk around the markets and stop at bookshops large and small, and art supply stores wherever we found them. In the evening we'd watch new films at the cinema, attend concerts, or spend time with friends.

I scheduled my time to keep myself busy during Rafa's work hours. I went out in the mornings following breakfast to explore the area and purchase what we needed by way of food. I discovered many places, including a shop selling the latest music recordings and houseware sold right on the street. Ziad also guided me to markets for shopping. In an adjacent area called the Village, I came across an English bookshop where I purchased a number of poetry volumes and novels that I was very pleased with, and which led me to split my time between reading, writing, keeping up with my email, and walking around. During this period Dr. Ferial Ghazoul asked me to conduct an interview with Rafa on his artistic practice for *Alif: Journal of Comparative Poetics*, of which she was chief editor. The journal is published by the Department of English and Comparative Literature at the American University in Cairo, and this commission took up a lot of my time. I kept up with my diary, describing our daily activities in this great city, and also wrote a few literary texts.

During our three months in Paris, Rafa completed a splendid collection of works. Etel was incredibly eager to view his output, and this was the first time she and Simone Fattal visited us in our Paris studio, as we always met in their home or one of their favorite restaurants. It was a cold and rainy day that brought us together in a warm atmosphere of love and excitement, complete with a Baghdadi lunch starting with lentil soup.

Before having lunch, we sat down in the studio for some red wine and a typically expansive exchange of conversation. Etel loved Rafa's work, and always described him as the leading Arab abstract artist. She emotionally sat before his new paintings laid out on the table and rested her head on her palms as though in a state of worship, attempting to contain her trembling upon encountering them. There was a spiritual tie connecting Etel and Rafa, one of a passion for nature and a shared affiliation with it as teacher and friend. They belonged to the same poetic universe. With all humility, Etel asked Rafa, "How can I possibly write on these illuminations?" And yet she produced a dense and remarkable text titled "Poetic Abstraction."

Meeting Solange and Peter (Pierre Olo)

One morning I went to Rafa's office at the University of Bahrain and found him reading a letter, his eyes filled with tears. He handed it to me and said, "This is from my Swedish friend Peter, read it." The letter was highly emotional, with Peter expressing his great concern for us during the Iraqi wars, which he'd followed in the news. He wrote how he'd cried with joy when he saw Rafa's name, and images of his works, published in *Le Monde diplomatique*, thus gaining proof that Rafa was safe, and how he looked forward to seeing him as soon as possible.

Peter had read that issue of the French paper in the company of

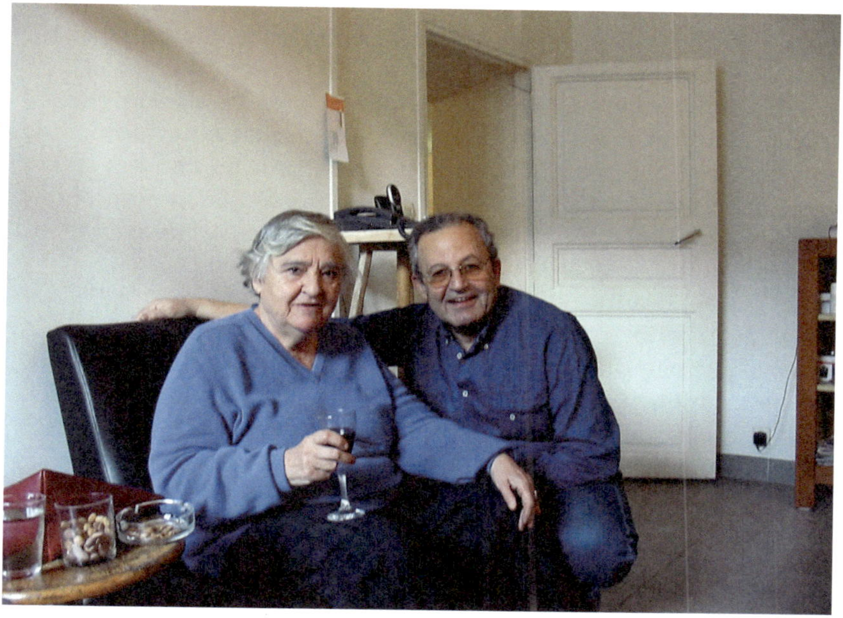

Rafa Nassiri with Etel Adnan at Cité internationale des arts, Paris, 2003

Solange, who he'd known from his days in China when Solange had joined the paper's office which opened in Beijing in 1966. Peter had returned to Beijing to complete his studies, specializing in East Asian arts. He and Solange met there and felt an affinity with one another, but their relationship was cut off when Peter returned to Sweden. Decades later, when Peter was in his sixties and had lost his wife, and Solange, who was younger, was feeling lonely, they started communicating again, sparking a mature love that consumed their hearts.

Solange and I communicated by phone and email, holding an extended conversation in which I assisted with information she requested. She said my name was familiar, for as she'd researched the history and civilization of Iraq, she'd referred to many historical, political, and literary sources translated into French, including the selected stories on war compiled and edited by Inaam Kachachi, which included a story I wrote. Solange's great sympathy for Iraq was clear from her tender tone and her newspaper's humanitarian position toward Iraqis and disapproval of American policy. This paved the way for warm relations between us that further developed.

As the publication of the Iraq issue approached, Solange called and asked me to write an English text expressing my personal feelings toward my homeland's destruction, with the damage incurred through the devastation of its built environment, cultural institutions, museums, and historic libraries. The published issue bore a humanitarian message decrying the war and occupation, with texts on Iraq's history and the global value of its heritage, interspersed with sixteen of Rafa's works.[1] I was pleased to see my testimony occupy a prominent space in the layout.

Rafa and Peter had a historic reunion during our trip to Paris in 2003–04. Peter came with Solange, who, for the sake of their love, had decided to leave her long-standing job at the close of 2004 and henceforth share her life with Peter between Stockholm and Paris. We met regularly and spent an intimate New Year's Eve with this marvelous couple in Solange's small and lovely home. Solange had told us that the paper's chief editor, Egyptian-born Alain Gresh, wanted to meet us, so we had lunch together, which was a memorable opportunity to meet this renowned journalist occupying such a significant place in world media.

Then something unexpected happened. Before Solange left her job or took the once-in-a-lifetime trip to Aswan that she and Peter had planned, Peter had a severe stroke that initially incapacitated him. Solange traveled to Stockholm to take vigilant care of her beloved, alternating shifts with his only daughter, the beautiful Johanna. Peter partly recovered but spent the rest of his life in a wheelchair. What's truly sad, as I learned in Solange's calls and emails, is that the stroke damaged the emotional part of his brain, transforming him from a tender, sensitive soul into an unaffected and cruel man. Yet Solange cared for him with utmost tolerance until his death, finding solace in his daughter Johanna. Solange later accommodated her in an apartment she owned when Johanna fulfilled her aspiration of studying fashion design in Paris.

We met Solange again during our second visit to Paris in 2008. She had somewhat overcome her plight and was preparing to travel to China to publish a photography book on the cultural revolution. A few years later she completed the project and sent me a copy after Rafa had passed away.

Paris – Cité internationale des arts 2008

In 2008, we received another residency invitation to the Cité internationale des arts, this time from the end of April to mid-July. Rafa seemed freer with his time than in the previous residency, and had greater desire to enjoy Parisian life. Himat Mohamed Ali was the first to welcome us, helping to provide everything we needed, and accompanied us to many exhibitions. We enjoyed the rich company of Etel Adnan, Ziad Dalloul, and Laila Muraywid, as well as Adonis, Sheherazade Qassem Hassan, Inaam Kachachi, and other friends. Among the indispensable outings we made was crossing over to the left bank, passing by Notre-Dame, and walking to Rafa's two favorite stores for art supplies: Magasin Sennelier for painting supplies, and Charbonnel, which was established in 1862. Rafa described Charbonnel in his diary as "the favorite of printmakers the world around." In his May 28, 2008, entry, he wrote of purchasing art supplies there as acquiring "everything your heart loves and desires."

It was a rich season filled with concerts, operas, films, and major exhibitions at the Centre Pompidou, the Grand Palais, the Bibliothèque nationale de France, and the Jeu de Paume, all of which we paid frequent and lengthy visits to. It was a wonderful coincidence that the Louvre was holding a large and impressive exhibition of Babylonian antiquities in collaboration with the British Museum, the Pergamon Museum, and the Metropolitan. As always, Sabah Nasiri visited us from Limoges on the weekends, and his knowledgeable company added a rich and interesting dimension to our experience. With his vast and deep knowledge of Mesopotamia's history, arts, and literature, not to mention his ability to read cuneiform, he acted as our guide to the Babylonian exhibition. He spoke with me about his work supervising doctoral candidates studying connections between Aramaic and Arabic poetry.

There were two important exhibitions at the Centre Pompidou that year. The first was by the internationally acclaimed sculptor Louise Bourgeois, who was ninety years old at the time. Visitors were greeted at the entrance with a black spider occupying the northern corner, extending its legs and casting its web over a large area that practically covered the ground floor, which was open to the second. Rafa did not care for her work, but it amazed me. The second exhibition took up the entire top floor and was an extensive visual study of the sacred and the sacrilegious, expressed through works ranging from painting, sculpture, and printmaking to interdisciplinary contemporary art. The exhibition concepts were covered widely and diversely, including religious and mystical imagery of all kinds, as well nonreligious subjects, and addressed any kind of focused seclusion, whether for worship, self-flagellation, or self-restraint in living with the beast, as in the work of Joseph Beuys and others. We visited the exhibition several times, and I watched its unique video works in full.

It was also our good fortune to attend another important art event, the Umm Kulthum exhibition at the Institut du monde arabe. Documenting the art of this vocal legend, the large exhibition was rich in photographs, films, and sound recordings, but unfortunately poor in texts. It included a few studies of her art and life, the most prominent of which was Neamat Ahmed Fouad's book and two secondary sources in French, in addition to interviews and Egyptian entertainment magazines contemporary to her artistic productions. In conjunction with the exhibition, in which you could listen to any of her recorded songs or monthly concerts, there was a program of symposia and concerts by Arab groups. Truly moving was the image of Umm Kulthum, with the phrase "The Fourth Pyramid" hanging on the façade of the Institut du monde arabe overlooking the Seine.

1 The issue was published in 2003, immediately after the start of America's occupation of Iraq and its allies.

Our Baghdad Home and the Productive Years

"I'll take you today to see the land I've decided to buy," Rafa told me. We took a road just outside of west Baghdad, turning onto another that had been forged but not yet paved, and drove deep into virgin land. The car bounced over pits and potholes. I kept my calm and listened in silence as he excitedly told me about plans to populate this area. We might have passed one or two humble homes, and traversed a very long distance, or at least that's how it seemed, before finally turning right, where I saw two houses under construction. Rafa told me they belonged to the filmmaker Yassin al-Bakry and his brother. They were near a eucalyptus grove, a field of wheat stretching before it. "This field will not be built upon," Rafa said.

He turned left, and then switched off the motor and asked me to get out, for this is where our house would be. I found myself standing in a 400-square-meter plot of land, mesmerized by the beautiful space. The golden wheat billowed in waves beneath the gentle afternoon sun, as birds flitting above cried out in sweet chirps. I couldn't fathom how this distant, undeveloped location could be transformed into a populated residential area, or how long it would take for that to happen. We were as far as you could be from west Baghdad, and thirty kilometers from Bab al-Sharqi!

We'd been living in the cottage for a long time, and it gradually got too small for us. Rafa had never thought of owning a home, and always spoke of refusing great offers in beautiful areas of Baghdad, justifying it with the idea of travel. Yet, he'd supervised the construction of his father's house in al-Qadissya, the home that housed us for eleven years, and he knew through experience the costs and effort involved in construction.

Years after having settled down together, and having produced much artwork during this period, Rafa had grown convinced that Baghdad was the ideal place to live and work. He began feeling a need to own a larger space in which to do so, and an urgency for his own printmaking studio. As was his nature, he dreamed without putting effort into research. Then an opportunity arose in the late 1970s to purchase this land at a suitable price. It was in an agricultural area west of Baghdad known as al-Khadra, recently split into plots and owned by the family of his colleague, the talented *santur* (hammered dulcimer) player Hashim al-Rajab.

It was a lucky coincidence that our close friend, the architect Amin Muhieddin Youssef, who resided in Kuwait, came to Baghdad on a visit around that time. Amin was the brother of our friend Rajeh, my friend Anan's husband, and he'd designed their house on Palestine

Street in an attractive, modern style uncommon at the time. We asked him to take on the mission and visited the site together. He understood exactly what we wanted, and in the spring of 1980 we began construction with a down payment that seemed reasonable at the time.

The Iran–Iraq War

On the twentieth of September that same year, 1980, the Iran–Iraq war broke out. We were stunned as the fighter planes rained missiles upon Baghdad, and a state of emergency was declared. Cities were ordered to remain lights-out from sunset to sunrise, and we spent a week in a terrifying atmosphere of war, at the mercy of random missiles that took many innocent people victim.

It was our first experience with a modern war of this scope. We'd previously gone through a number of coups and the bombing of specific sites, incidents that would be short-lived, followed by a curfew for two or three days, after which we'd go on with our lives. But a war like this, as jets broke the sound barrier with their thundering boom, was a new and terrifying experience. After the first week an agreement was reached to halt urban operations and limit targets to the combating forces on the battle fronts. Life became calmer in Baghdad, although we also coexisted with the war through televised "news of the battle." Black signs began appearing throughout the city's streets, bearing the names of young martyrs and leading funeral processions in which the wailing of women sent the martyrs off like grooms to their graves. News of the war dominated life, with whispered questioning of its cause and futility, as well as predictions of it continuing or ending, whether made in pessimism or hope.

There's a long history of conflict along Iraq's eastern border, which stretches a thousand kilometers, and of military maneuvers between what is today Iran and Iraq. These conflicts continued after modern borders were drawn, but have typically been resolved through agreements made by experienced politicians. Mesopotamia's conflicts and wars have remained the same over thousands of years; it's an area that God made rich, the cradle of the earliest civilizations, and has been the desire of invading forces from all directions. Things shifted following 1979 with Iran's regime change and establishment of the Islamic state and the rise of Saddam Hussein in Iraq. War broke out, and Iraq entered a tunnel with no exit. I recall a cartoon published

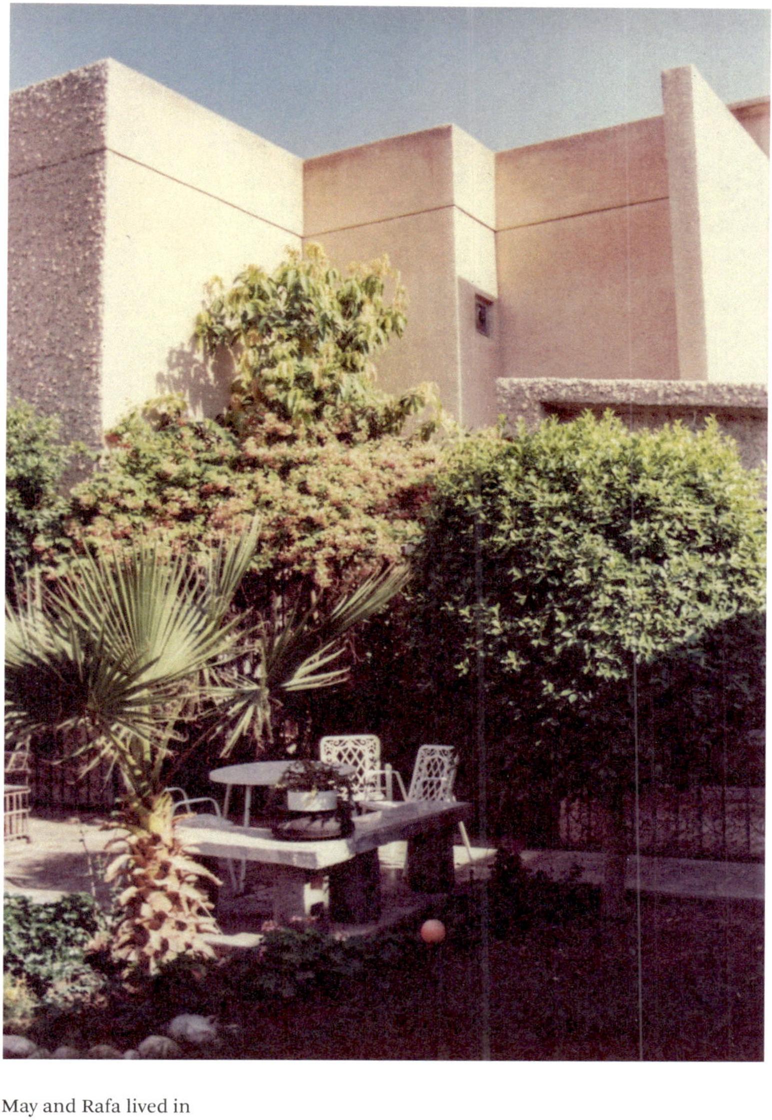

May and Rafa lived in
this house in Khadra
neighborhood, Baghdad,
between 1985 and 1991

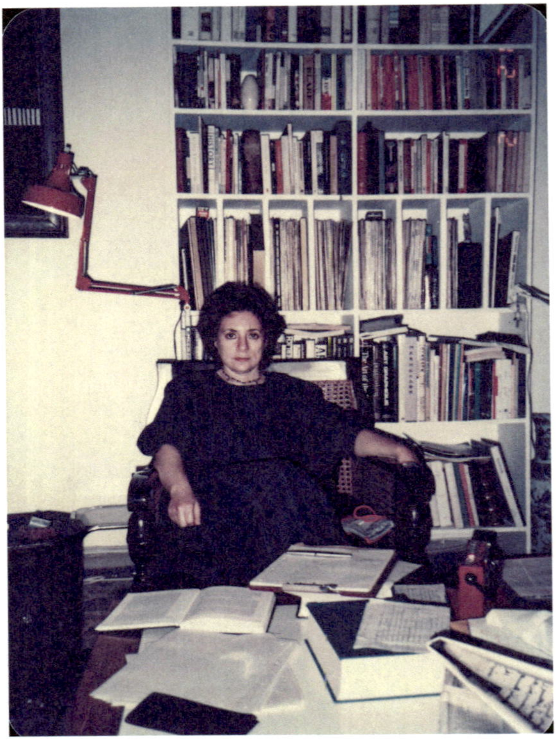

May and Rafa lived in this house in Khadra neighborhood, Baghdad, between 1985 and 1991

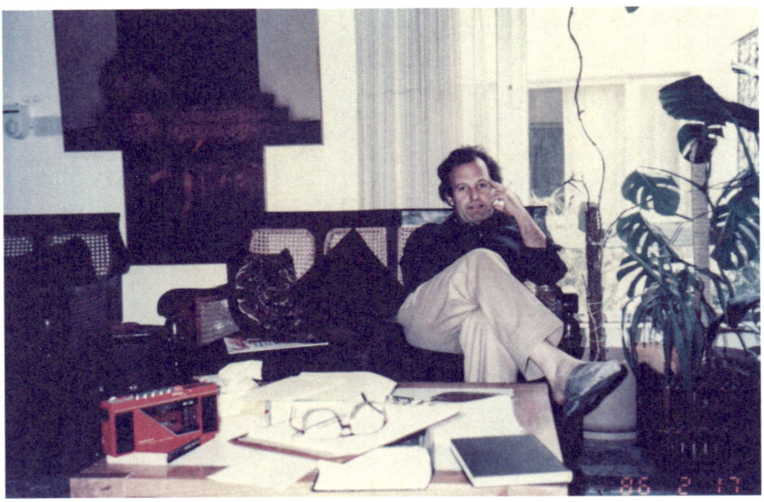

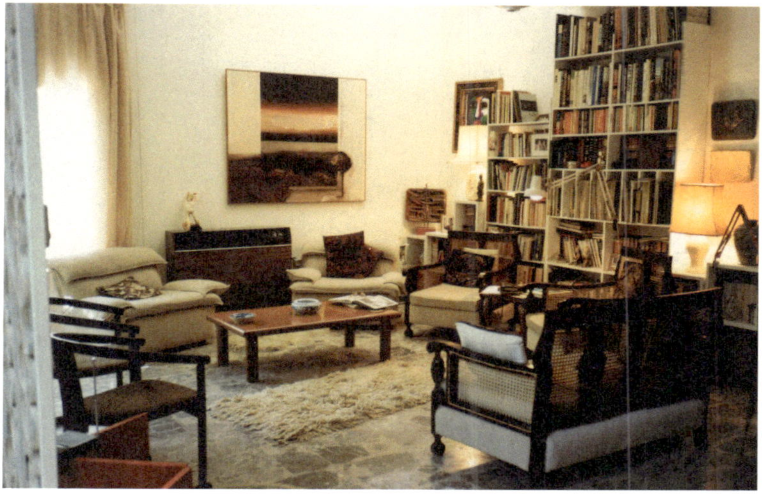

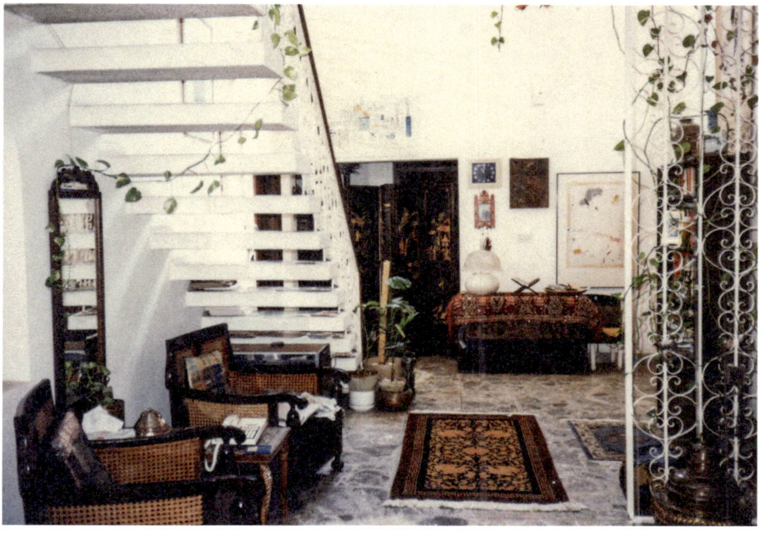

Top: May and Rafa's house, Khadra neighborhood, Baghdad, 1985

Bottom: May and Rafa's house, Khadra neighborhood, Baghdad, 1987

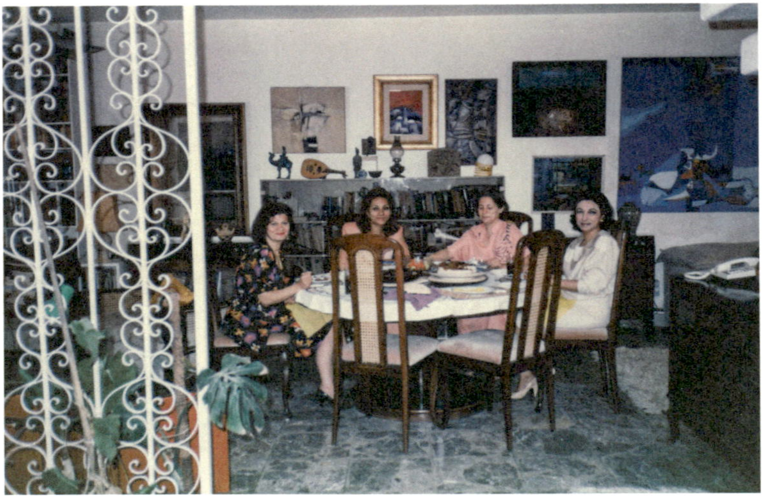

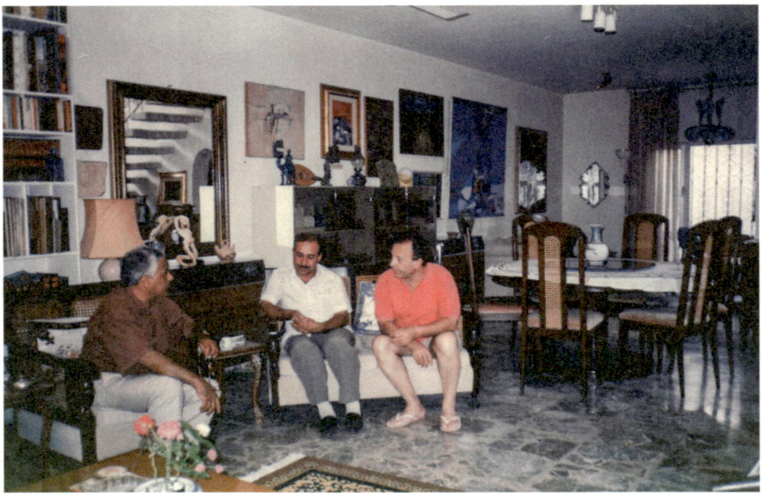

Top: May and Rafa's house, Khadra neighborhood, Baghdad, 1987

Bottom: Receiving guests at May and Rafa's house in Khadra neighborhood, Baghdad, 1990

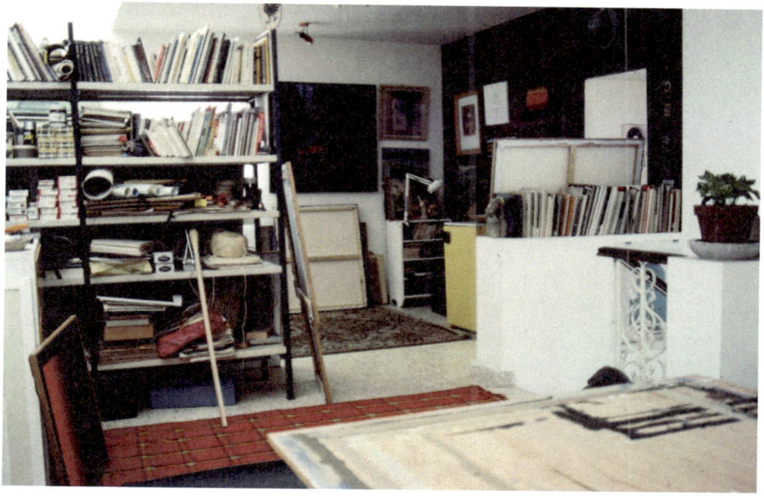

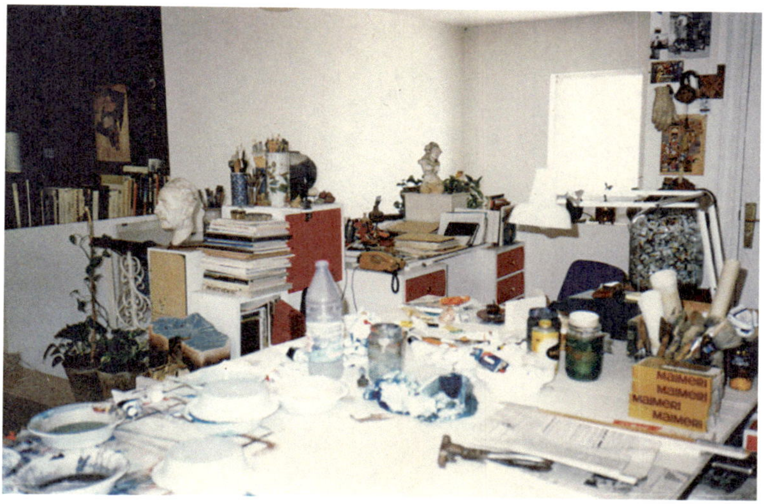

Nasiri studio at
the house in Khadra
neighborhood,
Baghdad, 1987

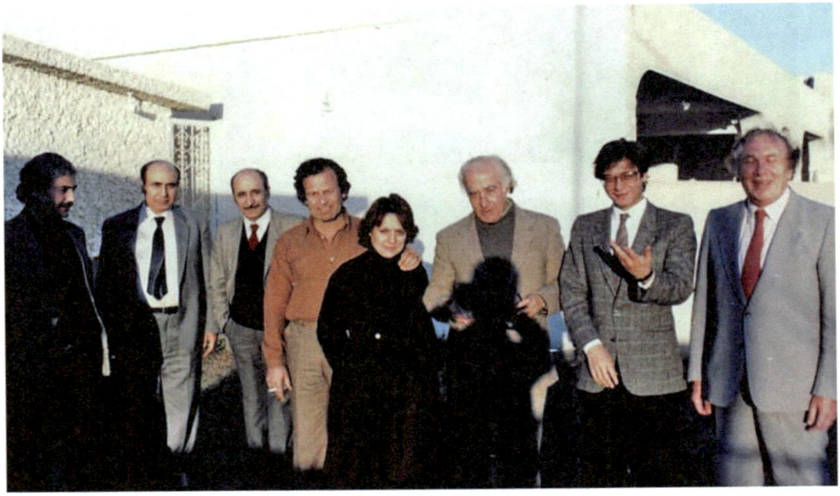

Ahmad Dahbour,
Nihad Al Takarli,
Jabra Ibrahim Jabra,
Mahmoud Darwish,
Nizar Qabbani, at
May and Rafa's house,
Khadra, Baghdad, 1986.
Photo by Charbel
Dagher

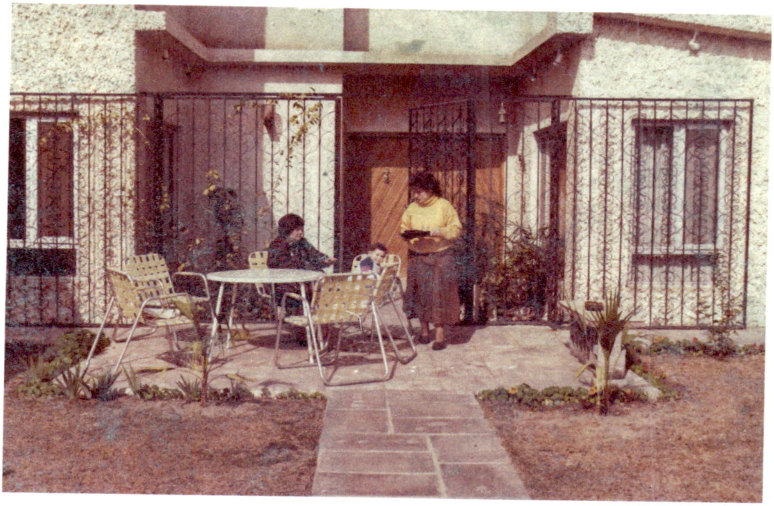

May with her mother, at the entrance of May and Rafa's house in Khadra, Baghdad, 1985

in *Newsweek* at the time showing an Iraqi soldier who'd crammed his boot into the rear end of an Iranian soldier and couldn't pull it back out.

The war compounded our everyday worries as the lives of all Iraqis came under threat. From time to time ground missiles would be fired at sensitive locations in the city, but they usually were off course and struck homes, markets, or areas crowded with people. It happened repeatedly that a family would go out, a missile would strike their home, and they'd return to find it rubble. Sometimes missiles would strike part of a house while another part would be spared, but typically some family members would be killed. Survival became a matter of luck. Many stories circulated at the time, including those told by fighters returning from the front with eyewitness accounts of brutal scenes. The more I heard of these, the more I grew convinced that our existence upon this earth is a matter of fate.

One day Rafa went to register for the purchase a car, as was required at the time. Typically, this was a lengthy process due to the long lines. He left at eight in the morning, and around noon a missile strike in that area was announced, with no further details. At the time, I'd left my job and was dedicated to my writing, having scheduled my time between light household chores and literary work. I was reading E. H. Gombrich's *The Story of Art* when news came of the missile striking Bab al-Sharqi. The world turned black before me and my throat went dry. My natural tendency to worry had me jumping ahead of things, assuming the worst. I left my desk and went to the sofa, paralyzed in thought and movement, staring into space and counting the minutes. It got to be three in the afternoon. I went out to the living room, hoping I could speak with the family, but everyone was taking their afternoon nap and there was not a sound to be heard. At 5:30, Rafa returned, exhausted and drenched in sweat. "I was worried about you and couldn't contact you," he said. I hugged him and placed my hand over his mouth to silence him. "Thank God you're safe!"

We thought this war was just a stage that would soon pass, and yet it didn't, so we carried on with our lives and adjusted to the new reality.

Here, I must trace things back a bit. In general, the life of Iraqis became quite comfortable starting in the mid-1970s. Iraq's economy was a leader among Arab nations due to oil profits, and the provision of major resources and a well-trained workforce led to diverse industrial and agricultural production. Statistics show that the average annual income of Iraqis in 1980 exceeded $3,000.00 when measured against the total population of Iraq, which was about 13 million. The

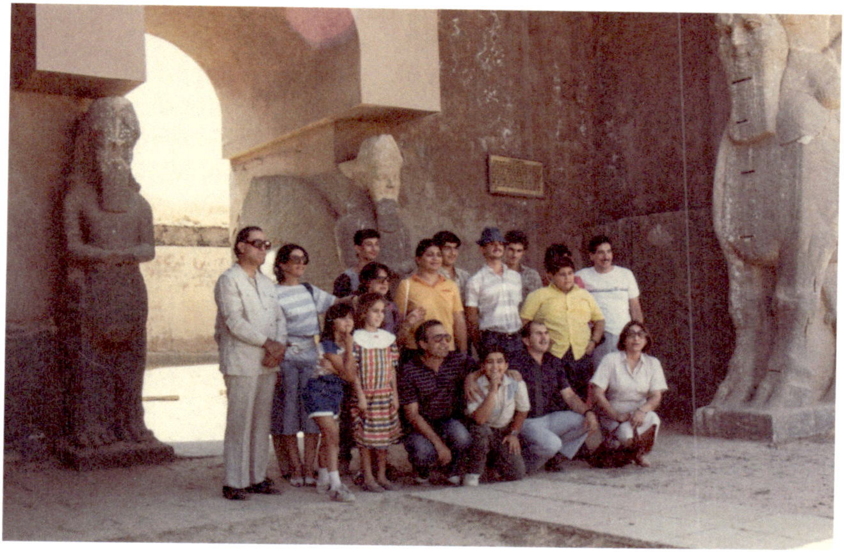

Friend's trip
to Nineveh, 1989

state controlled most everything that was vital, and subsidized water, electricity, and transit, and provided free healthcare and education. During this period, the Iraqi Development Board revived projects that had halted in 1958, and commenced new construction, renovated infrastructure, and supported education by building modern schools, universities, and institutes all over Iraq, as well as specialized hospitals, modern luxury hotels, and residential communities. For a few years Baghdad was turned into an open-air workshop for the construction of modern buildings, roads, and bridges. Subsequently, we could only find our way anywhere via the new traffic signs and main roads. This was accompanied by a boom in the construction of private housing in west and east Baghdad, significantly expanding the populated area of the city. This reflected on both public and private social life, which was always active and lively, and provided for the creation of new public recreation spaces alongside the local clubs and those allocated for certain professional groups that were popular among Iraqi families, in addition to regular cafés. Given the various cultural festivals hosted by the state in Baghdad, Basra, and Mosul, it can be said that this period was in fact one of the richest times in the social, economic, and cultural lives of Iraqis.

In the late 1970s, security restrictions and censorship of people's behavior and speech increased in intensity and cruelty. Arrest campaigns targeted the opposition in general and specifically leftists, while calls by party members to "Baathize" the youth were common. Intellectuals and leftists in particular were under pressure, leading many to leave the country, most of whom were from the 1970s generation. Fear became widespread and people cautiously avoided making slips of the tongue in public places. We all had to avoid mixing with the foreigners residing in Baghdad, for such relations became a subject of security questioning. The slightest rumors could send a person to an unknown fate. All of this encouraged those with weak personalities, and there were many, to exploit opportunities to gain the favor of authorities by offering information, whether true or fabricated. Rumor-mongering increased, becoming an intrinsic feature of the regimes in place since 1958, and anyone could be harmed by accusation of having insulted the authorities.

The night the Iran–Iraq War broke out on September 20, 1980, the Ministry of Information was holding an exhibition at the National Museum of Modern Art titled *Graphic Arts of the Third World* in collaboration with the Iraqi Cultural Centre in London. Many prominent artists, including close friends of ours, had works in the exhibition, and we were scheduled to attend the opening. Upon announcement of the war, however, the invitees left Baghdad by land for Amman.

With unabated urbanization and construction in preparation for Baghdad's hosting of the 1982 Non-Aligned Summit, the price of building materials rose, making people resort to the black market. Construction of our house would move forward at times, and halt at others, as we waited for the availability of materials or the necessary finances, on which we were sometimes short. It thus took us five years to build our house. During this period, we'd purchase basic electric appliances and other goods available at very reasonable prices from cooperatives and store them in my mother's house.

We moved into our new house on the first day of 1985. The area, which came to be known as al-Khadra, or al-Kafa'at, was now developed and attractive, populated with modern homes and boasting paved roads and basic services. Further aiding its rapid development, and assisting us in reaching downtown, was a wide road built by a French company for the opening of the international airport in 1982. By the end of that year, however, it had been decided to halt all flights and to bar travel for touristic purposes.

It was the house of our dreams, brilliantly designed in a modern Baghdadi style appropriate for a writer and artist. The studio on the second floor overlooked the double-volume living area. The house had two bedrooms separated by a bathroom, a large open reception and dining area, and a living area that looked onto an inner garden on one side, and on the other a small garden lined with an irrigation ditch and bitter orange trees. Annexed to Rafa's studio was a room he planned to make into graphic art studio, but he faced difficulties in making that happen and instead turned it into a storeroom. Linking the ground-floor reception area and the studio were stairs with a banister of wrought iron. To separate the entrance from the reception area, wrought iron painted white stretched up to the studio's bookcase. We planted crawling ivy here, and it grew extensively.

In front of the house, the pathway leading to the front door had garden spaces on either side. A tall wrought-iron barrier marked off a small inner garden in which we planted an Egyptian mango tree brought to me from Basra by Amer al-Kamel, the father of my sister-in-law Kholoud, along with a red Indian jasmine he kindly planted himself and which climbed all over the wrought-iron barrier. The Baghdad municipality stipulated that any new residential property be planted with olive trees and date palms, so on either side of the front entrance we planted Maktoum date palms, and on the edge of the garden orange, apple, and apricot trees. As for the olive tree, we planted it beside the sidewalk in front of the house. Because it was agricultural land, the garden flourished in a short period, and by the third year we began harvesting the splendid mangoes and then the delicious dates, which ripened after we left Baghdad, and which were brought to us in Jordan.

The house was stylish and unique in its design, appearance, and simplicity. We were overjoyed by the accomplishment, which became a symbol of our stability and perseverance on our land. I would sometimes get up early, or in the middle of the night when I couldn't sleep, and walk around, filling my eyes with this beautiful dream we'd long awaited. I saw it as the most beautiful home in which I'd ever stepped foot. Our life seemed complete now that Rafa had the studio he needed to produce large-sized works, and space in which to store the many supplies he bought in Baghdad or brought home with him from trips.

Starting in my childhood, I made a habit of holding onto records of my experiences and memories, some of which filtered into my writing. From time to time, I wrote down what I was experiencing and feeling, if not in the consistent manner I followed in later years. I often took my diaries as a friend in which to confide what I would not otherwise share. I also held onto what I could of letters and family documents, some of which belonged to my father and grandfathers and went back to Ottoman rule.

Yet Rafa surpassed me in his preservation of private papers and letters. He was always conscious of, and careful to document, his experiences and artistic legacy. He saved practically every paper he sketched on or letter he received, not to mention every sketch or print he produced from the start of his studies, all the artworks given to him as gifts or exchanged with friends, the photographs he took everywhere, and his diaries and other observations he wrote from time to time. He had a remarkably strong visual and mental memory, and did not forget a face he'd encountered, a work of art he'd been drawn to, or an exhibition or museum he'd visited. He knew the works of Arab and non-Arab artists better than he knew his own relatives.

Rafa was accustomed to keeping two paintings from each stage of his life's work, and at least two copies of each print. Then he began to include me in the selection-making. Before sending works to a gallery, he'd ask me to select with him what we should keep, and he'd say, "This is for you," meaning that we wouldn't let it go. We rarely differed in our selection of his work. We kept up this tradition wherever we went, and whenever Rafa was embarrassed by the insistence of a friend or collector, he'd say, "This is the property of May and it's out of my hands." When we moved into our new home, I told Rafa, "We'll make this house our private museum."

Our Professional Life and the Graphic Art Studio

We spent six years in our house, settled down with a good balance between creative work and an active social life. Rafa now had a large space in which to paint with the freedom he'd longed for and in the sizes that suited his projects. But he continued to wish for an independent space in which to practice printmaking, and could only do so in a separate studio, a wish that came true in 1987.

In 1983, the artist Widad al-Orfali opened a private gallery in a large residential complex in al-Mansour. The gallery occupied the ground floor of a building whose owner lived on the second floor, and formerly had been a nursery. Orfali Gallery was a special project that brought private initiative back to the art world, following efforts made in the 1960s when architects Henry Zvoboda, Said Ali Mazloum, and Rifat Chadirji had opened Al-Wasiti Art Gallery, and then Chadirji opened his own gallery called Iya. Each of these two galleries had celebrated the works of leading modern artists, and each closed down a few years later. In the early 1970s, Dia al-Azzawi, Rafa Nasiri, and Ismail Fattah opened a small art gallery in al-Mansour that did not last long, and which was subsequently taken on by the sculptor Ittihad Karim. None of these efforts were destined to last long due to the economic situation and various personal matters.

The opening of Orfali Gallery came at a time allowing it the support and encouragement of artists and lovers of art. Of course, the lively and engaging personality of Widad al-Orfali also played a large role. The gallery and its activities brought a sense of optimism to social life during that difficult period and opened the door to artistic activity, becoming an oasis in Baghdadi society.

Next to Orfali Gallery, Rafa found an empty and neglected garage with an area of eight by eighteen meters. Its rent was very reasonable, and he didn't hesitate to lease it and use it as a graphic art studio. During this same period other buildings in the complex were used for commercial enterprises of an artistic nature. Businessman Ali al-Kindi and Siham Mekkiya set up a fashion house called Tasmeem, and Widad rented another building nearby that she used for painting and music courses.

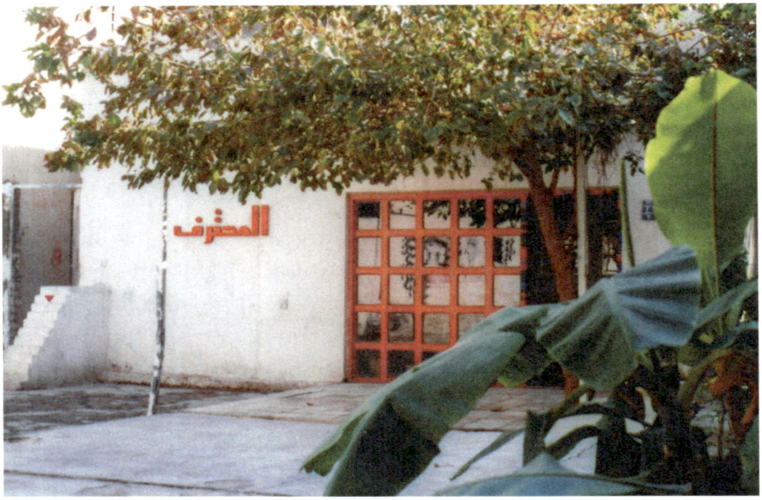

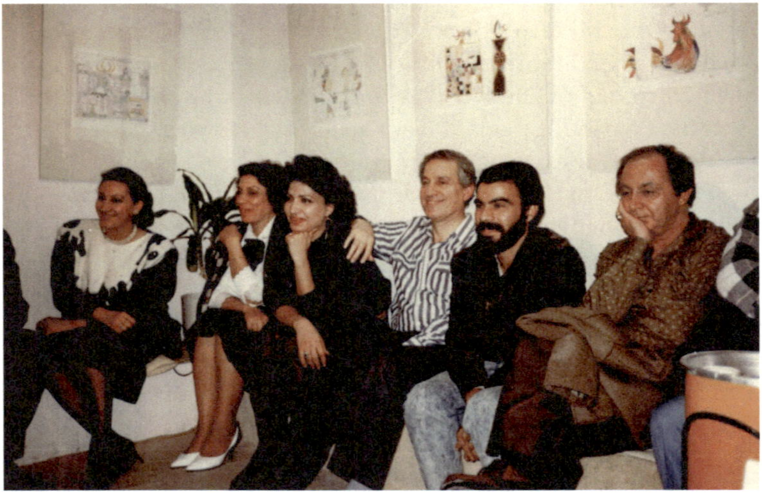

Top: Al Muhtaraf, Rafa Nasiri's Graphic Studio in Al Mansour neighborhood, Baghdad, 1987

Bottom: Dia al-Azzawi's works on paper exhibition at the Graphic Studio (Al Muhtaraf) during a poetry reading evening, 1989

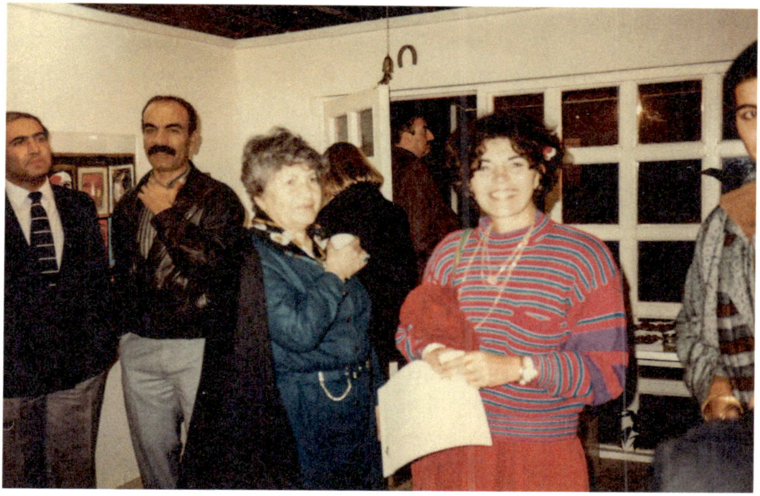

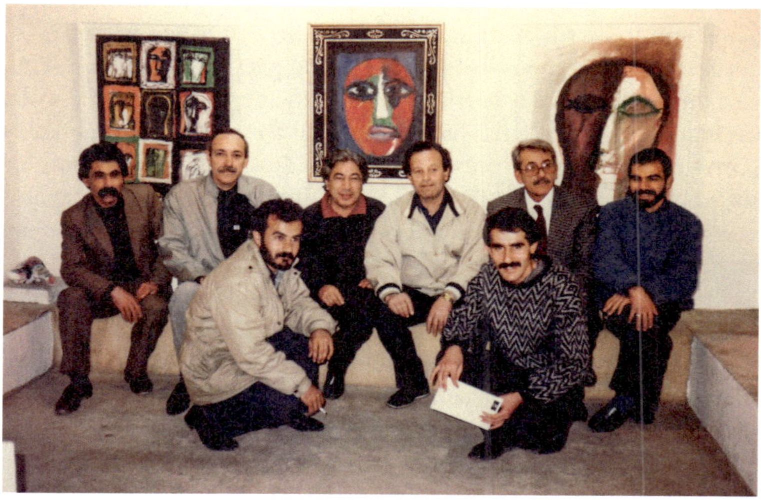

Ismail Fattah al Turk exhibition at the Graphic Studio (Al Muhtaraf), Baghdad, 1989

The garage was virtually in ruins and required some effort to make it ready to work in. Upon consulting our architect friends, Ghassan Raouf, who was working with Hisham Munir, nominated civil engineer Ghazi al-Badri to renovate the space, and he agreed to do so. Ghazi had supervised construction of the Ishtar Sheraton that had recently opened.

Following extensive effort, but with simple solutions and low costs, the garage was transformed into a beautiful and cozy studio ready for use by the summer of 1987. Rafa now had a large space for printmaking and brought in his press that had been stored away for years, later adding another press on loan from the Ministry of Information and Culture. The studio was split into two spaces, the rear with a large work area and a central space for plastic tubs to hold printing paper and chemical solutions. Shelves were fixed to the wall to hold inks, dyes, and books. In the front area Rafa placed a large work desk, and the entrance was designed as a small exhibition space for displaying up to sixteen paper prints (fifty to seventy centimeters). The ceiling was finished with papyrus reed to give the studio a unique touch. To maintain independence while working and prevent him from being disturbed, Rafa placed a barrier between the entrance and the workspace made of a white curtain with a metal chain. I had a small desk in the corner of the exhibition space. The studio's exterior was painted white, and Rafa designed a glass door split into squares with red wooden frames. The space, with its entrance, display area, and work room, was quite impressive.

At first, Rafa intended to limit the display area to his own paper drawings and prints. A few months after opening the studio, he held an exhibition of his paper works, including those that he'd produced in the studio. Later, however, he decided to hold exhibitions of other select paper works, including an exhibition of Dia al-Azzawi's work and two exhibitions of works by Ismail Fattah, as well as an exhibition by a group of Iraqi artists, in addition to other exhibitions of his own paper works.

We were still in the midst of the Iran–Iraq War, which was ongoing on the front. Yet life went on with its cultural and social events. During the period in which Iraqis were barred from traveling abroad for touristic purposes in the 1980s, Baghdad hosted cultural festivals for the visual arts, poetry, and theater. Many artists, writers, intellectuals, and journalists came to attend these events held by the Ministry of Information and Culture, such as the annual Marbid Poetry Festival, the Babylon Festival for Arts, and Arab Theater Festivals. There were also two large international art events held in 1986 and 1988, the

International Baghdad Biennale: "Art for Humanity." Well-known international artists participated in them, and while some only contributed artworks to the exhibitions, such as the sculptor Eduardo Paolozzi (1924–2005), others attended in person, including the famous sculptor Kenneth Armitage (1916–2002).

These occasions provided an opportunity for Iraqis, in particular lovers of poetry and art, to become acquainted with a wide variety of Western and Eastern experiences, especially important for the younger generations who had come of age during the war. Many of the visitors to these events came to visit both Orfali Gallery and the Nasiri Graphic Art Studio. During the 1989 Marbid Poetry Festival, we organized a poetry reading in the studio and invited poet friends of ours to take part. Friends would gather at the openings of exhibitions we held, sometimes lingering until after midnight. There'd also be private invitations and feasts held in our home and the homes of friends, and these gatherings would be attended by Arab and Western intellectuals, poets, and artists. One night during the 1988 International Baghdad Biennale, participating artists and friends came to our house and probably exceeded forty people.

Rafa continued to be invited to art events and group exhibitions all around the world. During that time, it was not permissible for spouses to travel together; this unannounced restriction was instated following several cases in which highly skilled people traveled with their families and did not return. We received an invitation from Mohamed Benaïssa, the Moroccan culture minister at the time, to participate in the 1985 Moussem culturel d'Asilah. An official invitation was sent to the Ministry of Information and Culture, and we were notified by phone that a personal letter had also been sent to the minister requesting we be permitted to travel to participate in the festival's studios and symposia, alongside its painting and printmaking workshops. After waiting for some time, approval was issued only for Rafa's travel. To ask about the matter, we met the minister in person, and he apologized for the delay in my permit's issue, assuring us it would be ready soon. In all confidence, he told Rafa, "You go, and May will arrive the following week." Yet weeks went by, and as the festival came to a close, I finally received the response: "Permission not granted." It was difficult to communicate by phone with Asilah, but Benaïssa had known from the start this was a preventative measure meant to keep one spouse in Iraq as a pawn so that the other would return.

With the ceasefire announced on August 8, 1988, life felt optimistic, and people went out in hordes to express their joy over beginning a new life in peace. Yet, we were not permitted to travel together until the autumn of 1989 upon an official invitation from Princess Wijdan al-Hashemi to attend the contemporary Islamic art exhibition held in London at the Barbican, in which Rafa participated with two large paintings and I contributed a chapter on the roots and history of the modern visual arts movement in Iraq. It was published in an English-language book titled *Contemporary Art from the Islamic World* edited by Wijdan Ali (al-Hashemi) and published in conjunction with the exhibition.

In 1989, Rafa completed his service in Baghdad's Institute of Fine Arts, and at last was free to devote himself fully, day and night, to a life of art, just as he had long aspired. He dedicated the mornings to painting in his home studio, and evenings to printmaking in the graphic art studio. He produced a plethora of remarkable creative works, continuing to develop his visual approach, skills, and vision. All of this was reflected in his work through an incredible rapprochement between printmaking and painting on canvas and paper, particularly when Rafa began creating his artist's books in the summer of 1990.

My own production from 1985 to 1990 was diverse, including art studies in Arabic and English, the publication of two poetry volumes, and many poems and short stories, which I'd pen on a daily basis, in addition to translation projects for the Ministry of Information and Culture. I translated four books, *Poetry in the Making* by Ted Hughes, *Painting and the Novel* by Jeffrey Meyers, *The Art and Science of Visual Illusions* by Nicholas Wade, and *Painting and Poetry: Form, Metaphor, and the Language of Literature* by Franklin and Mary Ann Rogers. This last book was published in the fall of 1990, and its content formed the greatest challenge I'd faced in translation. Yet, I was not in the mood to celebrate its publication or reception, as we'd fallen under the weight of nightmarish sorrow, worry, and an incapacity for joy. Iraq was facing its most uncertain future and severest threat ever upon its decision to invade Kuwait in August of that year.

Our house, and prior to that my mother's, was robbed twice. We'd moved to Jordan in late 1991 and left our house without a guard, for we felt reassured by the presence of our neighbors, none of whom had yet left Iraq. After two years in Jordan, however, we had to employ a guard when our valuable items, with the exception of our books and artworks, were stolen. We thanked God that cultural theft was not among the thieves' interests. They were highly selective, taking electronics such as the television, video player, and modern music deck, the cameras and advanced lenses, smoking paraphernalia including the pipe and lighters, expensive rugs, pretty decorative items, and Bohemian crystal chandeliers. They even took new clothes of mine and Rafa's. As told by my mother and our friend, the ceramicist Tariq Ibrahim, the house was left in a heartbreaking state that provoked tears.

As our home and its contents were of a private nature, we didn't want the guard to reside in the house itself. We built him a private room in part of the garage, leaving enough space to house one car, and provided him with all he needed in terms of cooling, electrical wares, and a phone. We agreed with him to guard the house in return for our covering the costs of his residency in addition to a monthly wage.

Our guard Leith was a polite young man without a family who was in dire need of shelter at the time. He owned a taxi and chauffeured several of our friends' families, and my mother relied on him for her transport. After settling at our house, the neighbors got to know him and he was trusted with taking their daughters to the university. We'd continuously check in on him to see what he needed, especially after the 2003 occupation. In 2006, as the Eid holiday approached, we tried to reach him to no avail, calling both his mobile phone and the land line. By then our neighbors who were friends had all left, leaving their homes rented, sold, or in the trust of Leith, so we had no one who could inform us of his fate. Sectarian strife had broken out in Baghdad and the city was split into districts, some areas Shiite and others Sunni. Shared transport vehicles would stop at the border of an area and passengers would have to catch another to reach their home. After a year of worry and bewilderment, a friend informed us that a strange car was parked in our garage. We made great effort to determine what had happened, and eventually learned the awful news that Leith had been killed at a security checkpoint on the airport highway, and that a stranger was now living in our house.

With the occupation, Iraq fell into utter chaos. The borders were left wide open with no surveillance or conditions for crossing, and anything could be brought in or taken out of the country regardless of its worth. As we believed the place for Rafa's artworks was Baghdad, and our house in particular, we'd left them in the safekeeping of our guard friend. But after he was killed, we found ourselves in a predicament. The area we lived in had become one of the most volatile and dangerous there was, and only local residents could enter. We therefore conceded to our fate.

When things first calmed down, we were able to get the phone number of the person living in our house. It turned out he was a peaceful man who'd had to flee his own home and took refuge in ours.

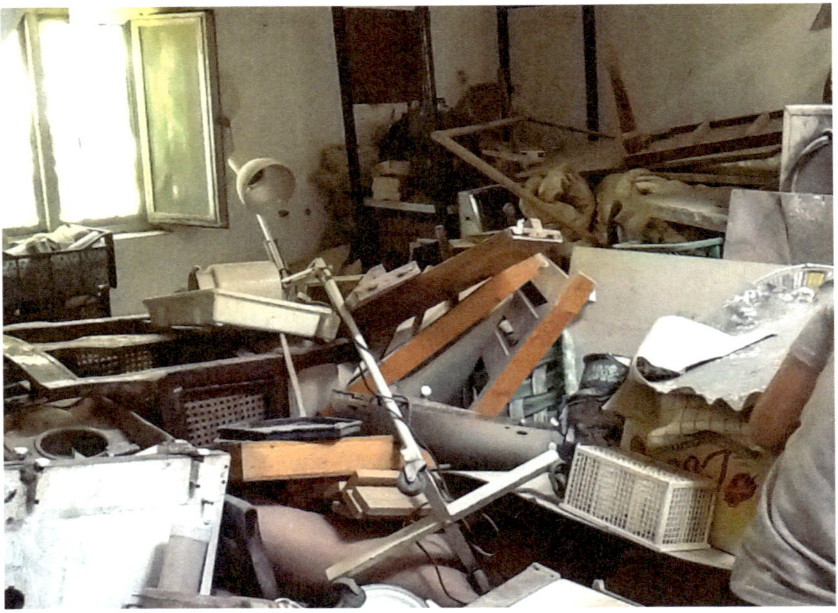

May and Rafa's house and Rafa's studio, in Khadra, were destroyed after the fall and occupation of Baghdad in 2003

He described to Rafa the state of the house when he'd entered it, how he'd found the door wide open and the house full of rats and bugs, and how he and his family had cleaned the books and paintings. "This house is a treasure and I want to protect it," he said. Rafa could tell Abu Mostafa was worried, perhaps thinking we'd either ask him to leave or pay rent. He was relieved to learn we only desired protection of our home and wanted nothing in return. As a safety measure we signed a contract with him.

When things calmed down even further, Rafa sent his relative, the engineer Yasser al-Duri, to inspect our house. Yasser had renovated many of the homes damaged in the area. Upon inspection, he told us it was in very bad shape, and that dampness had spread throughout the second floor, which had been completely neglected, and advised us to sell it rather than take on its costly restoration. The area had changed completely and was no longer comfortable or even feasible to live in. The news was crushing for us. What might have survived of the cultural legacy we'd left behind, and how could we save it?

Rafa agreed with Yasser to undertake the necessary renovation after collecting the artworks, the large paintings in particular, and storing them in his house. The studio contained a large number of Rafa's works: paintings on canvas and wood, and paper works stored in sliding drawers, including academic sketches, graphic art prints, and watercolors from different stages of his life from the early 1960s through to the early 1990s. He kept them as his archive, and it included his prints produced in various studios abroad, as well as what he'd produced in his Baghdad studio. He also had a large collection of artist's books he started making in the mid-1990s. And the list went on. In addition to all this were works he'd exchanged with artist colleagues, leading painters, sculptors, and potters, all of which were produced in an earlier period and bore great historical significance.

In early 2013, cancer was spreading viciously through Rafa's body, and the costly treatment was starting to debilitate us, so we decided to sell the house. Before we could take this step, however, we needed to secure our rich library and the artworks stored in drawers, Rafa's legacy of over fifty years, as well as our papers, letters, diaries, and photographs. The artist Khalid Wahal, one of Rafa's former students in the Institute of Fine Arts and very close to him, undertook the mission of transporting his works to Amman. Rafa had previously used Khalid's assistance in printing graphic artworks in the Baghdad studio, and he'd often come to our house in al-Kafa'at, so he knew what was there. In order to get the works out of Iraq in an official manner, Rafa spoke with Princess Wijdan al-Hashemi, head of the Royal Society of Fine Arts, and she suggested holding a large retrospective exhibition in Jordan, for which she wrote an official letter to the Iraqi Ministry of Culture requesting permission for transport of the works.

In May, Khalid Wahal went to Baghdad and gathered what he could of Rafa's works in the house (as well as Rafa's printing press and his metal etching plates).[1] He also contacted Yasser to pick up the large-sized works he'd promised to keep and placed them in wooden boxes to ship. As for the paper works, documents, and other items still in their wooden storage spaces or elsewhere in the house, Khalid collected what he could and placed them in cardboard boxes, securing a driver to take them in stages to Amman. There's no need to elaborate here on the obstacles encountered. The paintings scheduled to arrive by land in May only arrived in mid-August, and by plane via Kurdistan. They had not been allowed to leave Baghdad despite their official permits. The cardboard boxes arrived by land in stages, and included Rafa's academic sketches produced in China, a few watercolors and prints, the artist's books, and some letters, official papers, photographs, and a few small souvenirs Rafa had collected. Despite the losses incurred, we were delighted with what arrived. As for our extensive library filled with literature, nonfiction, and art books, I secured it with a close friend who was a writer and librarian.

By that time we'd purchased an apartment in Amman that freed us from having to rent workspaces, thanks to our friend Fikrat Abdel Qadir Totonji, who offered us an apartment in Luweibdeh in a building still under construction. Rafa designed the interior, and we paid for it in installments. The artworks arrived at a time when Rafa would leave the hospital only to return again a few days later; movement was extremely difficult for him, and disease was spreading viciously through his bones. Yet, he was overjoyed to retrieve this legacy of his. He attended his retrospective exhibition in a wheelchair, pleased to see his legacy on display before him, hung on the walls of the Jordan National Gallery of Fine Arts in the presence of many of our friends, acquaintances, and lovers of his art.

After having removed our artworks from the house, it was now possible to hand it over to its eventual purchaser. This procedure took place with the assistance of our loyal friend, the architect Faisal al-Jibouri, who contracted a young lawyer called Yasser al-Hashimi, whom Faisal himself had worked with and whom he described as honest, a characteristic that had become extremely rare in the new

Iraq. Faisal followed the sale with Yasser, but unfortunately the volatile area was becoming more and more dangerous, and the house declined in value day by day.

Once our family left Baghdad, either through passing away or by moving elsewhere, and after our house was sold, nothing remained for us of our city and home other than an image etched in our souls and in our memory, one that would nurture our lives until the end.

1 The graphic art studio was later maintained by Rafa's nephew, architect and printmaker Muhanad Nasiri.

It’s a Dirty War

In the summer of 1990 we were guests of the twelfth Moussem culturel d'Asilah in Morocco. That year, we were accompanied by our dear friends, architect Wijdan Maher and poet Farouq Yousef, along with his wife Sanaa and their son Amr. We were also pleased to meet again, after so many years, artist Mehdi Moutashar, who'd lived in Arles in southern France, once making his way there after leaving Iraq in the 1970s. He is a well-known Iraqi artist residing in Arles and married to French scholar, Michel Moutashar, who was at that time working at Musée Réattu and became the director of the same Museum. It was a touching meeting, as he still held intense longing for Iraq.

The day after our arrival, we began the routine we'd followed ever since first visiting this beautiful coastal town. Wijdan and Rafa and I stayed in Hotel Al Khaima, which to our surprise had been expanded with new wings overlooking the ocean. As for Farouq and his family, they stayed in Tangier, which was thirty or forty kilometers to the north, and they'd come every day in small busses that transported festival guests between Tangier and Asilah. Rafa spent his mornings in the graphic art studio, and I went to the Hassan II Center in the Casbah, which was the main meeting place for all the festival delegations. Usually, I sat in the courtyard and read or wrote, or might attend the cultural symposia accompanying the artistic events. The festival that year was set apart by the company of Wijdan Maher, who was attending for the first time, and we spent much enjoyable time together.

Every year the festival is attended by a group of artists and writers who are invited according to a curated art and culture program. There were certain guests we were used to always meeting there, including Tayeb Saleh, Buland al-Haidari, Mohammad Omar Khalil, Charbel Dagher, Pierre Abi Saab, and the Sudanese researcher residing in Canada, Ibrahim Al-Shush. Usually, they would be invited for the festival's entire duration, like the artists working in the printmaking studio. Among those invited that year was the Syrian artist Ziad Dalloul and his wife, artist Laila Muraywid, with their lovely child Bady, as well as the accomplished Syrian artist Fateh Moudarres, who was the guest of honor and had a wing allocated for his solo exhibition. We were all guests at Hotel Al Khaima and would meet every morning to have breakfast on the veranda overlooking the pool. There, in a friendly atmosphere, we'd exchange both serious and frivolous conversation, especially with Fateh, whom we'd compete with on secretly circulated jokes about our similar situations in Syria and Iraq. That year the festival also invited female Arab sociologists,

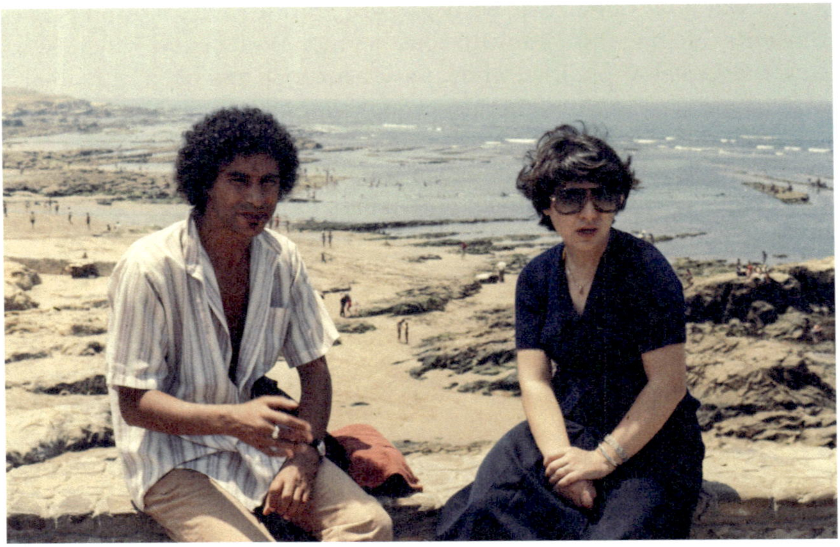

Top: With Moroccan
artist Mohamed Kacimi,
Asilah, 1992

who participated in a symposium organized and moderated by the Tunisian researcher al-Taher Labib, alongside other art and theory symposia. As every year, the festival also included a program of plays, performances, and concerts, and the guest of honor was the renowned Iraqi oud player Salman Shukur.

Politically, tension between Kuwait and Iraq had reached its peak, yet we were distant and in the gracious company of beauty and safety. On the morning of August 2, we gathered like every morning on the hotel veranda, and Fateh joined his family at the table beside ours. I noticed some concern on his face when he opened with, "Joking is permitted, but should it really reach the point of occupying Kuwait?" We couldn't believe what we heard; I thought it was Fateh who was going too far with his joking and objected. He immediately retracted his statement, saying, "No, I'm just joking with you!" But it was true, and Fateh later told me that my reaction made him want to protect me from the shock.

I don't know how to describe those difficult moments in which shock, anger, and sorrow coexisted. We Iraqis from Baghdad gathered together, away from the others who avoided sitting or speaking with us. Some even avoided greeting us, simply whispering and shooting us venomous looks. Our friend Charbel Dagher joined us in our bewilderment and sorrow, with Farouq Yousef, with his constant cheer and mockery, lightened our gloom. How had the crisis reached the point of a military attack?

Most of the world's nations soon joined an international coalition led by America, and full sanctions on Iraq were declared. Most of the Arab countries, with very few exceptions, were quick to join. Mohamed Benaïssa came to the hotel to see how we were doing and informed us that Morocco had immediately announced it was joining the coalition. There was only one television in Hotel Al Khaima, in the main reception hall, and I don't recall that we'd ever sat before it, even once. But now we began watching it, seeing the jets gather in military bases in Qatar and Bahrain, landing rapidly like striking hawks. Their appearance alone was sufficient to incite terror in one's soul.

Two days later, our dear host whispered to us that he'd made a special request to the prime minister to host us in Morocco. We thanked him for this noble initiative, but the decision was not that easy to take. Frankly, we were at a loss. How could we stay, how would we live, and what kind of life would this be? Would it be easy to let go of our life, our family, and our home? We received sympathy from some of our friends there, including Western foreigners who worked with Rafa in the studio and offered for him to travel to London or Paris. This bewildering situation sent Rafa into one of his spells of silence that he'd always fall into when facing serious crises. They'd turn him into a slab of stone that only I'd dare to hurl myself against.

My attachment to Baghdad and my family was nonnegotiable and my return was certain, but I didn't share this for fear of influencing Rafa. A week of silence between us went by in a state of near complete alienation. One afternoon I saw him lying on his back, his eyes focused on the ceiling. I knelt beside the bed and kissed his hand and asked him to tell me what he was thinking. He swore he was unable to decide. I was certain, after nearly twenty years together, that Rafa could no longer let go of Baghdad, especially after having accomplished all he'd striven for personally and professionally. It was no longer an easy matter to forego everything and begin anew in a foreign, uncertain place. Yet in Iraq we were also facing an uncertain future.

When Benaïssa noticed we hadn't responded to his invitation to reside in Morocco, he asked to speak with me alone. In a concerned tone he warned, "You don't know what's going to happen in Iraq. There'll be a war, and everything will be affected. Rafa is a big responsibility, and you must protect his life. If you decide to stay in Iraq, he'll have to stay too, because he won't desert you." I told him, "Have faith that Rafa will only be convinced on his own. I'd sacrifice my soul for him, but I won't take a decision for him."

I was well aware of Rafa's concern, and his fear of an unstable and uncertain life. I'd known him when he couldn't imagine any future for his life except outside of Iraq, and yet he'd continued to avoid a life away from home. So, what could I expect now? When I told him of Benaïssa's concern, and to lessen his burden, I suggested he stay in Morocco alone, and he smiled but did not reply.

Among those attending the festival that year were Iraqis working for the United Nations, and some of them stayed until the end of the festival. The most prominent among them was Salah al-Shaikhly, an old-school Baathist who'd refused to return to Iraq following the assassination of his brother Abdel Karim al-Shaikhly, the former foreign affairs minister, in Baghdad in 1980. Al-Shaikhly was well informed on the matters taking place, and he knew the Baathist leadership well, including President Saddam Hussein himself. We'd listen to his detailed explanation, rational analysis, and expectations of what might happen. He advised us, like many others, not to return to Iraq under such difficult circumstances. Our friend Dia al-Azzawi

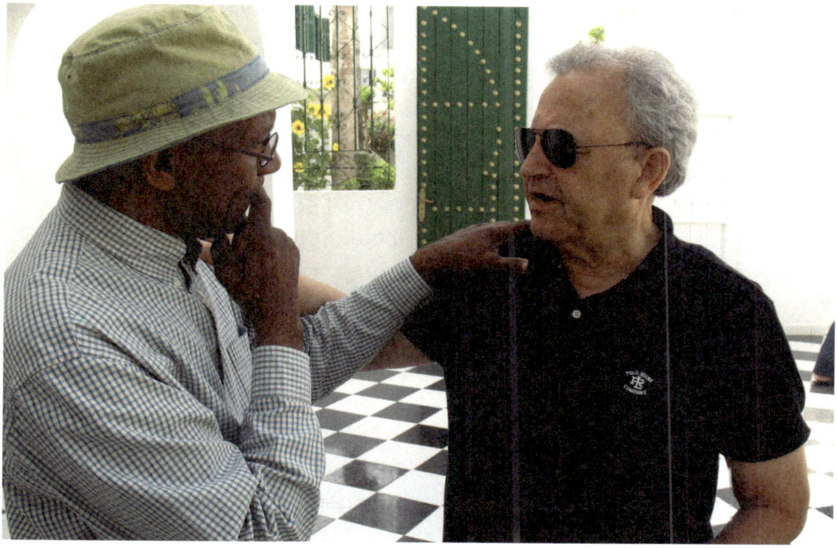

Bottom: Rafa with artist
Mohammad Omar
Khalil, Asilah, 2010

also advised us not to go back. But being away from my family in such circumstances was a terrifying nightmare.

We'd realized a countdown to the end of Saddam Hussein's rule had begun with the end of the Iran–Iraq War. After having praised Iraq's development and its army's strength, the West began a fierce countercampaign in the media. We'd noticed this in the summer of 1989 when we were in London. The British papers were inciting great indignation over the arms-to-Iraq affair underway in Britain with the knowledge of the government. They were filled with incendiary articles opposing Saddam's brute force and the strength of his army, and warning against his aggressions. This was followed by another fierce campaign when the Iraqi judiciary condemned the British spy whom Iraqi intelligence had uncovered, Farzad Bazoft, and handed him a death sentence. Then came the attack on Kuwait, after it had encroached on Iraqi oil fields and vetoed the aid grants Iraq desperately needed to recover from the war-driven economic crisis. The road had been paved for America to destroy Iraq and depose its regime. It adopted the media war and never looked back.

The festival was on the verge of ending, with only a few sessions remaining, the final of which were poetry readings that Farouq Yousef and I were invited to take part in. Mohamed Benaïssa moderated the session, introducing me with a touching statement. I read my most recent poems, which I'd written under the emotional weight of the Iran–Iraq War, the psychological pressures of everyday life, and fear of monitoring and censorship. The audience clouded over before me, and all I could see were Rafa's shining eyes, through which I realized the effect of my performance. It appears my poems surprised even those close to me, and strongly affected the poetry lovers in the audience, as Rafa conveyed to me with the comments he received.

As the days passed, and due to continued dialogue with Farouq and Wijdan, Rafa relaxed some and began speaking about our return as though it were a natural and given fact. This is how Rafa dealt with pivotal decisions: he only listened to his inner voice and usually left matters to take their course and dictate the outcome themselves. We practically cut ourselves off from the remaining festival participants, with the exception of those sympathetic to our predicament, including Charbel Dagher, Mohammad Omar Khalil, and Moroccan and Arab friends, among others. Time passed, and Rafa continued calmly working in the studio, immersed in his artistic production, while I remained in a state of suppressed worry. Wijdan was torn between returning to Baghdad or traveling to London, while Farouq continued to lighten the atmosphere with his amusing wit.

Wijdan was eager to visit her ill brother in London, and this was her only opportunity to do so, but permission to enter Britain had become nearly impossible. She asked me to discuss with Mohamed Benaïssa if he could mediate with the British ambassador, in hopes that he'd respond to this humanitarian circumstance and assist her. After some hesitation, Benaïssa said that he'd try. Thank God the effort was a success and Wijdan gained permission to travel to London. We went to bid her farewell at the Tangier airport, feeling as though we were all heading to our ultimate fates and not knowing if we'd meet again.

We waited longer. None of the festival participants remained, and the hotel emptied except for us and Farouq, who came with his family to stay in Asilah. We were informed that the last Iraqi flight would leave from Casablanca to Amman and then Baghdad on August 30. At eight in the morning we were at the airport, where a private area was set aside for us and filled with Iraqi families who'd been unable to travel. We spent about five hours in this closed-off hall, with small children and no food or drink, in keeping with the directives of the sanctions. Likewise, it was not permitted for the Iraqi plane to load food or drinks until landing in Tunisia, which had not yet joined the embargo, and only there were we able to obtain food and water.

Jordan remained one of the few Arab countries that did not cut off relations with Iraq. We reached the Amman airport at three in the morning and found it filled with Iraqis returning from various places, men, women, and children spread out across the floors with their bags. The scene made it appear as though the war had indeed begun. We only had a few hours until we traveled on to Baghdad, and Rafa was exhausted and needed to rest, so we spent the time in Alia Hotel near the airport.

In Baghdad we found things calm, life continuing as usual except for people's whispers of worry. Those with relatives abroad were urged to leave the country. We knew the war was imminent from the warnings, threats, and guidance broadcast on foreign radio channels, as well the Iraqi civil defense's instructions to distance ourselves from central Baghdad should military operations commence. Many people therefore prepared to leave Baghdad once an attack began, and to seek refuge outside the city in rural areas, villages, or small towns.

We returned to our professional and social lives with our family and friends, although apprehension remained our constant companion. We continued our daily trips to Rafa's graphic art studio in al-Mansour, continuing, like our neighbors there, to frequent the residential and art complex.

During that period before the war began, numerous delegations and brokers from East and West visited Baghdad, all trying in vain to convince Saddam Hussein to withdraw from Kuwait. Among those delegations were journalists who came to witness events, observe cultural and social life in Iraq after its construction boom, and get to know the opinions of people firsthand. Most of the time they arrived with negative conceptions of life in Iraq. The al-Mansour complex became one of the locations that media professionals visited, and the wonderful Widad al-Orfali welcomed them in her private gallery with her usual cheerfulness. She invited some to her home to introduce them to this peaceful community, aspiring to gain their sympathy and support in hopes that they'd view the fate awaiting Iraqis with objectivity.

Among these media professionals was an American journalist working for the *New York Times*, as I recall, who visited Orfali Gallery. His last name somewhat resembled her family name, and Widad welcomed him warmly, insisting they were related. She and her late husband Abdel Hamid al-Azzawi invited the journalist to their home, and on his return he wrote an elaborate and moving article on the situation of Iraq as it anticipated war, including a beautiful description of Widad's spontaneous and generous welcome, and her insistence that there was a connection between their families. He described her art gallery and the beautiful works by Iraqi artists exhibited there, praising her generosity as a host and her humbly playing the piano and singing for him. His article reflected how touched he was by the friendliness and goodwill he experienced with Iraqis, and in particular with Widad, who strove to embody this ancient people's love of peace, culture, and beauty. He concluded the article with an admonition to the American government that the war would only target peaceful and innocent people such as Widad al-Orfali. There's no need to mention the many similar articles published in the West, nor the demonstrations held against the impending war by millions in America, Europe, and countries around the world. It was all to no avail. The American coalition's decision was decisive: Iraq must be destroyed.

During those days of cautious apprehension, Rafa continued working tirelessly. Work was his refuge, in which he could release his pent-up worries and fears over what was to come without losing his external calm. He believed in living in the present and continued his life as actively as possible. We were aware of the imminent danger facing us under the threat of war, and our destiny seemed vague and uncertain. Rafa concealed his concern under a shell of calm and silence, and when I was with him, I gained a sense of security, only feeling threatened when we were separated. Our presence together guaranteed that our fate would be shared, no matter what form it took.

One evening, the threat of war drawing near, we were, as usual, in the graphic art studio. Rafa was immersed in his work, and I was calmly reading Umberto Eco's *The Name of the Rose*, completely absorbed in its plot twists filled with intrigue as a search went on for a rare Arabic manuscript. The writer Kheiry Mansour passed by to see us, as he often did. He stood before me in shock, asking in a low voice, "In the name of all that you hold dearest, will you give me an honest reply?" I said, "Of course, and with no need to swear."

"Are you two taking tranquilizers?" he asked. I laughed with all my heart. "I seek refuge in God! Why do you ask?" And he said, "By God, tell me how you two maintain such a sense of calm! Don't you hear what's happening all around us? That such and such and so on." I told him there was nothing we could do but, like others, await our fate.

I'd like to linger at this pivotal point in our life. After we moved into our house and set up the graphic art studio, and Rafa was freed from his job responsibilities, he reached the peak of his contentment and sense of stability. He'd become the master of his time, traveled a great deal, and produced art prolifically. I only saw him sorrowful following the death of his father, when he went through a period of deep silence reflected in the images and texts he left in his diaries.

I was accustomed to going to the graphic art studio twice a week to take care of a few matters and see Rafa's new work. Usually, I'd spend the time reading, or reviewing texts I'd written if I was not working on something new. I always found him fully immersed in his art, seemingly lost in a distant and mysterious world. He might raise his eyes suddenly and smile at me, but then he'd disappear again into his private state of working. I wouldn't interrupt him until I heard him sigh out loud as the customary sign that he was finished. As the political crisis intensified, Rafa insisted I accompany him daily to the studio.

Sometimes friends would stop by, or our beloved neighbor Widad al-Orfali would come with her oud to play and sing for us. We welcomed many friends in the studio: Ismail Fattah, Ali Taleb, Alaa Bashir, Farouq Yousef, and Rafa's students who were close to him, such as Samer Osama, Hiyan Abdel Jabbar, and others who might visit by chance. When cultural events were held in Baghdad, there'd typically be a group of our friends and acquaintances in attendance, artists, writers, and journalists. Sometimes a friend would come by without prior arrangement, bringing with them one of the visitors in Iraq for various reasons. I recall Kheiry Mansour's visit with Mahmoud Darwish, in the company of Yasser Abed Rabbo and Bassam Abu Sherif, who'd come to take part in the meetings of the Palestine Liberation Organization. That was in the fall of 1990. We were delighted with their visit, and they enjoyed seeing Rafa's works, especially Mahmoud, who loved art. We all had dinner at Shumu‘ (Candles) restaurant in Karrada.

On the eve of the attack on Baghdad, we were, as always, in the studio. The complex was bare and desolate, with no one there but us. From time to time I'd look over with concern, wondering when Rafa would finish, when our neighbor Siham Mekkiya and her son-in-law Ali Al-Kindi looked in on us as they were checking on their fashion house opposite the studio. Siham stuck her head around the door, looking at us in surprise when she found Rafa focused intently on his work. "Haven't you heard the news? What are you doing here?!" she cried. Rafa laughed in response. It was after 9 p.m. and Baghdad was apprehensively awaiting zero hour.

The Night of January 16–17, 1991

At 2:20 a.m. we were awoken by the horrific thunder of bombing. So, this was the war under whose threat we'd been living for months now. The ground shook beneath us as the terrifying roar of jets broke the sound barrier and rained missiles upon Baghdad. Pitch-black darkness fell. We peeked out from behind the curtains and saw flames raging in the distance. We lived near the outskirts of Baghdad, and the heart of the capital was aflame, as described by the British correspondent John Simpson. Watching the view from his room in the Meridian Hotel overlooking the Tigris, he said Baghdad looked like a fireworks display. This is how the experienced journalist saw the coalition attack led by America. Power plants and reservoirs were among the primary targets. Yet, why bomb cities? Why terrify the people? These were my naïve ponderings at that moment, perhaps alerting me that the war to liberate Kuwait, with its catchword "shock and awe," in fact aimed to destroy Iraq, both its structures and its people. This was and still can be seen today in the implications of both previous and subsequent events that produced the horrors continuing to affect Iraq to this day.

At that moment, in which everything seemed uncertain, we felt nothing but desolation, bewilderment, and shock. Yet, we held ourselves together and gave in to the shaking of the earth below us, waiting for the dawn's sun to rise. I don't know when or how we fell back asleep, but when I awoke at 8 a.m. I found that Rafa had woken before me and bathed and dressed, looking as nicely put together as always. We used up our last drops of hot water, and with them ended our life of comfort. We were going through an intense cold spell that winter, and temperatures plummeted to below zero at night.

With the new day, the air raids came to a halt. I put on a red blouse and combed my hair, filled with a strange sense of boldness and a readiness to face whatever fate might bring. I was with Rafa, and that was enough. At 10 a.m. I found the neighbors gathering in front of our house, which was opposite a newly built home owned by engineer Mohamed al-Mawsawi. He and his family were preparing, like many others, to move to a safe area outside of Baghdad, and he offered for the neighbors to stay in his fortified shelter. He left the key with our neighbor Salah al-Malaak, who'd been my colleague at the reinsurance company for seventeen years. I went out to join them, and Rafa greeted me with a look of satisfaction on his face, as the clear and radiant January sun shone upon us, and I smiled and wished all a good morning. Our neighbor al-Mawsawi was surprised by this and stared at me, not returning my greeting but remarking, "Look at her!" In turn, I was surprised by his disheveled appearance and worn-out attire. He was overcome with terror and anxiety. "I don't want to meet the face of God except when I'm smiling and well-dressed," I told him.

Salah al-Malaak, along with his wife and daughter, who was eight months' pregnant, were the first to move into the shelter. I understood his fear and concern as he faced this harrowing responsibility, especially as his daughter's husband was in the military service like most young men. Another neighbor joining us that morning was the businessman Talib al-Tahhan, with his wife and three children. They seemed composed, and tried, like us, to exchange jokes about the situation, although al-Tahhan was suffering from advanced cancer. He'd had major surgery to remove a tumor a few years earlier, conducted by a brilliant Swedish surgeon working with a full team at Ibn al-Bitar hospital, and had undergone chemotherapy. Al-Malaak insisted that we all join them.

Al-Mawsawi's house had been constructed in the most up-to-date fashion by a Japanese team he'd contracted to build the amusement park north of Baghdad. The shelter was located on the ground floor and consisted of a large, furnished living room, with two bedrooms and modern facilities. Yet I felt out of place and oppressed in this dark basement, despite it being attractive and comfortably providing everything one would need. As usual, however, I didn't say a word, waiting to hear Rafa's opinion first. We left without comment, to be embraced by the sun's brilliant, unfiltered light, inspiring within us a sense of optimism and warmth despite the bitingly cold breeze. Rafa let out a long sigh. "The place is stifling, what do you think?" I thanked God and said, "It's a beautiful grave, but I don't want to be buried alive."

Telephone communications had not yet been cut, and I called my brother to check on them. Their house was in Karrada 'Arrasat, and our mother was in al-Sa'adoun. He told me he'd taken our mother and aunt to stay with him and asked me to join, but we didn't go. Around midday, Rafa's younger brother Talal came over, asking to borrow our car to take their mother and the wife and children of their brother Maath to Tikrit, for they'd been absolutely terrorized by the bombing at night. When he returned from this journey, it was almost 6 p.m. and pitch black. Talal was unsettled and looked despondent. He hadn't expected to find the gas stations empty and apologized for returning the car with only a quarter tank of gas, which alarmed Rafa. Before leaving, he asked us to not stay alone and to join my brother. Yet Rafa remained unconvinced, as it wasn't easy for us to get around.

We spent the night in a corner beside the kitchen that we used as a sort of fortress, seeking shelter beneath the studio on the upper floor. We followed the civil defense guidelines, including placing tape on the windows. The street seemed deserted, and the night was more forlorn and terrifying than we could have imagined with the air raids and intense bombardment. We were certain the house's door would be blown off its hinges at any moment. In candlelight we followed the events as broadcast by Monte Carlo on our transistor radio. We were the target of a military force intent on the total destruction of Iraq, land and people. Thirty-three powerful nations led by the United States of America had positioned their armies, jets, and weapons on Gulf bases under the pretext of liberating Kuwait. Injustice and gloom prevailed.

So as not to again face the desolate night and angry skies alone, we decided in the morning to move to my brother's house in Karrada

‘Arrasat. I called and told him before the lines were cut. At 8 a.m. our neighbor al-Malaak knocked on the door, trembling and imploring us to join them in their shelter. “Saddam made an air strike on Israel,” he said, “and the retribution will be even fiercer.” I grabbed him by the shoulders, pleading with him to calm down so that he could hold his family together. This shocked him and he rushed off. We spent time gathering our clothes and what we could transport in terms of water, gas, and the stores we had in our refrigerator and freezer, as Iraqis tend to store food. In the afternoon we looked in on our neighbors in the shelter and had no regrets about declining to stay with them. We laughed a bit with our neighbor al-Tahhan and his family, with their easygoing attitude and calm composure.

We left our home in the afternoon, after having entrusted our deaf gardener, Nasr, to come every day to check on the garden. Rafa chose to avoid the airport highway and we took the back roads to reach the hanging bridge, which had not yet been bombed. The roads were not deserted, but neither were they busy. Midway across the bridge we saw a plane flying at low altitude in the direction of the Daura refineries, ground defenses trying in vain to intercept it from every direction. Even more shocking was the sight of many people standing at the bridge’s railings, some of who’d stopped their cars and gotten out to watch, pointing at the plane. Then, in a flash, flames rose from the refinery, followed by the thunder of a massive explosion. We could barely believe we made it in one piece. My very worried brother and his three children were in the middle of the street, hollering with joy at our arrival. This welcome alone made us feel reassured.

The family was together, and Namir and Rafa found a familiarity in each other’s company. Luckily, we all had high spirits, and an ability to adjust to the situation we found ourselves in, meaning that while we held deep pain and sorrow for our fate and that of the children, we weren’t paralyzed with fear. This positive attitude reflected on the rest of the family, which included a young man, a teenager, a child, and two elderly women: my aunt, who was partially paralyzed and not prepared to give up any of her routine, and my mother, who was younger and more aware of the circumstances but filled with fear. We lived our life according to the circumstances imposed on us, and which busied us with constant work.

We lived a harmonious life, cooperating to acclimatize ourselves to extremely cold weather and regulating the use of everything. We were nine people living in a house with no electricity and no water other than that in the tank. In the morning we’d busy ourselves preparing food, using what we had in our stores and especially the red meat and chicken. Like everyone else we'd hold grilled feasts in the garden under the sight of monitoring satellites. We rationed the use of water, candles, and gas to prevent their depletion, and tried maintaining order despite the difficulty of convincing those accustomed to a life of waste and chaos.

During the period we stayed in my brother's house, the nights were hellacious, with jets breaking the sound barrier and intense bombing countered by endless ground missiles fired from rooftops and striking random targets. There were rarely raids during the day, but the possibility was always there. Public bus services and smaller private vans continued to transport people all over Baghdad. My brother and I took a double-decker bus to our mother's house in al-Sa'adoun to empty and clean the refrigerator and freezer, and make sure its narrow windows were firmly shut. Luckily there were of the old Baghdadi style from 1930 and did not require being taped.

The next day we had to do the same thing in our home. We took our car and returned to my brother's home before sunset. While I was busy with housework, Rafa spent the time in his studio working on his artist's book titled *It's a Dirty War* in one of his folded Chinese notebooks, its pages spreading six meters by thirty-two centimeters. He consumed himself with pouring out his anger and grief that he'd been concealing beneath an exterior of calm. This was his second war artist's book and the most important, and he completed it over stages by January 23, to be followed by other artist's books of different sizes.

We'd spent about a week in my brother's house when the Karrada 'Arrasat neighborhood was bombed during the day. We rushed out of the house and found people running toward the luxurious villas lining the river. Then we saw teenagers, led by the son of Salwan Baban, heading toward us, their faces terrorized. "A missile struck our garden, creating a huge, deep hole, and people have been injured with the flying glass shards and shrapnel!" they told us. Then we heard ambulances heading to the site. We later learnt that international television stations were covering news of the battles as they occurred, and they covered this random, or perhaps intentional, strike. A CNN correspondent interviewed local residents on this specific incident, and the experienced diplomat Soha Mohamed al-Tarihi gave the most eloquent and scathing interview, addressing it to America. She was among the people terrorized by this bombing, and her home was severely damaged.

From the very start, the Iraqi civil defense had issued citizen guidelines that included staying away from central Baghdad and relocating to the suburbs. It made more sense to move my brother and family to our house, but he preferred we gather in his as he had a small adjacent villa on his property, which meant more room and more water tanks. But following this strike on a dense residential area, we chose to all move to our house in al-Kafa'at, where the atmosphere was calmer and there was hardly any of the antiaircraft artillery that we only heard from afar. My brother had two cars, which allowed us to take our stores of water and gas. Rafa and I were happy to return to our home and went ahead of them to prepare their sleeping quarters. We prepared a place for my brother and his wife in Rafa's second-floor studio and allocated the second bedroom to my mother and aunt. The boys only felt safe beside my mother, so they slept side by side on the floor. The first night was more comfortable than the previous nights had been, except for the thundering air raids. The next morning my mother told me that, thank God, she'd at last been able to sleep.

I now bore great responsibilities that began with the first hours of the day. It was my task to prepare hot water for Namir and Rafa to bathe with every morning. As for the women and children, we set a schedule for bathing once or twice a week, and by turn. After breakfast I'd prepare lunch and do other housework, and check on the neighbors still in the area, the dearest to us being the archeology professor Walid al-Jadir (1940–1996). We'd exchange our sorrows and concerns, examining and reexamining the events, asking why and what if? All questions of no use. As dusk fell, we'd close the doors and pull the curtains, then light the Aladdin kerosene heater. The whole family would gather around it to bake the balls of dough I'd prepared in the morning. It was an entertaining ritual with which we killed time, while providing the family with essential food. I'd roll the balls out and place them on a metal grill Rafa fashioned for me and framed in wood, held over the stove with its lid removed. I had to prepare enough bread for three meals. The children would gather around me, eager to devour the hot bread once it had puffed up and cooked through, exuding its sweet scent. Due to my great love for the smell and taste of homemade bread, I continued preparing it even after the war ended and electricity returned in record time.

The nights seemed incredibly long. Namir and Rafa would kill the time and drown their worries and sorrow with drinking until numb and sleepy. We'd talk about many things, some of them serious and led by Namir with his vast knowledge of history and war in general, analyzing our situation jestingly at times and more often with anger. The conversation might be colored with memories, experiences, and stories about trips. It was a lovely flow of conversation, but usually cut off by the warning siren, followed by an air raid that would shake the house and those in it. Silence would fall and a sense of apprehension would rise, followed by curses on those responsible. We spent ten days with my brother and his children in this manner, and it was an experience filled with busy work, worry, vigilance, fear, and also pleasure. As for the ongoing war between the children, it only subsided with the air raids, when, upon hearing the warning siren, little Mohammed would throw himself into the arms of his terrified brother Ali, nine years his elder, always asking the same question, "Is this the beginning or the end?"

We began limiting our gas reserves for cooking, and sufficed with only one kerosene heater, as we bought its fuel at exorbitant prices from itinerant vendors. When we'd nearly run out of gas, we started reserving kerosene for cooking with too. Then we decided to go into central Baghdad, specifically to al-Shorja market, to buy a kerosene cooking stove (they were referred to as Chola, which I believe is an Indian name, but also known by their English-language brand name, Primus). That day, Namir, Kholoud, and the children went to check on their home, and Rafa and I went to al-Shorja. We had to walk a few kilometers to the al-Adel quarter, where we caught transport from the bus station to the main square not far from the market, which we ultimately reached by foot. We had to return before the busses stopped at four in the afternoon, and the entire trip took seven hours there and back. And we couldn't believe that the dark thoroughfare we traversed there was al-Rashid Street.

In the 1980s, Baghdad became a modern city with wide, clean streets, regulated traffic, modern bridges, beautiful buildings, and sound infrastructure. Despite the city's expansion and the construction of residential communities in various areas, al-Rashid Street remained the city's main artery and symbolic center with its mosques, cafés, arcades, storerooms, and cinemas. It was the beating heart of Baghdad, and from there we'd branch off to the various markets for books, crafts, clothing, gold, and other goods. Overnight, however, this street was transformed into a dump in which the wind blew about discarded papers, cardboard boxes, and all the merchants' trash. Cars disappeared and were replaced with carts drawn by horses or people. I felt as though we'd left the age we'd lived in and traveled in H.G. Wells's time machine to the era of our forefathers. The sidewalks were filled with merchants spreading their old-fashioned wares, and men and women sat before large pots selling all kinds of popular Baghdadi dishes. Vendors displayed old hand-operated tools and other items that might have been used in a previous age, in addition to new necessities such as candles, matches, and kerosene lamps. I was surprised to witness their quick readiness to take advantage of the situation to earn a living; merchants found it a good opportunity to sell off their old stock.

When we entered al-Shorja market we were plunged into darkness save pale rays of light shining through openings in the interlaced roof. We made our way through with difficulty, tripping on plastic packaging piled up in the middle of the market, trying to avoid getting our feet caught in ropes, sharp metal wires, and garbage mixed in with mud the entire length of the narrow street. Most of the small shops were closed except for two or three owned by the top merchants, where we found exactly what we were looking for. We purchased a small blue Primus stove, made in England, and a large number of candles that we later discovered sputtered when lit, quickly going out because they were still full of water. We filled our arms with purchases, and the time came to make our way home, exhausted, by sunset.

This was our first experience leaving our house to cover great distances on public transportation. The journey was filled with action, adventure, sorrow, and laughter, and I described it in "The Bus Driver," in my short story collection *Texts on a Gemstone*, alongside other scenes from those days. This story captured the driver's behavior so filled with contradiction, and how he yielded his authority over the passengers in a typically Iraqi tragicomedy.

It was our first trip but not our last, as we repeated the experience from time to time when we needed to purchase something, check on a friend, or merely wanted to take a look at the state of the city. We might cover around ten kilometers on foot there and back just going to relatively nearby areas such as al-Jami'a. Taking a bus or microbus (called "rockets") required walking five kilometers to the al-Adel neighborhood. From there, we could take a bus to al-Maydan, and from there get to Bab al-Sharqi via fast little microbuses in which we encountered crude behavior from the driver and his assistant, not to mention new popular songs with insanely fast beats played at high volume and in poor quality, the drumbeat piercing your ears. In the opposite direction, we could take a bus from a location near our house, in al-Ghazaliya, to al-Kadhumain, where there were markets of all kinds. This was a much easier and safer trip.

We'd take these outings with my brother and his wife and children. Just about every time we went out, we'd wonder about the location of a fierce bombardment that had shaken our home until dawn, thinking it had been closer than our own breaths. But we never found any indication of destruction on the main roads, except on al-Rashid Street, whose public spaces, bridges, and beautiful buildings had all been bombed, including the post office designed by Rifat Chadirji, and the Ministry of Planning overlooking the river. The ministry had been designed by the Italian consultant Gio Ponti and was one of the Iraqi Development Board's projects built by the state. Then we learned that the strikes were targeting vital sites such as factories, communications centers, and electricity and water stations, and bombed repeatedly simply to terrorize people.

Once we'd depleted our food stores, we also went to nearby areas to purchase what we could. We'd see Jordanian trucks on the main roads distributing bread, milk, and canned goods for free. Despite having armed myself with faith and patience as we faced our uncertain fate, one day I found myself breaking down in tears despite myself. We were on our way to make some purchases when a large Jordanian truck passed by on the main road. When the truck driver saw me, he stopped and his assistant threw two bags of Jordanian milk powder to us, crying out to Rafa, "Take this for the lady!"

When it became clear the war would not be ending soon, Namir decided to return to his home, and we agreed that my mother and aunt would stay with us for the sake of their comfort. It was a difficult decision for everyone even though it was the right one, for it wasn't feasible to leave their house empty. But nor was it easy to check in on one another, as paying visits took up an entire day. We again faced the long hours of the night without them, reading by candlelight and listening to the news reports on Monte Carlo.

Gradually, the families who'd fled Baghdad for the suburbs and smaller cities began returning, due to the difficulty of life elsewhere. Most of Baghdad's residents spent the nights in public shelters provided in various areas, seeking safety and fleeing the horrible sound of the planes. We heard much about these families' nightlife as they sought protection in each other's company. At sunset they'd take their tastiest food and spend the night together singing to recorded songs or playing frame and goblet drums, seeking an escape from the terrifying night and the sounds of missiles, as if practicing magical rituals to dispel djinn and demons. This would have been the case for those taking refuge in the al-Amiriya shelter when they all met a horrific fate in one of the most heinous war crimes in history. American intelligence had concluded that this shelter, fortified against ballistic missiles, was the meeting place for the Iraqi leadership, and so it was pelted with enough missiles to penetrate it, trapping hundreds of men, women, and children in a fiery oven with no means of escape. Yet the world, aligned with America, remained silent on this catastrophe.

Rafa's passion for artistry and creating beauty led him to fashion an oven from handcrafted clay vessels we'd bought from the Institute for Popular Heritage and Arts to decorate our garden. Following several trials, he succeeded in creating a brazier by adjoining two clay disks of the same size, one as a base, its walls perforated with ornamental openings through which to place charcoal, and a similar one above it. It was open at the top and closed at the bottom to collect soot. We were delighted with the experiment and now had a beautiful oven for baking with the flavor of charcoal. Rafa assumed the duty of preparing it for use, laboring over it in the slow stretch of time heavy with cautious anticipation.

One evening I'd taken up my position in a corner of our shelter space. I had no room to move, as the tray of dough balls was beside me and before me was the low wooden table on which I rolled them out. Rafa came in, graciously carrying the prepared oven, and as he set it down the upper part flipped over, its hot coals emptying onto my thick gown and scattering across the Persian rug. Since I wasn't able to move, I submitted myself to my fate. Rafa was hysterical, grabbing the coals with his hands and returning them to the oven. This, in turn, terrified me, and worried about his hands, I screamed, "Your hands, be careful! Your hands!" Yet Rafa continued picking up the coals as my mother rushed to put them out with the blanket she was covered with. Luckily my gown was pure cotton and insulated, and this protected me from catching on fire. It was a nightmare, however, watching Rafa tremble as he carried the clay oven outside to smash it, emptying into it his terror and fury. Then he rushed back to inspect me, repeating his apologies and making sure I hadn't been harmed, as I hysterically inspected his hands in a state of shock. Thank God they were only inflicted with superficial burns that I immediately treated with an ointment. Rafa threw himself on the sofa to calm himself by drinking, and my mother and aunt concealed their shock by praying, while I carried on baking with the kerosene heater that Rafa had been dissatisfied with.

We probably never witnessed in our modern times the solidarity, cooperation, and closeness between people as we did during the war, and that included domestic security. Many people left their homes for locations outside Baghdad, and yet robberies did not take place except for the theft of gas canisters and rooftop water tanks. The robbing of both vacated and inhabited homes did not take place until later, after military operations had ended, in what came to be more like organized crime. At that time, a wave of robberies swept over a large area and grew in scope, expanding to also target cars and car parts. People began thinking twice before leaving their homes empty, even for a few hours. Greed even drove robbers to commit murder if they encountered resistance from homeowners. My mother's house was robbed twice while she and my aunt were staying with us, and upon investigation, the neighbors were suspected, but the valuables including silver, rugs, and antiques were never returned. With the continuing pressure of sanctions and their domestic implications, a basic sense of humanity began gradually eroding in the most painful way. Bribery became common in the security agencies and among government employees, and this increased all the more following the 2003 occupation of Iraq, becoming a phenomenon obvious to all.

Our relations with the neighbors were limited and mainly restricted to a number of homes, those of Salah al-Malaak, Talib al-Tahhan, Ghalib al-Uraibi, and Yassin al-Bakry, who all lived right beside us, as well as the archaeology professor Walid al-Jadir (1942–1994), who lived relatively close by. We'd check in on each other every day and shared news of water, gas, petrol, and kerosene, and whether meat or vegetables were available in such and such location. With the start of the war, trucks arriving from Jordan distributed free foodstuffs, bread, and milk, as I mentioned previously. A few days after the war started, the Bunniya company began sending refrigerated trucks all over Baghdad to sell frozen meat at reasonable prices, and this was a wonderful service. The food subsidy program started in response to the sanctions also assumed an important role in the survival of Iraqi families who had fallen into need. The Iraqi currency had collapsed, making it difficult for people to acquire the goods they used to be able to afford. Families began selling their valuable belongings, each according to their abilities. First to go were artworks collected over time, silver and porcelain dining sets or any valuable houseware, all of which were sold at private auctions, and well-established libraries sold on al-Mutanabbi street to booksellers every Friday, including rare books and old manuscripts.

Walid al-Jadir, may he rest in peace, was a close friend of ours. We spent pleasurable time together discussing shared interests, most notably stories of Baghdad with its people, places, and traditions. Whenever he went to the market with his shopping basket, he'd stop at our door to ask if we needed anything, and if he didn't find us at home, he'd chat with my aunt, who usually sat in the fresh air under the warm sun. He'd listen to her old tales of Baghdad and bitter complaints of our house, which she called "the exile" and the "Bastille prison," because it was located in a new and distant neighborhood lacking the activity and noise of areas like al-Sa'adoun and al-Bataween, where she'd lived since the 1930s and everyone knew her and she felt secure. Walid asked me in surprise, "How does your aunt know the Bastille prison?"

My aunt had not completed her education and hadn't been successful in what she did complete; she left school in fourth grade, unlike her older and younger sisters, who gained more of an education before their early marriages. In fact, my Aunt Fadhila was among the first Iraqi women qualified to teach in the late 1920s. And yet my aunt Tali'a's education had enabled her to read, and she loved the popular romance novels translated into Arabic at the time, filled with adventures, chivalry, and love. These were the books that first whet my appetite for reading. As for my grandmother, who was illiterate, she loved listening to these stories as much as she loved film and its world of magic. She'd ask my aunt to read her a few pages every night, and I think my aunt liked to leave her hanging, reaching a suspenseful point in the plot and then feigning sleepiness. My grandmother loved staying up and listening to the radio once people had them in their homes, and she was sure to listen to Umm Kulthum's concerts every month. Among the books my aunt read and was moved by was Victor Hugo's *Les Misérables*, and she watched the film with her mother when it was screened in the 1930s, as I believe. She told us how a man would stand at the theater entrance distributing handkerchiefs, which was customary at tragic films. She often narrated to us what she'd seen and read in her own dramatic and suspenseful style colored with comedy. This is what drew Walid to her.

During one of our morning walks to check on people, we visited the graphic art studio in al-Mansour. The complex was practically deserted, for Orfali Gallery and Tasmeem Fashion House were closed. We opened the door to find a great deal of dust covering the studio, and a bullet on Rafa's worktable that had penetrated the roof. In the front display area, a shard had damaged the bench and then settled in a large portfolio occupying the center of the exhibition space, piercing the twenty different prints it held. Rafa kept it as a material reminder of the war, and it was later filmed by Italian and German television crews in a campaign against the military aggression.

Rafa remained hesitant to use the car, even after it became possible to obtain limited amounts of gas, for which he'd have to leave at seven in the morning to wait in the long queue, only returning at five in the afternoon. He took our responsibility toward my mother and aunt seriously, for they couldn't return to their own home until after the situation stabilized and electricity was reinstated to a few hours each day. This great accomplishment was made by Iraqi teams in just two months.

On February 26, 1991, an end to the military operations was declared and some degree of reassurance entered our hearts as the air raids came to a halt. On February 28, we were scheduled to attend a family wedding. My maternal cousin Said Na'el Basri was marrying Abeer, who'd waited for him throughout the years of his captivity.

Said had just graduated in the top ten of his class at the University of Baghdad's medical school, and been appointed to al-Yarmouk Hospital, when he was conscripted into the military service and sent to the front during the 1981 Iran–Iraq War. His experience, like that of other young civilian men, was extremely difficult, as he suddenly found himself face to face with cruel scenes of disfigured corpses and injured people wailing in pain or struggling between life and death. During his first vacation to Baghdad, he made his engagement to Abeer official before returning to the army. Then all news of him was cut off, and a year later we found out he'd been taken prisoner. News of prisoners came via the Red Cross and television programs in which prisoners of war sent messages to their families, and we found out from people who saw the program in London. They informed his brother Mahmoud, who was living there, and who in turn informed their parents. It was a brutal shock for his father, a military man, and for the eight years Said remained captive, worry and pain spread through his body and soul until he passed away from cancer in mid-1990, a few months before Said returned to Baghdad in the last group of prisoners released by Iran.

We had to cover a distance of over thirty kilometers to reach Abeer's family home on al-Rabi' Street in east Baghdad. First, we took a microbus from al-Adel to Karrada, and from there another microbus to the wedding location. In the microbus, we heard whispers of an attack in Basra or an army rebellion, something vague that didn't make sense at the time. It later became clear that this was the uprising called for by the Americans and the opposition, who'd promised to back the rebels. Yet the movement was marked by extreme violence and infiltrated by terrorists. The Americans rescinded their support and in fact allowed the state to use force in order to achieve security. The "uprising" was thus a failure, with more victims falling to chaos and random killing.

It took us three and a half hours to reach al-Rabi' Street. Namir and his family had arrived before us, and we were surprised to find a large number of guests who'd come from different areas of Baghdad. Some had come on bicycles, which were being widely used for transport. For this exceptional party the garden had been set up with a large circle for men, and another for women and children. The air was filled with a joy we'd missed and thought we'd never experience again. Jubilant celebration of life beamed from the faces of those present. Friends of the bride and groom documented the event with video cameras, and faces were filled with hope as we danced to Iraqi songs played on loudspeakers. We chatted and joked about our circumstances and our acclimatizing to the difficult living conditions. There's no need of course to describe the bride and groom's rejoicing over their new life, especially after the groom had survived his captivity. To make it back to our neighborhood by sunset, however, we left right after lunch, rushing to catch our transport home.

Rafa returned to working in his home studio, taking advantage of the daylight and producing more of the war artist's books he'd commenced with the early days of the war. He invented a new game with which to amuse himself and provide an outlet for his anger, and worked on it daily. "I'm going to take revenge on this filthy war," he happily told me one day. Among his collection of art books was one on erotic art that symbolized fertility and the life cycle across world civilizations, creatively expressed by artists over the ages in the form of wall reliefs and three-dimensional sculptures. From his paper supplies he selected a large notebook with white pages and tore images from the book and pasted them in, drawing in pencil beneath them parallel images of the sexual positions. He worked on this notebook, which he titled *Greetings to Desert Storm*, from March 17 to May 30, 1991, producing 148 images in which he fiercely and adamantly expressed the victory of love over war. This he reinforced in an accompanying text, in which he wrote, "Don't curse the darkness / Light a candle / then draw a man and woman / in a state of love / thus restoring life."

Our poet friend Farouq Saloum came to check on us from time to time. He was also a media professional, and immediately after the military operations halted, he came to tell us, that an American crew from the ABC channel wanted to interview intellectuals about their reactions on the war. Initially, I refused outright, telling him I would never allow an American to cross the threshold of my home. He stressed that this was different, that the crew held great empathy for the Iraqi people and that this would be an opportunity to get our voices out to the world. The following day, two correspondents came to our house with Farouq, who at the time was an Information Ministry official. We welcomed them in the garden, the gentle Baghdad sun hidden beneath the dark clouds filling the sky after the petrochemical laboratories had been bombed and as the oil fields burned in the south. It was said the smoke rising from the oil wells covered a distance of 350 kilometers, causing rain as the exhausted Iraqi army retreated beneath a downpour of American bombs targeting the Highway of Death.

The American correspondent sat beside me on a stone bench as black drops of rain intermittently fell upon us. I told him, "Perhaps you're pleased now as the sky rains oil?" He looked at me and asked, "Would you allow me to borrow this line of poetry?" I gestured my agreement with a mixture of nonchalance and mockery. Then I said, "Have you at last accomplished your aims? I never expected that I would allow an American to enter our house."

"You're right to feel so and I'm embarrassed, as what has happened is unforgivable," he replied. He went on, telling us that he and his crew had arrived a few days before the start of the war, thinking they were coming to face a "fierce, murderous, oppressive people threatening world security." He said they'd go out in the morning to the city center and walk around the markets, getting to know people and learning their opinions. They were surprised by the warm hospitality they received, realizing Iraqis were a peaceful people tolerant of the West and even of their killer, as he put it. This made him realize that the bombs sometimes hitting markets or residential buildings, whether by mistake or intentionally, were targeting these same people seeking to make a living and insistent on continuing their lives. "We're staying at the Sheraton Hotel," he said, "and I've been surprised to witness weddings held at night, young people starting new lives together despite the events taking place on the ground. Some of them return the next day to the front, so just who are these people we're fighting?"

The correspondent was preparing daily coverage for "The Red Line," broadcast live to America after midnight Baghdad time. Rafa suggested that I speak first. I went on for over fifteen minutes, expressing my great disappointment with the principles of justice and humanitarianism propagated by Western civilization and stressed in its literature I'd been raised on since my youth, only to discover decades later that matters differed in reality. "Are humanitarian values limited only to your own people? In your view—and the view of your people, who know nothing beyond their own country's borders—are we creatures unworthy of remaining on this land so filled with abundance, and must we be eradicated for the sake of your luxury and comfort? This is what I've learned from your unjust war." I fell silent when I saw the correspondent's eyes filling with tears.

Then Rafa spoke, saying, "I won't add to what May's said, but rather will suffice with showing my perspective through this work. I swore after completing it that no one would see it until a decade had passed. It's my response to the destruction of my country, and the murder of its people, in an aggression that has no convincing justification." With this he opened the tie on the artist's book and placed it on the table, spreading out its long Chinese accordion pages (three meters by sixty-five centimeters) and revealing powerful strikes by his palm dipped in acrylic, as he'd emptied his anger onto the pages dated with the war's forty-two days. Unable to conceal his awe at this work expressing the tragedy of war, the correspondent sufficed with saying, "It gives me the creeps."

When he left, the correspondent shook our hands and said that this had been the most important interview he'd held in Baghdad, and that he'd broadcast it without edits that evening. Farouq Saloum later informed us that it was the longest interview they broadcast in full.

Leaving Baghdad

We were at a loss as to what to do.

Life in Baghdad resumed, and everyone returned to their jobs. But it was no longer a life to live given the stifling social and economic conditions created by the harshest international sanctions ever placed on Iraq. The entire world spoke, to no avail, of how inhumane this unprecedented measure was, causing the greatest damage yet to Iraq's social structure. This is not to mention the subsequent occupation that mercilessly violated the country and its people, and whose effects are still felt to this day.

We submitted ourselves to fate as we always had in difficult situations, through revolutions and wars, for there was always a way out. At least that's what my faith told me, and we never diverged from it, always living in the present with optimism for what was to come. I asked Rafa if he regretted our return from Morocco, and he burst forth, "I couldn't! Impossible! It was unreasonable to stay on promises with no clear horizon before us." Then he stroked my hand and said, "Don't worry, we're fine." I had no doubt as to Rafa's attachment to Baghdad and our home and studio, or his ability to make a living with his creative work. In fact, I wasn't worried about anything but his creative production, for he'd never had to exploit it to survive. Rather, he'd always created in response to his inner self, his senses, and his research. I found comfort and security in this.

A few months later we were both in the graphic art studio when Milia, the wife of musician Faridallah Weirdi, came bearing a letter and calling to me from afar. It was a letter from Amman, from Princess Wijdan al-Hashemi, head of the Royal Society of Fine Arts, via UNICEF, where Milia worked. The letter was an invitation for me to attend the Jerash Festival of Culture and Arts, and an offer for Rafa to teach at Yarmouk University. I felt a sense of relief mixed with some uncertainty. Rafa remained silent, except for a passing expression on his face indicating comfort with the letter's friendly tone and expression of appreciation for us both, but he also seemed hesitant. A return to a full-time job?

In mid-July, we traveled to Amman in comfortable business-class busses and stayed in Quds Hotel with the other festival guests. A meeting had been arranged for us at Yarmouk University, which offered the only art education degree in Jordan at the time. We arrived in Irbid on an extremely hot and dust-ridden morning, it appearing to us like an expansive village. Yet the large, landscaped campus of Yarmouk University had been recently constructed, and was surrounded by pine and olive trees, creating a distinct setting that we found endearing. We were welcomed by the education and arts dean, Mohamed Sabrini, who was incredibly kind. He praised Rafa's CV with all its accomplishments, looking through it before handing it to the head of the visual arts department, Insaf al-Rabadhi. Flipping through Rafa's CV, she outlined his future responsibilities as if he had no prior experience. Rafa listened calmly, and when she finished, he stood up and thanked her, ending the meeting. "But you didn't say a thing!" she cried in surprise. He politely informed her that he'd convey his decision shortly. When we got into the car, he happily squeezed my hand and whispered, "Oof! We're returning to Baghdad." We were both pleased with this choice.

That evening, the dean came to the hotel to ascertain Rafa's decision. He explained to him the nature of the contract, with its conditions appropriate to his experience, expressing his pride in having Rafa join the college faculty. We chose to live in the university housing, which seemed pleasant and comfortable. Because we were only two people, we were allocated a small apartment with one bedroom and a modern, furnished living room, and Rafa remained doubtful about this small space designed only for dining and rest.

Throughout our years together, we'd always believed in the necessity of adjusting to life wherever we were. We were always armed with an ability to protect ourselves and maintain our very cores, and to decline work offers we found unsuitable. Rafa had turned down all the job offers he'd had in Baghdad following his early retirement. Returning to teaching had not been expected, but it seemed a temporary solution, or so we thought, in light of the difficult economic circumstances.

When the Jerash festival ended, we returned to Baghdad to prepare for our new life. Our friends received our decision with regret and sorrow, and we assured them that we'd return, for it was difficult to leave our warm social life that had embraced us for years, the house we'd worked so hard to build according to our specifications, and the studio Rafa had dreamed of for decades. The night before we left, all our friends gathered in our house, some of them lingering past midnight. It was a sad and moving farewell, even though we were only moving to the adjacent country that had opened its borders to us.

On the business-class bus we met our dear friend Amel al-Sharqi, who'd opened a publishing house focusing on translation, along with her assistant Sukaina. We sat together and Amel's sweet spirit and rich and amusing conversation added a sense of friendly fun to the trip. We

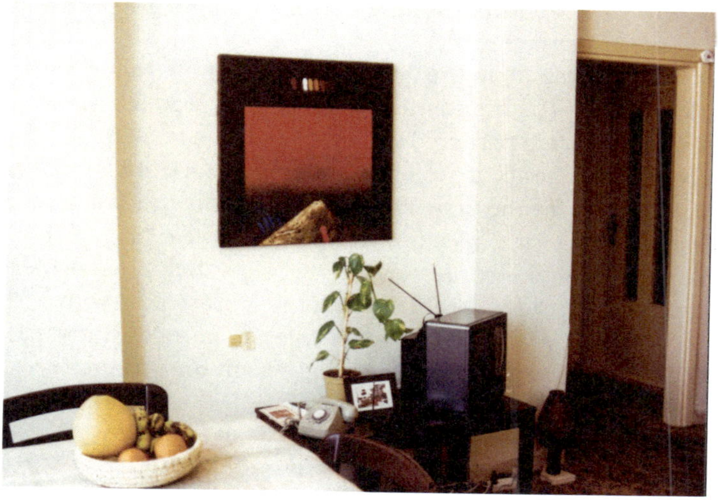

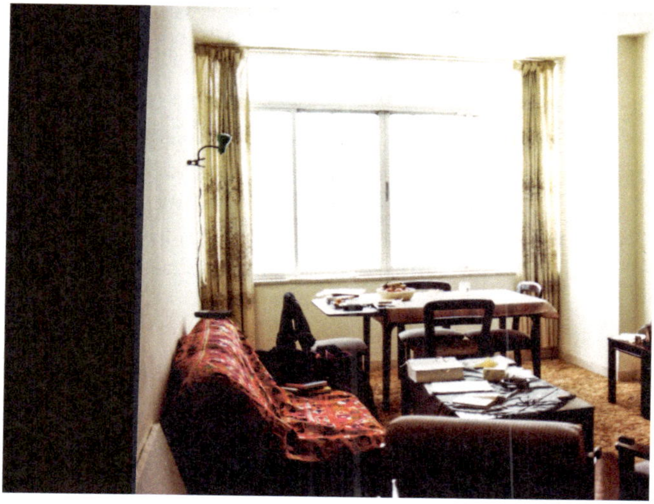

May and Rafa lived in an apartment on the campus of Yarmouk University, Irbid, between 1991 and 1997

shared the food we'd brought, including delicious Iraqi kofta, which has reminded me of her ever since.

Rafa joined the university in the first week of September 1991, and was quickly followed by his friend Ali Taleb and other Iraqi artists of various specializations. He prepared what he needed, as well as possible, before the students arrived on September 22. He'd planned a course in printmaking for the first semester. During the first week of teaching, he expressed to me his pain: "If during this year I can just raise the students' level to zero, as they're way below that, I'll consider this a major accomplishment." Rafa was extremely frustrated with everything in the university that he found professionally substandard. These shortcomings, however, were the main reason the university had sought the aid of experienced Iraqi teachers.

In 1974, when Rafa established the graphic arts department in Baghdad's Institute of Fine Arts, he was intent on selecting his students from those with advanced skills in drawing and sketching. He did not have this luxury at Yarmouk University, yet he retained a sense of optimism, gradually adjusting to the situation through his students' affection for and attachment to him. He wrote in his diary from day one, recording his impressions and his evaluation of the classrooms and students. He found a glimmer of hope in just a few students who could be counted on one hand. The comments in his diaries touch on an array of administrative and humanistic issues during his first months there. I quote from an entry on September 23: "I came to change for the better, and to create a new style of teaching, if I'm able to."

Sunday, October 2, 1991

Autumn shyly made its start this morning. There was a breeze bearing the scent of pine trees, rain, and earth, and I was slightly intoxicated by it. Yet this intoxication dissipated a few moments after I entered that horrific spiraling corridor on my way to the lecture hall. I was irritable and explosive, and I rebuked the first student I caught making a simple mistake. I quickly began the lesson, and in order to teach them how to engrave wood, I grabbed the knives and started engraving a sample for them on the wood plate. My outburst helped, for although I was irritated, I engraved with power and skill, and the outcome surprised me, granting me some peace and satisfaction. From the corner of my eye, I could see

> the students in a state of deep admiration. And from among them, the breeze of autumn returned to me, but from a distance, from a great distance this time.

Most unfortunately, the rapidly expanding classes of skilled Iraqis in Jordan started getting sidelined within the first few months of their arrival. While high-level Jordanian officials sought to make use of their expertise and talent, professionals could nonetheless feel their marginalization, leading the best of them to seek opportunities to emigrate, and gradually they left, leaving a vacuum. We witnessed hordes of Iraqis lining up for hours outside the UNHCR office. There were also strangely bold cases of young Iraqis escaping to Amman because they were unable to pay the large fees of Iraqi departure permits. Some of them crossed the country by foot to avoid the border points between Iraq and Jordan. Many of these young people later made use of smugglers to transport them from Amman to places around the globe. I don't think there exists a place in the world without Iraqi migrants.

The first year of our residency in Jordan was equally negative and positive with regard to both place and people. Making things easier was the presence of Iraqi and Jordanian friends in Amman and Irbid, and as time went by, we created a social circle. Even more comforting was my brother Namir moving with his family to Amman. Due to his experience and qualifications, he'd been employed in the office of Prince Hassan bin Talal.

Rafa missed having an appropriate space in which to paint, so we decided to rent an apartment in Amman in which to spend our weekends and other holidays. We were led to a lovely apartment in Jabal Amman, and Rafa thus resumed his artistic activity, preparing for a joint exhibition with Ali Taleb in a gallery belonging to the Abdul Hameed Shoman Foundation in May of 1992. The opening was attended by a large audience, all of whom were Iraqis residing in Amman, and it left an influential mark on the cultural scene.

The Iraqis arriving in waves to escape embargoed Iraq and seek asylum elsewhere in the world included creatives, and their presence rejuvenated Amman's cultural and artistic life. In addition to exhibitions held in the first half of the 1990s, many poetry readings, roundtable discussions, and lectures were held in the Jordan National Gallery of Fine Arts, the Royal Cultural Center, the Abdul Hameed Shoman Foundation, and, once established in 1993, Darat al Funun. In the first two years of Iraqi immigration, the opportunity to hold art-related events was invested in by each the Jordan National Gallery of Fine Arts, thanks to art history professor and painter Princess Wijdan al-Hashemi, and the Shoman Foundation, under the initiative of artist Suha Shoman.

Suha Shoman sought the aid of artist Shaker Hassan Al Said to organize a weekly cultural program for six months in 1992, and later collected its outcomes in a book titled *Hiwar al-fann at-tashkili* (Discussing visual art). The Shoman Foundation hosted remarkable exhibitions that year, both solo and group exhibitions for Shaker Hassan Al Said, Himat Mohamed Ali, Rafa Nasiri, Ali Taleb, Mohamed Muhereddin, and Ismail Fattah. Her efforts were crowned in 1993 with the establishment of Darat al Funun, one of the most important, and most beautiful, art centers.

Skilled Iraqis continued arriving in Amman throughout the 1990s to live and work, or to use as a base from which to seek immigration in other countries that had opened their doors via the United Nations. Among them were artists, poets, and teachers from different generations, many of them from the 1980s generation, and some spent three to ten years in Amman before migrating like their colleagues who'd preceded them. Each of them was seeking a better future and more professional art training than what was possible to achieve at the time in a place of limited activity and experience like Jordan. Young people came with ambitions and dreams that the wars had nearly aborted, seeking new windows of opportunity. Among these were students of Rafa's from the Institute of Fine Arts who found refuge with us as much as we found company in them after having become their teacher's friends.

The art market in Amman was thus invigorated with a constant flow of Iraqi works, most of which were of a commercial nature or imitations of leading artists, while important artworks were smuggled out of Iraq, soon continuing their journeys to distant locations. However, serious initiatives were also taken in the art scene to establish galleries, the most prominent of which was the 1992 opening of Abaad Gallery, owned by an art-loving Jordanian businessman and run by the young artist Mahmoud Obaidi. It focused on select works by Iraqi and Jordanian artists. This was followed by other galleries with a range of artistic quality, spearheaded by Orfali Gallery, which soon became a second home for Iraqis and their various activities. In the early 2000s, galleries of similar artistic level were established, such as the 4 Walls Gallery owned by Majida Muasher, and after this closed down, Nabad Art Gallery, run by Mona Deeb

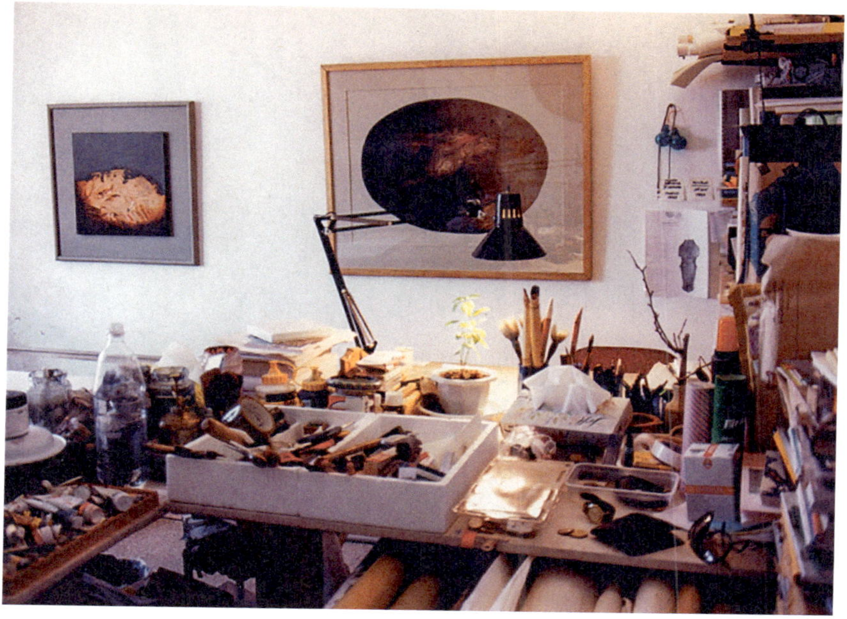

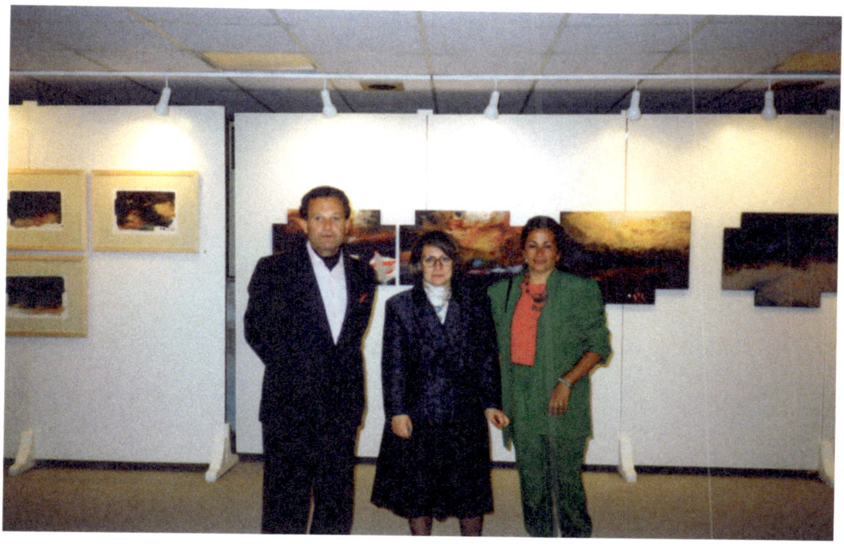

Top: Rafa's studio in their apartment in Sweifieh neighborhood, Amman, 1995–2000

Bottom: With Suha Shoman at the opening of the two-artist show by Rafa Nasiri and Ali Taleb at Shoman Foundation, Amman, 1992

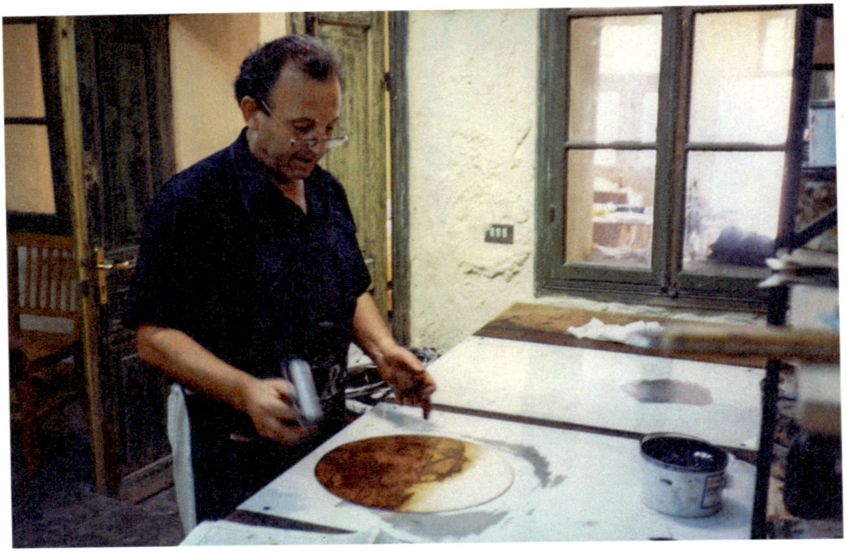

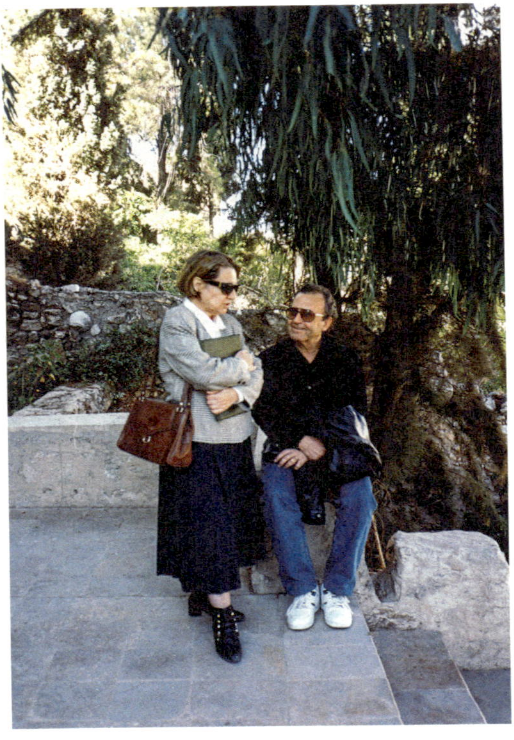

Between 1993 and 1995, Rafa directed the printmaking workshop at Darat al Funun, Amman and Nadia Zacharia, which was among the most important galleries in Amman.

In parallel to these endeavors in the art world, other cultural initiatives also took place in Amman, the most significant of which was the opening of a café in the al-Gardens neighborhood called Phoenicia, which hosted cultural programs and lectures, and invited Iraqi writers, poets, and artists under the directive of Palestinian poet Kheiry Mansour, who'd spent many years in Baghdad. The café soon became a refuge for artists and poets who gathered around the poet Abdel Wahhab al-Bayati, who'd adopted the café as his base.

In the autumn of 1993, Darat al Funun was opened by the acclaimed artist Suha Shoman to serve as a home for the Arab arts and a museum for the Arab art collection belonging to her and her husband, businessman Khalid Shoman. It included a beautiful space for exhibiting select Arab works. Among the first projects taken on by Darat al Funun was setting up a printmaking studio. This is something Princess Wijdan al-Hashemi, head of the Royal Society of Fine Arts, had wanted to undertake at the Jordan National Gallery of Fine Arts since 1981, when she invited Rafa to hold a solo exhibition and proposed the endeavor to him. Finally, it became possible, in cooperation with the Royal Association of Fine Arts, when Rafa came to Amman, and Darat al Funun was established with its spacious area. This helped to invigorate an art form that had been practically absent in Jordan except for limited activities under the Ministry of Culture. Rafa set up the studio and outlined the conditions for its use, and he supervised it for two years.

At the same time, Iraqi artists and especially the younger generations found in Darat al Funun an arena for implementing modern art projects proposed by Suha Shoman. Among these artists were Nadim Kufi, Himat Mohamed Ali, Samir Osama, and Halim Karim, who was given a small corner of Darat al Funun in which to produce his pottery works called *The Shop of Extraordinary Items*. Darat al Funun became a beautiful refuge for us and young Iraqi painters and writers, with its gorgeous space, large, specialized library, and active art programs, and the printmaking studio became a space in which Rafa could breathe. He produced marvelous works there.

Among the goals of Darat al Funun was to foster an art culture by providing books and modern resources, workshops, and an art film library that held bimonthly screenings of films on European art history throughout its different periods. Soha asked me to assume responsibility for this program. The English-language films were sound academic productions, and to aid the local audience I translated their scripts and provided a brief overview of each artistic period with an introduction to the artists, explaining any necessary details. It was very well received, and I noticed a growing attendance throughout the months I ran it.

Despite all these activities, Rafa remained uncomfortable with the situation in which he found himself. He longed for freedom to work and was not enjoying what he was doing. In addition to the large works he produced on canvas in our Amman home, he began painting small pieces in Irbid, taking advantage of every window of time he found. He also drew many sketches, in black and white or colored pen, of female nudes in his diaries.

Friday March 13, 1993

In a room only a few meters in size, I look around, angry, for the evening is stifling with the sounds of the wind, banging glass, the television, and the internal voice screaming, "What are you doing in this corner of the distant world?" I feel so far from every person and every human center. Everything is distant in memory and spirit. Nothing remains tangible other than smooth walls and a small window looking out onto the contrived world. I paint in the daylight, and at night feel the desire to inspect color and form. I rush to draw in black and white, pursued by the bodies of women, and so I draw them, but they're not what I want, and I know it's only a playful distraction. It's a desire to capture pleasure with an old act, and even reassurance that the line is still strong and the color is still as pliant as it was. These distractions are not sufficient, however, for time stretches and passes slowly, destructively, inhumanely. Daily writing is short and always cut off, for my memory does not flow, as the components of life are few and not interesting. I'm like a truncated tree; it will not grow new branches unless the soil remains the same and it continues to be watered and breathes air again, thus returning to its original form.

We spent seven years in Jordan. In the beginning, Rafa told his students he wouldn't stay longer than a year, and at the end of every year we'd be advised by friends and family to remain there due to the poor living conditions in Iraq. Following one of our visits to Baghdad, Rafa wrote a farewell to our beautiful house and beloved city:

Baghdad, January 27, 1992

> I bid farewell to my mother, the *hajji*, today at noon, her eyes shining with love and prayers. Parting is easier this time. The last time she asked why I traveled and left the family, house, and nation. I told her, "The nation is always in my heart, as you are." At the studio we bid farewell to many friends and loved ones. They gathered as though it were an exhibition opening. Love is our treasure.

The years went by and Rafa moved between teaching and his practice, participating here and there in events, although we couldn't travel except by official invitation. Together, we attended the Moussem culturel d'Asilah two years in a row, and then Rafa had a solo exhibition in Beirut during the autumn of 1993. We had a sad reunion with the beloved city so destroyed nearly twenty years after our last visit. In 1995, Rafa was asked to join the jury of the Norwegian International Print Triennale and spent two weeks in Fredrikstad.

As for me, I scheduled my time to spend the mornings working at home and going to the university library. I published my third short story collection, *Texts on a Gemstone*, and my third poetry volume, *Nocturnes*, and reprinted my Arabic translation of *Life with Picasso* by Françoise Gilot and Carlton Lake, the first printing of which had been published in Baghdad in poor quality and full of mistakes. I was extremely pained when the Iraqi media was scathing toward me. All the more embarrassing was the book's good reception by readers, as I noticed in our last visit to Baghdad in 1995, for all the youth on al-Mutanabbi Street thanked me for it wherever I went. I therefore decided to reprint it in Amman.

During that time, I also frequented the library of the Royal Academy for Islamic Civilization Research, where I looked at books on Islamic art aesthetics to complement my study of the history of art in Iraq. This was after I'd been accepted in 1990 by London's Royal College of Art to work on a dissertation on the history of Iraq's modern art movement, exploring its connections to the roots of Iraq's ancient civilization. I'd been accepted to work under the supervision of professor Keith Critchlow, but had to finance my studies myself. When we moved to Amman I wrote to him, and he assured me that my acceptance remained standing, but that I had to procure funding. Unfortunately, we weren't able to meet the condition of paying for studies, which was beyond our means at the time, especially as we'd lost all we had due to the devaluation of the Iraqi currency.

To my good fortune I turned to the eminent scholar Abdel Aziz al-Douri and asked him to guide me as I continued my research. Al-Douri was a follower of art and a close friend of Hafidh al-Droubi, who set up the first open studios in Iraqi universities, starting at the College of Education where he was dean, and where Jewad Selim oversaw the studio. Then he set up and supervised a studio in the College of Arts and Sciences, and then another at Queen Alia Girls' College, under the supervision of Khalid al-Jadir. Al-Douri left Iraq after the 1968 coup, and was welcomed by the University of Jordan, where he continued to work until he passed away in 2010. I asked him to assist me in completing a short, methodological study, and when I began consulting him, I discovered how wonderful it was to work with a professor who grants you basic keys to work with, not only in the manner of conducting research, but also in the details of language. This makes a researcher put in great effort to achieve the comment of "good" or "not bad" that means so much when stated by a scholar like him. It was he who directed me to the academy library, for he was on its board. I went often and met leading scholars there, including Mohamed Rashid al-Fil, the Iraqi scholar of Islamic geography.

The head of the academy at the time, Nasser al-Din al-Assad, asked me to work with them part-time, granting me another opportunity to strengthen my experience as a writer and researcher. I had met him in 1965, when the Arab Literary Convention was held in Baghdad, but now worked with this great figure directly. He entrusted me with collecting his studies and publishing them in three books, the last of which was on Palestinian literature in the second half of the twentieth century. It was an arduous task, as I had to compile three books, editing out anything that was repeated, in one volume. He later recommended me to the Egyptian-Lebanese Publishing House to write about him and his published works to introduce him to young readers. While in Amman I also strengthened my relationship with the eminent professor Ihsan Abbas, whom I'd also met at the 1965 Arab Literary Convention, and thus became close to yet another influential writer.

In the early years of Iraq's embargo, theft grew widespread and included house and car robberies. People began getting creative about protecting their homes and cars, to the extent that one person placed his car on the roof of his house. We'd secured our car in the garage of Rafa's father; it was a Toyota Super Sedan, which was very popular with car thieves. When things got worse and became violent, Rafa decided to sell it. Then, in early 1993, my mother informed me that our house had been robbed, and the expensive household items had been taken but the library and artworks had not been touched. We thanked God that the thief had not been interested in cultural plunder. In fact, we were not much concerned about what we'd lost, as the losses of Iraqis, sometimes including their lives as they tried to protect their wealth, made us grateful for the safety of what and who had survived. On our next visit to Baghdad, we placed our house in the hands of a trusted guard recommended by a friend. I spoke of him and his horrific fate in chapter eight, "Our Baghdad Home and the Productive Years."

In May of 1995, we received news that Rafa's mother had passed away in their family home in al-Qadissya, where she'd been in the care of Rafa's younger brother Maath and his family. Rafa's pain was compounded by his inability to see her before she passed away, and her departure continued to cause him grief and despair. When we'd first moved to Jordan, we would travel to Baghdad on holidays to visit family, enjoy living in our house, and see friends. But with the loss of his mother, Rafa lost interest in going to Baghdad. It also became more difficult to do so after we moved to Bahrain, requiring us to travel to Amman first and from there continue by land in the hot summer. Yet, we continued to enjoy the dates and mangoes sent to us every season from our garden.

Moving to Bahrain

Contrary to what we'd hoped for and wanted, the winds carried us even further. For in the fall of 1997, Rafa's contract at Yarmouk University ended, and we moved to Bahrain.

Our friends, artist Sheikh Rashid Al Khalifa and businessman Jamal Fakhru, had made an offer to Rafa to work at the University of Bahrain and establish a visual arts curriculum there when he held his first solo exhibition in Bahrain in 1996, but Rafa had declined due to his commitment to Yarmouk University at the time. When his contact ended, Rafa contacted Jamal to tell him he was now prepared to take on the task, and they asked him to travel right away to Bahrain.

We moved to Bahrain and spent six comfortable and luxurious years there from 1997–2003. Yet it was not satisfying for an artist with the experience of Rafa, who longed for greater freedom to realize larger art

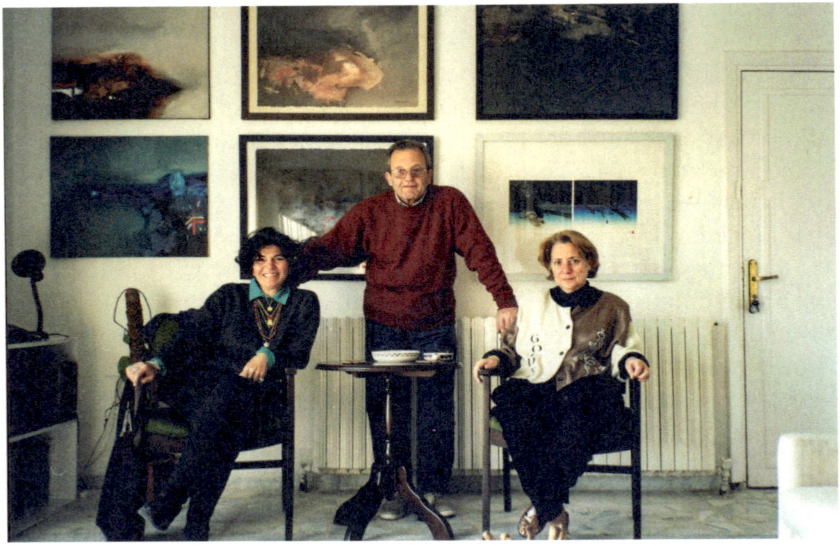

With Nuha Al Radi, in May and Rafa's villa, Al Rashidiya Compound, Manama, Bahrain, 2000. May and Rafa lived in Bahrain from 1997 until 2003

projects. When his contract ended at Yarmouk University, he had two choices: either to return to Baghdad, which he was advised against due to the conditions of its harsh sanctions, or to rely on freelance work with no guarantee of how that would fare. The idea of traveling to Bahrain to develop a curriculum pleased him. At the time the Gulf lacked methodological art education, and if he could create an educational endeavor there, it would make Bahrain an appealing center for the Gulf region in general.

The University of Bahrain had been established in 1986. Its main campus was in the northern al-Sakhir area, in a modern building designed by a brilliant Japanese architect. This campus held the College of Arts, with which Rafa was affiliated. Art classes were merely elective, but the university president at the time aspired to develop them into a specialized department. Rafa worked in a spacious oval hall that was well lit and looked over the university gardens lush with tamarisk trees. To the side was a teacher's office with luxurious furniture, adjoined by a space for the secretary and open to the main hall. As fate would have it, two years later I temporarily worked in this space while I was working as an editor for the cultural journal *Thaqafat* (Cultures), which I'll speak of shortly.

Rafa found himself in professional circumstances even more miserable than his experience in Jordan. Art was simply an elective class that students resorted to for reasons bearing no relation to art. Some of them were perhaps surprised to find a stern professor asserting that his class would be serious for those willing and able to learn. Rafa had to teach the fundamentals of painting and color to students who had no foundation in art whatsoever. Yet, the passion of most of them to learn at the hands of a professor of Rafa's stature made them put in great effort to earn his satisfaction. In the end, Rafa produced marvelous results, and selected the best works with which to hold an official university exhibition in which the students could take pride at the close of the academic year.

The Bahrainis' interest in the arts did not surprise us, for Bahrain had long been known for its art events and its people's love for acquiring the finest works, as well as their great appreciation of Iraqi artists. Some of them owned notable collections by Arab artists. The large attendance at Rafa's first solo exhibition in Manama in 1996 was a perfect example of their interest in art. Bahrain had an active art movement led and mentored by the distinguished artist Sheikh Rashid Al Khalifa, who'd studied art and architecture in Britain and possessed experience that was unique for the Arab world. Yet, despite the activity of Bahrain's art scene, few of the artists at the time had had the opportunity to study art in Cairo or Baghdad, fewer still had studied in the United States or England, and the rest relied only on their own potential.

With his typical optimism, Rafa began his work with enthusiasm and devotion, in hopes that he could turn this simple space into the creative hub that the art-loving administrators were anticipating. Among these were the university president at the time, Mohamed Jassim al-Ghatam, may he rest in peace, who was clearly pleased with our arrival and personally told me during our visits to his office that he'd like me to work with them at the university.

Among the first of Rafa's personal initiatives was contacting close artist friends and inviting them to donate print works with which to create a private university collection and a core for a future modern art museum. Many of his distinguished printmaker friends in fact sent their works, and to mark this step Rafa held an exhibition in the university department, sponsored by Sheikh Rashid Al Khalifa and attended by the university president and professors, as well as a number of Bahraini artists and art collectors. At the exhibition opening, Sheikh Rashid announced that Rafa was being appointed the head of the Arts and Heritage Association in addition to his work at the university, and that the university intended to establish a department specializing in art.

When the media announced this, the university, and us personally, were immediately inundated with calls asking when the application process would open. Rafa's first task was to submit a plan to the university administration for establishing a fine arts department within the College of Arts. Unfortunately, the endeavor was delayed year after year with different excuses. With subsequent changes in the university administration and the change of its presidency, it became clear that such an endeavor was out of reach. Six years later, when Rafa ended his work at the university, it was still being delayed. Yet the collection of works gifted by Arab artists continues to decorate the art hall in Bahrain.

The University of Bahrain had given us housing in a spacious private villa in the al-Rifa'a area near the university. It was newly constructed and built in the traditional Bahraini style, but furnished with bulky luxury American furniture. The narrow windows were designed to limit the sunlight shining in with its heat, and this formed a great challenge to Rafa's work. The living room was open to the dining room and constituted an appropriately sized space, so Rafa chose to work there, near the small window allowing in a limited amount of morning light that soon faded out by noon. He cleared the space, and to protect the dining room table placed large boards over it. Then he prepared his supplies: paper, canvas, and paints locally available in the best quality global brands, which quenched his thirst for materials and whet his appetite to work. I placed my desk in a corner of this area.

Around that time, we learned there was a joint effort underway to open a new exhibition space in Manama, the initiative of two Iraqi friends, artist Ferial al-Adhami and Bayan Al Barrak Kanoo. At the time there were no proper galleries except for the Ministry of Information's Art Center, which is where Rafa had held his exhibition two years earlier. Rafa was optimistic about this gallery and suggested it be called Al Riwaq Art Space, and he designed a logo for it. It was announced that it would open in January 1998 with a joint Iraqi exhibition by Rafa Nasiri and Suad al-Attar.

Rafa eagerly began working and produced a number of paintings on canvas and paper, which he loved. It was a beautiful and harmonious exhibition, and well attended. It also pleased us that our friend Nashwan Ali was managing the gallery. Nashwan was serious and dedicated, and she'd worked with Widad al-Orfali in her Baghdad gallery and gained good experience there. Al Riwaq gallery remained active for twenty years and hosted many outstanding exhibitions by Iraqi, Bahraini, and other Arab artists, and we were always pleased to meet our Iraqi and Arab friends there.

I spent the first two years in Bahrain focusing on my own work at home and occupying myself until Rafa returned from the university. Sometimes I'd go with him and spend time in the spacious and comfortable university library. Some months after we'd settled in, Nasser al-Din al-Assad contacted me. The Egyptian-Lebanese Publishing House in Cairo was launching a book project on the life of major Arab writers, with the aim of introducing them to the younger generations in a modern and appealing style appropriate to the times. He'd nominated me to write on him. I was taken by surprise and not sure how to respond, but he left me with no option when he said, "No one but you is capable of such a task."

The work took me a few months, during which I read some of his private papers and had him tell me his life story, including memories of his childhood in Aqaba, where he was born, before his family moved to Amman. I asked him to grant me freedom in language and style, which he did, only interfering on purely linguistic matters in his review. When I completed the book, I discovered that the material I'd produced was twice the length set in the contract. I discussed this with Nasser, and he wanted to publish it in full as he was so pleased with it. He contacted the publishing house director, Mohamed Rashad, who agreed on the condition that the book remain in keeping with the series format. So, I rewrote some of the chapters and adjusted some of the others to fulfill the conditions of the publisher. Upon completing each chapter I'd send it by fax to Nasser for his comments, and he'd express his surprise that the same topic could be conveyed in two different ways. Nasser continued to praise this work and said to Rafa every time we met, "I take the book with me wherever I go and give it as a gift. May doesn't write, she paints with words!"

Our life in Bahrain settled down nicely thanks to the presence of Iraqi and Bahraini friends and other visitors. It was good fortune that I met colleagues I'd worked with in the reinsurance company who'd settled in Bahrain to work, like Piercy Squeira, Muwafaq Hassan Rida, and Qais al-Mudris, and we also met wonderful people such as Yousef al-Maamar and Hakim al-Adhami and his wife, the artist Ferial al-Adhami, among others. We met in the evenings and all gathered from time to time. Then the Iraqi artist Nuri al-Rawi, who was in his eighties, came to Bahrain for six months and joined us. Al-Rawi worked tirelessly, holding a solo exhibition and producing large works on commission. We spent pleasant evenings with him and his amusing stories in our home or in al-Sharaa' Café overlooking the sea.

The following year, Rafa held a solo exhibition in the Bahrain National Museum *titled Ten Years . . . Three Locations* that included examples of his works produced between 1989–99, including those he'd produced in Bahrain. I wrote the introduction to the exhibition catalogue. The large exhibition covered the walls of the spacious museum, and an event was held in which he spoke of his artistic journey and the effect of place on his experience. Yet, he left the exhibition frustrated, and it was the first and last time I witnessed him in this state. To start with, the exhibition space hadn't been appropriate due to its overly large size and dim lighting. And the museum did not receive many visitors, so its reception was largely limited to the opening night. Rafa remained incredibly worried, considering this a failure unprecedented in his professional life.

Working in our al-Rifa'a home continued to dissatisfy him due to its lack of natural light, which except on Fridays left him with no choice but to paint in the evening. We began seriously considering moving to another house at the insistence of our friends, for we lived far away from them and the city center. We had to cover tens of kilometers from north to south, meaning we practically crossed Bahrain in its entirety in order to go out, shop, or attend cultural or social events. Our rent contract, however, required us to stay two years. And thus Amman became the ideal place for us during the summer holiday, when Rafa would dedicate the mornings to working in a comfortable atmosphere. We'd maintained our rented apartment there to spend our vacations in, especially once my mother moved in with us after my aunt passed away. This meant we had to give up visiting our beautiful Baghdad home during summer holidays, due to the lengthy journey by land and the power outages for hours at a time during hot Baghdad summers, until the situation got even worse following the occupation in 2003.

One day, in the autumn of 1999, Rafa came home happy—we were always pleased with small things—for he'd bought me a small, old book with lovely typesetting that was a volume of al-Mutanabbi poetry. It was a small version of the Amin Hindiya print published in Cairo in 1923, and Rafa had found it in a large collection of stored books the university was selling at very modest prices. I was delighted, and we decided to buy a number of copies to give to friends.

One Friday morning our friend Lubna al-Amin, who was married to Jamal Fakhru, stopped in to see us, as she often did. Lubna loved antique furniture and took us on outings to the old parts of Manama and al-Muharraq. She also loved art, and collected Arab art with her husband and took private painting lessons. That day, she brought with her an old table, and asked Rafa to turn it into a piece of art for the annual group exhibition benefiting the Bahrain Cancer Society. He liked the idea but set the small table aside and postponed working on it, as he had no idea what he might do with it. Then he began placing on it his constant cups of coffee and cigarettes while he worked. The copy of the al-Mutanabbi poetry volume remained nearby and he'd read from it from time to time, fascinated with its expression of alienation from one's homeland.

I don't recall how much time had passed when Lubna contacted us to ask what he'd done with the table, as the exhibition date was approaching. Rafa had completely forgotten about it. He turned to the table and emptied it of everything but the poetry volume, and stood there looking at it calmly and smoking, as the music we always played continued in the background. In delight and excitement, he cried, "I'll make this a desk for al-Mutanabbi!" He went to the kitchen clapping, prepared his black coffee, and lit a cigarette as he sat down to contemplate his subject.

He began by repainting the worn-out brown table in acrylic, and then chose a corner of it to host the poetry volume. Then he began randomly tearing pages from a second copy and plastering them in stages over the table, and then fixed the entire volume onto the left side of the tabletop, painting its cover in shades of brown using ink and watercolor. It was an astonishing and innovative piece, and intrigued attendees of the exhibition with its amusing idea, beautiful execution, and multiple meanings. Our friend Sheikha May bint Mohamed Al Khalifa, a sponsor of the Bahraini culture and heritage movement, kept raising her offer until she purchased it in the auction. She placed it in the historic home of Sheikh Ibrahim Al Khalifa in al-Muharraq, which following renovation had been turned into a cultural center.

This experience lit a flame of excitement, inspiring a series of subsequent projects that continued to generate others until the very end of Rafa's life, including many dreams that did not materialize. He was inspired by al-Mutanabbi, and produced a number of related works over the following years, including paintings on canvas and paper, prints, and also artist's books. Rafa regularly read al-Mutanabbi and also read some studies on him, and he listened to the professional recordings of his poetry produced in Abu Dhabi. He connected with the sense of alienation and sorrow in al-Mutanabbi's poetry in his despair over ever returning to Iraq.

With the start of the new century we were able to change our residence and moved to the al-Rashidiya neighborhood near our friend Yousef al-Maamar, who put great effort into helping us move and assisted us in renting an appropriate home in the lovely al-Rashidiya compound. This neighborhood had homes of unified design in different sizes, all built like English bungalows separated by roads planted with Tamarisk trees. Each house had a shrub fence, like the houses built by the English in Basra and Baghdad. They'd been dubbed the railway houses in al-Karkh and Andalusian Square in al-Rasafa, but were later demolished and replaced with modern buildings, including the Kamal al-Samara'i Hospital.

We were pleased with the spacious house, and its courtyard and gardens, which Rafa's lovely studio overlooked. I chose to place my desk in the open living room. The house was unfurnished, so we selected modern and comfortable Danish furniture, and found it an appropriate house for us. The residential compound included a medium-sized swimming pool, tennis courts, and a considerable area for walking or biking. My mother moved with us and fit in well with the family lifestyle. She found herself amid Iraqi and Bahraini women enchanted with her company and charming conversation.

After al-Mutanabbi had become Rafa's portal to a new stage of creativity, he produced in his new Bahrain studio a number of works of a Sufi nature, and held a solo exhibition titled *Homage to al-Mutanabbi* in Al Riwaq gallery in Manama in 2002. Through his diverse treatment of this topic in terms of content, vision, and technique, he called upon all his experience and skills acquired in the East and West. In fact he employed Eastern arts more, including the use of gold leaf and Arabic font in his compositions. In this exhibition he displayed for the first time an art book he'd created on the same topic, and which illuminated the spirit of Islamic arts in a modern style.

He'd started working regularly on these art books during the summer of 1990, after he'd been able to purchase handmade folded notebooks during his visit to China in the autumn of 1989. He'd gone by invitation of his professors and held a retrospective exhibition of twenty-five years of his print works in the Central Academy of Fine Arts, in which he'd studied. His first experience working with these notebooks had been in 1973, when he surprised me with a printed volume of my poetry titled *Is There a Space Between a Movement and Stillness?* He'd handwritten the poem on blue-gray cardboard and chosen birds as a subject, depicting them in different settings and using black Chinese ink and wide brushstrokes in the Chinese style. Rafa had wanted to print the volume through facsimile, before realizing that was not possible at the time due to the cost. Yet he chose an image from it for the cover of my first poetry volume, *Bird of Fire*. Until this day, the texts and images remain trapped in this beautiful notebook and have not been published.

From the very start of our residency in Bahrain, our social life was active with the presence of Bahraini and Iraqi friends, and this provided a pleasant atmosphere. Among those we were pleased to meet there was the well-known journalist Ahmed al-Manna'i, who was respected and liked by all due to his fine character and long history in journalism. Every Monday he held a literary salon in his Manama home, inviting Bahraini and Arab intellectuals and writers, men and women, and notably his closest friend, poet and scholar Alawi al-Hashimi. He'd welcome these friends with his generous wife Aisha in his library filled with stacks of books, newspapers, and Arabic periodicals on the shelves. Al-Manna'i was good with documentation and had a large archive of the Arab press. He often gave me published articles I'd written and did not have a copy of myself.

In the autumn of 1999, the president of the University of Bahrain approved the publication of a cultural periodical by the College of Arts. This was the initiative of its dean, Alawi al-Hashimi, and the editorial board members were selected from among its professors, including Rafa, who supervised the layout and production, and also produced a special section on the arts. In the search for an editor, al-Mana'i, who was on the editorial board, nominated me, with support from the chief editor Alawi, and soon this gained the approval of the university president Mohamed al-Ghatam, who expressed his pleasure with this choice. In the editorial board's first meeting, Rafa suggested the name *Thaqafat* (Cultures), and this became the journal's name. I began working in early October of that year.

I don't want to speak here of my work that lasted nearly three years, starting with laying the journal's foundations and creating a database of creatives and researchers, communicating with Arab writers, and reviewing the magazine's mail, until I later became the managing editor. I will simply say that it was serious and exhausting work that consumed most of my time and distanced me from my own work. Thanks to the joint efforts of the professors, the journal gained the trust and admiration of Arab cultural circles starting with the very first issue. Through my work on the journal, I gained additional experience that put me in direct contact with many Arab researchers, writers, and poets from all over the world. I had to reschedule my time for reading and writing, especially my work on my short story and poetry collections I'd written at the time, until I was finally able to publish my fourth poetry volume, *Predicament of Turquoise*, and my fourth short story collection, *Mail of the East*, in addition to continuing to write commissioned studies on art in Arabic and English.

When I first started working at the university, and until an office was set up for me near the office of dean Alawi, I occupied the space beside Rafa's office. During the few months in which I worked in this space, I was able to witness at firsthand the approach that Rafa followed in teaching his students. They varied greatly in their knowledge of art and practical background: some of them had never drawn a line, while others had some experience and talent. Rafa took preparatory steps with them, introducing them to the meaning of art, its rules, and its symbols, and illustrating this with images and videos. Then he moved on to the practical side, placing before them models to draw, until they reached the final stage of direct drawing. He'd ask them to collect flora from the surrounding gardens and to arrange them to serve as still life models. From time to time, he'd expand their education by showing them international and Arab artworks. At the conclusion of each academic term, he'd select a number of noteworthy works and hold an annual student exhibition with them on campus. Through my short-lived observations of his practical experience teaching, I was able to grasp the secret of his students' love for him.

In 1993, Rafa had written in his Amman diaries that an English friend of his had asked him one day, "Would you rather be a large fish in a small sea or a small fish in a large sea?" And he'd told her, "A large fish in a small sea." He understood her intention, which was to learn the extent of his willingness to reside in the West, or the big sea, in comparison to his homeland, the small sea. "It's the homeland that I never thought, ever, that I'd leave for any reason," he wrote. "Now I feel as though I'm a very big fish in a very small sea. Here there's an imbalance for two reasons. The first is that I don't want this feeling of being large, and the second is that this is not the sea I want to be in."

Despite our comfort and pleasure in Bahrain, Rafa was often restless. He spent long hours committed to his official work. Yet despite this he took advantage of free hours while at the university to write, or draw in ink or watercolor, hoping that his small dreams and projects might turn into larger endeavors.

Another factor contributing to our ultimate decision to end our residency in Bahrain was Alawi al-Hashimi's appointment as vice president of the university and his replacement as dean of the College of Arts with another academic as different from his predecessor as could be. Luckily Alawi continued as the journal's chief editor and my work remained attached to him. He gave me his undivided attention and was highly intent on maintaining us at the university by transferring us to another office under the university presidency. Yet, we'd decided it was time to return to Amman.

Between its content and its production design, with its openness to creativity and academia, *Thaqafat* (Cultures) had gained the trust of cultural circles around the Arab world. With the publication of issue five in the summer of 2003, we completed our jobs and bid farewell to Bahrain and its generous people.

The Last Ten Years and the Return to Amman

With the occupation of Iraq, our return seemed near impossible. In the summer of 2003, we left Bahrain and returned to Amman with the intention of staying there. We'd left Baghdad for over ten years at this point, and yet, unlike many of our friends, we hadn't bought a house, as we'd always aspired to return to our beautiful Baghdad home. My brother had settled the matter of his residency in the mid-1990s, buying a lovely apartment in Jebal Amman to safeguard a home for himself, his family, and his children, who were completing their education.

Throughout our residency in Bahrain, we'd maintained the apartment we'd rented in Amman. In this apartment we stored Rafa's art works he'd produced and continued to produce in Jordan, as well as the library we'd formed over those years after having left behind the extensive library in our Baghdad home. We often needed to reacquire certain reference books. This Amman apartment was spacious and included a spare room in which Rafa worked. In late 2003, we spent three months in Paris at the invitation of the Al-Mansouria Foundation to reside and work in their private studio in the Cité internationale des arts, which I previously spoke of in chapter seven. When we returned to Amman, we decided to rent a small apartment to serve as a work place in which we could welcome our guests with greater freedom. We found a small and appropriate apartment in Jabal Lweibdeh, an area we loved. And so our work and social lives began to fall into place.

Once settling back into Amman, we began seriously considering buying a permanent home rather than continuing to rent. We were not, however, able to find anything appropriate for our budget or needs. One day, an Iraqi man named Samir al-Jarrah came to our building and asked to visit us. He'd just arrived from Baghdad, and Rafa declined his visit as he'd become wary of strangers after the plights of our times had spoiled people's morals. One night, however, he knocked on our door and introduced himself. We invited him in and he apologized to Rafa, saying, "Sir, I only want to pass on my sister's greetings. She was your student, and very happy when she learned that you are my neighbor."

At this point. Rafa insisted he sit down with us, and we found before us a man of high morals with a depth of experience. He told us about his failed attempt at teaching in Iraq, for he'd gone after the occupation to help raise the level of this vital artery the embargo had destroyed. Yet, there he grew certain that neither the occupation forces nor the officials running the nation were serious about making

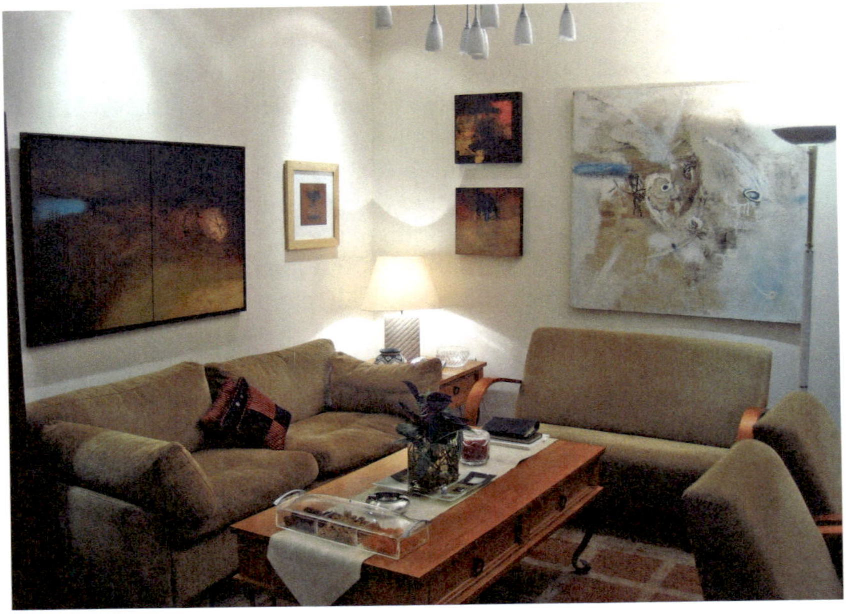

May and Rafa's
apartment in 4th Circle,
Jabal Amman, 2005

reforms to any state services. And so he'd left Iraq with the intention of returning to London, where he'd previously resided. He asked us how long it had been since we'd left and was surprised to learn that we still lived in a rented apartment. We discussed the issue with him, and it turned out that he had a lot of experience with the market. He immediately suggested to us apartments for sale at an appropriate price in Jabal Amman. I couldn't believe it, for this was one of Amman's highest-class neighborhoods, and I'd often dreamed of living there. He suggested we go visit it together.

It was December 2004, and a cold and rainy night. Samir stopped his car outside an attractive building on the hilltop, designed in a modern style with high-ceilings and open spaces. Rafa looked at the glass façade and balconies with wooden railings, immediately saying, "I've bought it without seeing any details." Rarely did Rafa take a decision so quickly. He contacted the number on the sign, and the owner, engineer Mohamed Qweider, informed him there was nothing left in the building other than a ground floor apartment with three rooms. The next morning we went to see it and happily discovered its balcony was in the back and overlooked the valley. We contacted our friend, engineer Munir Doghramji, to evaluate the building. Rafa fell in love with the apartment and its features and the area, and Munir praised it and encouraged us to buy it immediately. We informed our neighbor who'd descended upon us like an angel and visited the apartment together. He was an excellent guide, pointing out to me many comfortable and practical details. In the spring of 2005, we moved into our new home, which was also close to my brother's house. And we thus came to own a home that brought comfort and stability to our hearts.

In the summer of 2004, as we were celebrating the engagement of Ali, my middle nephew, and specifically the day that the men were going to the official engagement ceremony, Namir received test results that indicated he had a malignant and rapidly spreading tumor that must be removed as soon as possible. He indeed had surgery two days after Ali's engagement, just as Ramadan was about to begin, and then underwent chemotherapy. We were often left sleepless at the idea of chemotherapy and its implications, especially after the other cruel and bitter experiences we'd witnessed. Cancer had killed Rafa's elder brother Munir Nasiri when it was discovered he had an advanced-stage pancreas tumor leaving him less than six months to live. We worried that Namir would get blood cancer like my father, who died from it at the age of forty-eight. Namir was strongly built and healthy and had suffered from no disease other than a kidney stone that had been quickly treated and dissolved by laser.

I spent many nights in a kind of daze, fearful of losing him and at a loss before my mother, who was eighty-seven and in excellent health. Prior to the development of cancer, Namir had narrowly survived a heart attack that had occurred in the middle of the night. Our cousin, Dr. Said Na'el Basri, had gotten him into Jordan Hospital and supervised the saving of his life. It was a severe heart attack, and he was saved with electric shocks after his pulse and blood pressure had reached zero. Then the brilliant heart specialist Dr. Harran Zureiqat conducted heart surgery on him. A year later, signs of cancer appeared and did not leave Namir with much time.

During his illness, I gradually prepared my mother to accept the eventual loss of her son, whom she'd only seen glowing with health. As she witnessed his rapid loss of weight, she whispered with a mother's sense, "Is this truly my son?" In his final stages, he was admitted to the intensive care unit at King Hussein Medical Center and put on morphine. I'll never forget his flowing tears when he saw our mother the first time she visited him in the hospice room. After that, they closed his eyes and placed him under full anesthesia, for the disease had reached his spinal cord and he was in intense pain. I spent the mornings speaking to him and reciting the Koran as he lay there connected to machines. Rafa would join me in the evening and bring my mother. I'd ask her to speak to him, but she'd just look at him in shock and cautiously reach out to touch him.

I thanked God that her own suffering did not last more than a year, when she joined him in a calm and peaceful death in the hospital, in our company and under the supervision of her beloved doctor, Junaid Najeeb Mahmoud, and her nephew Dr. Said. The cause of her death was a fourteen-centimeter aorta opening that could burst at any moment. She passed away a few days after being admitted to hospital, on the same day and time as her son one year earlier, at 1 a.m. on August 10, 2006. Rafa was with me when she passed away, along with my nephew and dear old friends Anan and Rajih Muhieddin, supporting me and providing tender love and security.

Namir was not at all your average person. He was very social and greatly loved. He bore great knowledge, and I previously spoke of his qualifications. Following his return to Baghdad from London in 1964, and after completing his military service, he worked in the Basra oil company for about ten years, gaining great administrative experience before being transferred to the Ministry of Oil when the foreign oil companies were nationalized. Following his retirement in Baghdad in the early 1980s, he opened a translation office and was certified by the Iraqi minister of foreign affairs to translate official documents and contracts signed with the foreign companies coming to Iraq at the time. He took on translation as a profession and collaborated with al-Ma'mun Publishing House in Baghdad.

Following the 1991 Gulf War and the embargo placed on Iraq, he found it difficult, like many others, to survive with three children in various stages of their education. So, he and his family moved to Amman, where he was appointed to the office of Prince Hassan bin Talal as a researcher and translator. At the same time, he continued translating books beyond the scope of his official work, in agreement with the Arab Institute for Research and Publishing. He published a number of important translations that enriched the Arabic library, perhaps the most notable of which was *Democracy and Its Critics* by American researcher Robert Dahl (the translation was published in 2005). Yet, the most important translation he worked on, with the experience of a contemporary historian and researcher, was *Gertrude Bell: From Her Personal Papers 1914–1926* by Elizabeth Burgoyne. In this book he not only translated Bell's diaries and letters related to her role in Iraq, but also commented on some of the information she recounted that he saw as lacking precision. In doing so, Namir Abbas Muzaffar did not suffice with available references, but rather sought out the relevant Iraqis and listened to their accounts in order to annotate the necessary corrections. The book was published in 2002, and the novelist Abdel Rahman Munif wrote the introduction.

Starting in the 1990s, Amman became a center for meeting family and friends from East and West. The presence of a somewhat harmonious Iraqi community, and the ease of movement and travel after having been freed from official obligations, helped us to create a comfortable and productive life filled with a variety of activities and pleasant occasions meeting friends we'd been apart from for years, but with whom Amman had reconnected us. During the first five years, we accomplished a great deal of art and writing. Rafa held solo exhibitions in Amman, Dubai, Kuwait, Damascus, Cairo, and Bahrain, which we visited several times on official invitation. We did not, however, obtain permission to travel to Rafa's Dubai exhibition, despite our official invitation. We no longer traveled except together, and Rafa accompanied me to the symposia and poetry readings in which I was invited to take part. We easily traveled to Syria, Lebanon, and Turkey whenever we wanted.

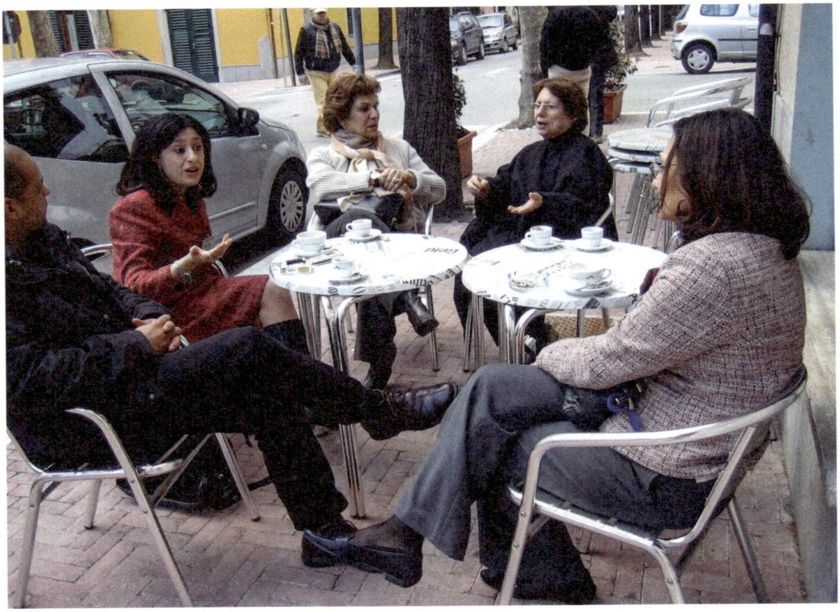

With Nada Shabout,
Princess Wijdan
al-Hashemi,
and Salwa Mikdadi,
Florence, 2006

In our previous planned travels, we always intended to spend a summer vacation together in Rome, where the Iraqi Airways stopped en route to London. Rafa had previously visited it several times on his own, and in the end he always preferred to spend all his time in London working in the graphic art studio. Traveling to Rome remained a dream, and after we moved to Jordan I was granted two opportunities to do so. The first was in 1996 with a delegation from the Aal al-Bayt Institute to attend a Muslim-Christian dialogue held annually with churches around the world. The program was suggested by Prince Hassan bin Talal, the president of the the Royal Academy for Islamic Civilization Research (Aal al-Bayt Institute) to respond to the controversy provoked at the time by Samuel Huntington in his book *The Clash of Civilizations and the Remaking of World Order*. The program's slogan was "Dialogue among Civilizations" as an alternative to the theory of the downfall of civilizations. The conference was held in the Vatican, presenting me with a rare opportunity, as I hoped to use the visit to see art I had long wished to view in person. Yet, I found myself restricted by a program that didn't end until eight or nine at night. The Sistine Chapel was just a few steps away from the hotel, and I'd gaze at it wistfully.

Then, the following year, my dream came true when I received an invitation to participate in the cultural convention for "disaster-inflicted" nations of the Global South organized in the historic southern Italian city of Alberobello. Rafa was not able to accompany me due to his commitments at the university, but during this trip I was able to visit Rome and Florence. I went to Florence on a guided tourist trip with a group of Japanese people who were not moved by anything—not the enchanting views on the roads to northern Italy, nor the art museums I was eager to visit after books had whet my appetite for them. It was a poor and lacking visit, but sufficient to raise questions that led to new convictions. For when I stood face to face with renaissance sculpture, that of Michelangelo in particular, and saw the greatness of the human form embodied in perfect proportionate figures, especially David with his beauty, and the massive Moses, half of him still encased in stone, I felt awe and intimidation. The exaggeration in glorifying the human—the god—through sculpture and painting, and the subsequent theories that such visions produced, is what turned humans into domineering demons. I'd call Rafa from there and convey my impressions, and he promised me that we'd go together some day.

This dream did not come true until years later, when Rafa accompanied me in 2006 to attend a symposium in Montecatini Terme, in northern Italy, under the auspices of the Association for Modern and Contemporary Art of the Arab World, Iran, and Turkey. The European University Institute's Robert Schuman Centre hosted the symposium in this beautiful holiday resort, organized by a group of female researchers specialized in Arab and Islamic art history, among them Nada Shabut, Salwa Mikdadi, Silvia Naef, and Princess Wijdan al-Hashemi. Rafa walked around the city enjoying his time, while we were trapped in a small room. He only attended to listen to my paper "Art in Exile: The 1980s Generation as an Example." When the symposium ended, we went to Florence and spent two days there, then traveled to Venice and then Rome, where we spent a few days. We stayed in a beautiful hotel that had been a monastery in old Rome, chosen by our dear friend Lubna Alman. She accompanied us on our walks, enriching us with her vast knowledge of the places, museums, and art exhibitions, most notable of which was an incredible and comprehensive exhibition of Amedeo Modigliani works. By chance, Rafa met a number of his students who were living in Rome and Florence, including the painter Ali Assaf and the sculptor Dara.

My well-scheduled life in Amman helped me to complete a number of books, including my fifth poetry volume, *From that Distant Land*, and my sixth collection of short stories, *Have None of Them Remained?*, which is a portrait of Baghdad. Then, in 2007, I published a book about a quarter century of Rafa Nasiri's practice, titled *Painter of Universal Scenes*, and contributed to editing an academic study of his practice titled "Rafa Nasiri: His Life and Art," written by his brother Sabah Nasiri and published in 2010. All of these books were published by the Arab Institute for Research and Publishing, Beirut.

Among the art studies I completed during this period (in Arabic and English) that I'm proud of is a study titled "Gender and Empire," which was part of a symposium by the same name at the American University in Cairo in 2006, as well as the English-language paper I presented in Montecatini Terme, Italy, on the migration of Iraqi artists, focusing on the 1980s generation mentioned above. I later presented this in Arabic at the Arab Visual Artists' Convention in Sanaa in 2009, after further developing and updating it.

Among the literary studies I'm proud of is "Poetry Resisting Oblivion," presented at the symposium held by Philadelphia University in Amman in 2007, and organized by the International Association of Contemporary Iraqi Studies. Rafa also took part in this symposium, with a study on resistance through creativity, in which he addressed the experience of Iraqi artist immigrants. Both of these studies were published in English and translated by professor Ferial Ghazoul, in the *International Journal of Contemporary Iraqi Studies* edited by professor Tariq Ismail. Another was a study on the literature of Lebanese poet and artist Etel Adnan, titled "Has She Been Created of Water and Light?," for an event honoring her that was organized by artist Nidal Al Achkar at Al Madina Theater in Beirut in the spring of 2010. I'd previously translated from English Adnan's brilliant book *Paris, When It's Naked*, published by Saqi Books, Beirut 2006. Included in the program was an evening of Etel's translated poetry and prose read by various writers and poets. At the end of each reading the name of the translator was mentioned, and they were not many. Yet, one of the participants read a long excerpt of my translation of Paris, *When It's Naked*, without mentioning the source, and another participant spoke on the Arabic translations of Etel's work without mentioning my translation I'd been so praised for. I was upset but made no public comment.

Alongside this and that, I wrote many short articles on places and memories, and studies addressing the experiences of Iraqi artists, which Rafa eagerly insisted I publish in a book. But his illness prevented me from doing so. A year after he passed away, I collected them and published them under the title *Continuation and Distinction: The Modern Art Movement in Iraq*, with the Arab Institute for Research and Publishing, Beirut, in 2015.

I can say that the last ten years, before the onslaught of Rafa's illness, were among the most pleasurable periods of our life. We grew both closer and more distant, each immersed in our own projects, and each delighted with what the other accomplished.

The Years Before Departure

Rafa rarely fell ill, but in April 2009 he began complaining of painful symptoms that worried him, and so went to see Dr. Said Na'el Basri, director of Jordan Hospital's international center. Tests revealed a prostate tumor, and this was a shock to Said, for he's my cousin and is close to us, and held great love and respect for Rafa. I could tell by his tone on the telephone that the news was not good. He wasn't able to inform Rafa himself, and said he'd write a report for the chief surgeon and head of the urology department, Dr. Nader Younis, and place him in charge. I told Said to leave the matter to me, but first I needed to absorb the news so as to be able to tell Rafa.

At the time, I was in our Jabal Lweibdeh studio, which had become a comfortable refuge. We were content in the studio, and Rafa had produced beautiful works there for a solo exhibition in Amman and several Gulf countries, beginning with Amman's 4 Walls Gallery. Yet, he'd continue to dream of owning a graphic art studio, for his printing press sat without use in this space not large enough for both painting and printing. After three years, once our life had settled down, he rented another studio with a space appropriate for painting the large-sized works he wanted to produce, and with a separate room sufficiently large enough to hold the large printing press that had been made for him by the Iraqi engineer Jihad Ghawi. He began spending most of his time in this larger studio and maintained the smaller one to serve as my office and a place in which to store his works, as well as to welcome friends and guests. I was alone there when I received the news, and had a few hours before I'd see Rafa, giving me some time to calm down.

I typically maintain utter calm upon hearing shocking news. This allows its bearer to continue speaking at ease, while I receive the news as though in passing, and not something affecting me personally. Then, when it later seeps in, touching every nerve and joint of my body, it triggers connections that manifest one after the next, as past experiences and scenes reappear before me. First, I saw the image of my father, and the broken look in his eyes as he was dying. This was followed by the image of Rafa's elder brother Munir, who'd been devoured by disease in only six months. Finally, I saw my brother, whose cruel agony I'd witnessed and not yet recovered from. I began trembling and felt powerless. My heart beat rapidly and I screamed at the top of my voice, "Mercy, oh Lord! Rafa's such a blessing to this world, and still has so much to give. Aid him to overcome this plight!"

I heard the door open and Rafa come in earlier than usual. He came over to my desk, cheerful as always, feeling satisfied at having completed an artwork or a stage of it. I hugged him tightly as he told me what he'd done that day, before asking, "Didn't Said contact you?" In a tone that was reassuring despite the discovery of a tumor, I told him about the test results and that Dr. Nader would review their details with us that evening. I felt him tremble in my arms despite maintaining calm. He seemed relatively at ease, perhaps due to my reassurance or his optimistic nature. I'd previously met Dr. Nader when he'd conducted surgery to dissolve my brother's kidney stone some years earlier, and I'd been comfortable with his wonderful and personal approach. He was one of his field's top specialists, and when he met us that night, his comfortable demeanor, detailed explanations, and medical advice all had an air of optimism that planted a great deal of hope within us.

Rafa underwent further testing and X-rays to determine where the disease was located and how much it had spread through his body. These showed that he was lightly afflicted in two areas, in the left shoulder and the spine. The doctor described these as secondary and reassured us, saying the disease was in its early stages and did not require surgical intervention or chemotherapy, and that it might go away with medication and supplementary treatment, especially since Rafa was in good health. Rafa began his treatment and at the end of every month test results would show that his body was responding. The percentage of disease kept decreasing, and we reached the point where Dr. Nader was certain that in another month it would be at zero.

What happened, however, was the complete opposite. Rafa's body began resisting the medication, and the disease increased month after month, until no option remained but chemotherapy. We implored the doctor to find us an alternative, and he prescribed another medication that didn't work. He told us chemotherapy was inevitable and referred us to an oncologist. At this stage, Rafa began suffering from weakness, especially in his left leg. This was in the spring of 2011.

All the doctors we consulted in Amman and Beirut, as well as those Dr. Said consulted in Germany, America, and England, concurred that chemotherapy was a must, and yet we traveled to Beirut for further consultations. On this trip we took with us Mohammed, my youngest nephew, who I called our seasonal son. Rafa adored him and had taken a keen interest in him since he was young, encouraging him to develop his skills in design and helping him get into the College of Arts at the University of Jordan, indeed becoming his close friend and mentor. Mohammed had joined us on a previous trip, bringing joy and enthusiasm.

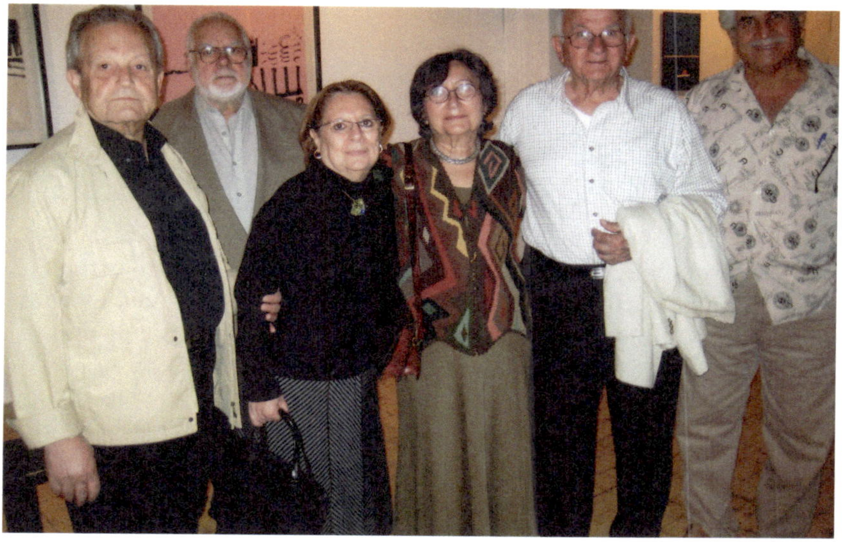

Seminar on Etel Adnan,
Al Madina theater
Beirut, May 13–16, 2010.
With Ferial Ghazoul and
Maath Al Alousi

On the surface, Rafa did not appear to have lost any of his intellectual or physical vitality. In fact, his activity had reached a peak in 2009–11, reflected in his rich production of paintings on canvas and paper, drawings, prints, and artist's books of various sizes that satisfied him on certain topics, including his collections *Homage to Ibn Zaydoun, After al-Wasiti*, and *Beyond Time*. He held a wonderful solo exhibition in Jebal Amman's Nabad Gallery, and also produced several portfolios of graphic prints.

Beirut held a special place in Rafa's heart, and he had his personal rituals there, starting with a visit to Librairie Antoine as soon as he arrived to purchase the latest international art books and periodicals. Then there were certain cafés and restaurants he liked to visit in Hamra, Raucheh, and Zeituna. We took to visiting Beirut with and without reason, spending a few lovely days meeting dear friends or attending special occasions. In 2010, I took part in a symposium honoring artist and poet Etel Adnan, previously mentioned in chapter eleven. The following year, during our daily walks in Hamra, Rafa's attention was caught by a collection of posters advertising various art, music, and theater events. Many of these had been affected by the elements, getting torn, their colors fading, or otherwise melding with the wall. Rafa photographed them, saying he'd turn them into print works titled "The Walls of Beirut." He was excited and spoke of it to our friend Wadah Faris, who was pleased with the idea. He also told our close friend Nidal Al Achkar, promising her he'd hold an exhibition in Nuha al-Radi's gallery in the same building as her theater space, Al Madina Theater. When we returned to Amman, Rafa asked his assistant Saver Jalal to create digital prints of his photographs, but he wasn't pleased with the results and tore them up, discarding his idea.

We had two days in Beirut before our scheduled consultation at the American University hospital, and decided to take a trip to the mountains with Mohammed, stopping in Zahleh and Brummana. Rafa was relaxed and cheerful despite the pain in his left leg that was beginning to bother him. It pained him when we stopped to rest at a café in Zahleh, due to his sitting so long in the car, and acted up again when we arrived in Brummana.

The next morning, we went to our appointment at the American University of Beirut Medical Center with urologist Dr. Raja Khouly. Upon reviewing the test results and X-rays, he advised commencing chemotherapy immediately, and referred us to an oncologist. Then he asked Rafa, "Do you have pain in your left leg?" He told Rafa to have his left leg treated with radiation, and this was confirmed by oncologist Dr. Ali Shamseddine, who also advised beginning chemotherapy with no delay.

Before returning to Amman, we paid a visit to the Beirut Exhibition Center to see the space for which Rafa was meant to prepare large-sized works as part of a group exhibition curated by Meem Gallery in Dubai and Beirut. The exhibition was held first in Dubai, but we weren't able to attend. Titled *Art in Iraq Today*, it included works by twelve artists from two different generations. Rafa stood in the middle of the exhibition hall, gazing at its vast space and high ceilings, looking all around and absorbing the challenge awaiting him. The exhibition was the idea of Dia al-Azzawi, conceived as a commemoration for Palestinian-Iraqi novelist, art critic, and painter Jabra Ibrahim Jabra, who'd set the foundation for documenting Iraq's visual arts movement, closely following it and writing on its artists. Rafa had been asked to paint large-scale works appropriate for Beirut's iteration of the exhibition, and he seemed both enthusiastic and awestruck as he faced the high-ceilinged walls and open spaces. Yet, in fact, he was facing the challenges of two intertwined situations affecting body and soul.

We returned to Amman, and Rafa's treatment was overseen by oncologist Sami al-Rabadhi, one of the best Jordanian doctors and cofounder of the cancer hospital later named the King Hussein Cancer Foundation. Dr. al-Rabadhi was a man of science and kept up with the latest developments in oncology. He was intent on informing his patients of the status of their health in a professional, polite, and reassuring manner. Our first appointment with him was comforting, as he quickly gained Rafa's confidence and raised his morale. He told Rafa that his general health was excellent, and therefore his body would respond positively to the treatment. Even more reassuring to Rafa was that the treatment would take place in his attractive private clinic.

Dr. Sami al-Rabadhi informed us that he would use an advanced treatment of one dose every three weeks. Despite his calm demeanor, Rafa seemed to dread the first dose. I asked the doctor if I could sit with Rafa and he welcomed the idea. He himself sat beside Rafa's arm receiving the treatment and held his hand and exchanged general conversation with him for twenty minutes, before standing up and patting Rafa on the shoulder. "Excellent. Your body is receiving the treatment without counterreactions." Rafa's face lit up with a smile and he took a deep breath to expel the worry in his chest, as he always did when facing a difficult situation, like the time I underwent major surgery in Irbid. The doctor turned to me and explained that some patients have a strong reaction when they first begin treatment, and their blood pressure drops to a degree requiring hospitalization.

The very next morning, Rafa woke up filled with energy. He took me to my office and then went to his studio, then went with his young assistant, Saver Jalal, to the University Bookshop in al-Gardens and bought a large number of canvases and art supplies with which to begin work on his new paintings. He'd just completed a collection of works titled *Homage to Ibn Zaydoun*. Two days later, he noticed excessive hair loss he'd shed onto his pillow and in the bathroom. He wanted to treat this before it advanced, so rushed to his barber Jalal in Shmesani and asked him to shave his head. The barber smiled and asked what degree he wanted, and Rafa insisted "all of it." Rafa's charisma, gentle character, and humbleness with everyone made him loved by all who knew him, and he noticed the change on Jalal's face when he learned of his illness, crying out, "But no!" To avoid similar reactions from others, Rafa preferred to keep the matter between us, with very few exceptions.

In the beginning, Rafa maintained his normal appearance with no changes to his face and body except for his shaven head, which he began covering with caps or berets. Initially the chemotherapy effects were limited to the first few days of a dose, and then he'd regain his natural state and remain active. Then a gradual but distinct change occurred in the fullness of his face and body due to the cortisone, that two-edged blade, giving him energy and vitality that quickly dwindled as his consumption of it decreased. He also experienced drops in electrolytes and red blood cells, among other effects. He'd often lose consciousness and we'd have to take him to hospital.

Rafa never stopped painting except on days when he felt exhausted. He continued to spend the evenings reading, in which he increasingly found pleasure, moving between novels, history, and art books, as well as watching films and visiting websites. In fact, his illness drove him to examine memories of the past and to document his life and practice in writing, as well as to share it in lectures, symposia, and private meetings.

Following a lengthy separation, in 2006 Rafa was able to meet his brother Sabah Nasiri in Amman. Sabah was Rafa's sibling closest to his heart and mindset, and decades apart had made them thirsty to revisit their past. This opened before them new opportunities to discuss not only personal matters but also cultural ones, as Sabah possessed a deep knowledge of visual arts and music and had great respect for Rafa's practice. Sabah was ten years his junior and had left Iraq in the early 1970s after completing his university studies in Arabic literature. He first went to teach in Algeria, and years later moved to Paris to complete his graduate studies, earning a PhD and then teaching in French universities. Rafa spoke admiringly of the wonderful letters he'd send to the family, and to him in particular. After a few meetings in Amman and Paris, Sabah decided to write an academic study of Rafa's personal and artistic journey. In the summer of 2010, we met in Asilah, Morocco, and Sabah brought a draft of the study we were so eager to see. Sabah had a vibrant memory of their family life, but due to the time and space that had separated the two brothers, and his lengthy absence from the family and Rafa's life in particular, I reviewed the book with him and we'd also consult Rafa. This very important resource was published in 2010 under the title *Rafa Nasiri: His Life and Work*, written with the expertise of an experienced academic and a writer well-versed in art, and specifically that of his brother.

And so Rafa found himself led to writing about his personal experience in China. He spoke of his fateful decision as a young nineteen-year-old choosing to travel to the Far East instead of Europe, which had enticed so many others. Since I knew well his ability to express himself in writing—from his letters and his dense, precise articles, as well as the poetry and prose he showed me in his diaries and notes—I found that he was avoiding exposition and sufficing with very little text. Brevity was in his nature and could be found in everything he did. When he traveled to Portugal to gain additional experience in printmaking, he fell in love with abstraction and quickly adapted it to his personal style in printmaking and painting, starting in 1968. Abstraction was highly compatible with his intellectual and temperamental makeup, yet prose writing is a different matter. I always pushed him to expand on what he'd written when I found that he could enrich it with different aspects, or if something required clarification. He'd protest at first, claiming he was tired and that what he'd written was sufficient. Yet, he'd later yield and resume working, and would be pleased as he found himself recalling details that appeared before him, images and events pouring out one after the other, until he completed *Rihlati ila al-sin* (My journey to China), which was published in mid-2012. It's a charming book and I believe it stands among the most interesting contemporary Arab autobiographies published.

During this same period, he also produced wonderful art works including large-scale paintings and prints that he compiled in portfolios in his large Lweibdeh studio, with the assistance of Saver Jalal and others, as well as the artist's books he created in various forms through to September 2013, just two months before he passed away.

When Rafa was diagnosed with cancer, I became the channel between him and the doctor, shielding him from anything that might affect his morale. Rafa had always had an aversion to illness and rarely got sick; I never saw him lose his patience or nerves unless he had congestion. When confronted with the serious illness of a relative or friend, he'd conceal his concern and take refuge in silence. This is how he reacted to his brother Munir's illness, and then his father's. In contrast, I'd lived with my mother's colds and severe asthma, taking care of her and doing what I could to relieve her, including cupping. Personally, I'd suffered from seasonal health problems since my youth and started treating myself to avoid burdening others. And I took care of my aunt when she had a severe stroke that paralyzed her movement and digestive system. I gained a great deal of experience as I followed her critical case with specialists, diligently carrying out their directives, to the point that the brilliant surgeon Abdel Karim al-Khatib asked me, "How did we fail to gain you in the ranks of medical school?" But I belong to the arts, not science.

It was with this experience and commitment that I became Rafa's spokesperson, in his presence or absence, offering detailed verbal reports referring to the date and hour of a symptom. My diary became a detailed record of Rafa's treatment, doses, and all the developments of his case, day by day.

Rafa's treatment, over nearly five years, was not all chemotherapy: the doctor constantly sought new developments for treating his disease. Whenever Rafa complained of not being able to bear it, his strength giving out, the doctor would begrudgingly discontinue it and temporarily replace it with widely available, yet ineffective hormonal treatments. At one point, Rafa was quite sick and the doctor told us about an effective hormonal treatment in capsule form (by the commercial name Zytiga) that targeted tumors anywhere they existed in the body. It wasn't available in Jordan but could be obtained in America. Following a brief silence, he added that it was very expensive. I looked at Rafa and wished I could say we'd sell everything we own. I found Rafa waiting for my response, and I told the doctor, "Nothing is more precious than Rafa."

I immediately contacted a lifelong friend, Khawla Hafiz Khalid, a pharmacist living and working in Boston. She'd left Iraq in the late 1970s to accompany her husband, engineer Anwar Naji Diab, and they'd created a life for themselves in Boston, where she continued to work in a pharmacy. Khawla contacted me a few hours later to tell me the treatment was exorbitant, and yet she promised to procure it despite the difficulty in doing so. She managed to purchase it through close ties to a Lebanese colleague holding a high position in the Dana-Farber Cancer Institute. She got us three boxes that would last three months, as prescribed by Dr. al-Rabadhi, and her husband sent it to us by express mail. When it arrived, Jordanian customs were suspicious as to what kind of medication it was and didn't allow it through until contacted by Dr. al-Rabadhi. He was thrilled with this success and told Rafa he'd be the first person in Jordan to use this medication. Rafa began taking it in November 2011.

During the first three months, Rafa took it four times a day, in addition to a monthly injection and medication for his symptoms. His medical tests showed an incredible response to the treatment, and it practically rid him of chemotherapy's harsh side effects, allowing him to eat with a nearly normal sense of taste. The three months passed, and we got more of the medication, but when he finished the fourth box, his health began declining and he experienced weakness in his left leg. The disease began spreading through his bones, and the doctor advised him to use a cane to lessen the pressure on it, as well as to undergo radiation treatment. We walked half an hour every day as it was good for him, and Rafa continued to drive and to regularly go to his studio.

I did not stop working during Rafa's illness. After publishing my last collection of short stories about Baghdad, *Have None of Them Remained?*, I worked on my poetry volume *Absence*, which I'd begun writing following my volume *From that Distant Land*, which was inspired by the loss of nation, home, and loved ones. At the same time, I focused my efforts on completing my studies on the pioneers of Iraq's modern art movement. Rafa pressed me to finish them and publish them in a book that would become reference material. He urged me, with some reprimand and blame, to complete what he saw as different from everything else written about Iraqi artists. I still had a lot of work to do on it and focused on completing it to please him. Yet the circumstances were not in my favor for the necessary contemplation, research, and follow-up.

In crises like these, I usually turn to translation. I'd acquired an old book on Iraq called *New Babylon* that was sold out in the bookshops.

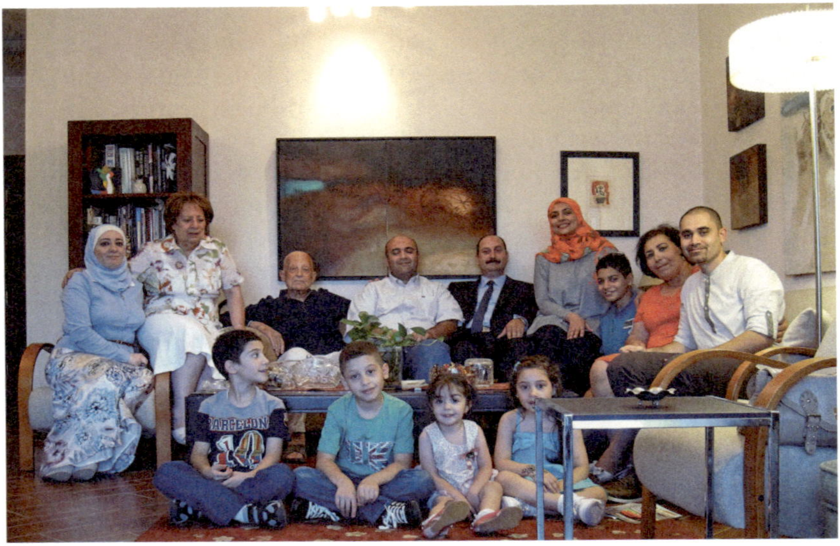

With family in the 4th
Circle apartment,
Amman, 2012

Published in London in 1957, it presented a portrait of Iraq in the mid-1950s, via the experience of two British professors who'd resided in Baghdad and held empathy for the land and its people. I obtained a photocopy of it from a dear friend, the economist Mahmoud Ahmed Uthman, who suggested I translate it. In the early 1950s, the Ministry of Education had contracted two professors to teach English and English literature, Desmond Stewart and John Haylock. After nearly five years in the country, the two had entered into Iraqi social fabric and realized the mistakes Britain had made, including its presumptuous policies toward the people whom the occupying force had made no effort to get to know. They were openly concerned about the political conflicts taking place, and which might undermine the efforts of this developing country, which they believed would be leading the Middle East once its five-year plan was fulfilled. When Rafa read the book he got excited and urged me to translate it. So, I began working, and found a safe refuge in translation. I completed half of it, and then it became impossible for me to work.

In February 2012, we traveled to Spain by invitation of the University of Granada, to present a paper on the relationship of poetry to painting, and to speak on the experience of the Jordanian painter Jihad al-Amiri, who was soon to defend his dissertation. Rafa was pleased about the trip and looked forward to it. The day before traveling we went to Dr. Adnan Qasim's clinic for radiation treatment on his left leg. The snow was heavy that morning, and we waited at the door for the doctor's arrival. Given that we were about to travel, he chose to delay treatment for Rafa's leg. "Frankly, you'll be away for a week and I won't know what happens with you during this period. And why should you pay the sum when we won't know the results of the treatment?" He was an earnest, straightforward doctor.

We were advised from the beginning to use a wheelchair at the large Madrid airport, which had been built in a postmodern style with intertwining pillars in a large open space with glass walls. But Rafa insisted on walking. We covered great distances to reach the floor for domestic travel, the electric walkways transporting us as we followed the signs to gate K92. Airport staff would stop and offer assistance and a ride in their buggies, but Rafa firmly declined despite how tired I could see he was. We waited seven hours in the Madrid airport, soaring, via its glass walls and roofs, through its panoramic views in which clouds and mountaintops intersected with a very low sky. It was a long day, and our journey had been tiring, starting at 4 a.m. and not reaching Granada until 9 p.m. Yet the warm welcome we received, and our great love for this historic city we were visiting together for the second time, raised Rafa's spirits and rejuvenated his tired face.

I woke up early, but the sun didn't rise until after 7 a.m. From our room overlooking the round garden, I saw in the soft dawn light bitter orange trees ripe with fruit, and the cacophonous activity of birds. The scene looked as though it had stepped from a miniature by the thirteenth-century miniaturist Yehyia al-Wasiti. It was a sunny day and bitingly cold. After breakfast, the poet Ali al-Amiri, who resided in Granada, came to accompany us to the Alhambra Palace. We were incredibly eager to see it again in person. In 2010, Rafa had been inspired by Andalusia in a project on Princess Wallada and Ibn Zaydoun, and he'd been consumed by passion for it, producing beautiful works in different mediums on paper and canvas of various sizes, the largest of which was two by two meters. It was a message of love and beauty to a world which every day was sinking further into horror.

As we drove on the road to Alhambra, we recalled how we'd taken the same long distance by foot forty years earlier, and I'd bought a guitar. This trip had a special effect on us as we moved from room to room and from the corridor to the garden, following history with our eyes and footsteps as the astonishing interior opened to a magical natural environment of utter harmony. Rafa was fully absorbed with the space, capturing images with an experienced eye that saw everything with the perspective of a lover. He photographed the details of the façades and the Arabic calligraphy ornamenting the walls, to enrich his photography collection and hoping to make later use of them. At the end of the tour, we sat on a wall overlooking Albaicín, the heart of the city shining under a gentle sun, and Rafa's face was lit up with joy and peace, having forgotten his pain and fatigue.

Our other main pleasure on this trip was the event in which we spoke before a large audience, including leading Arabists Pedro Montabith and Carmen Ruiz, who'd come from Madrid, in addition to other professors, including the archaeology professor Akram Thanoun, an Iraqi from Mosul who'd resided in Granada for thirty years. Rafa spoke on the artist Jihad al-Amiri's visual treatment of Mahmoud Darwish's poem "Jerusalem" and Lorca's poem "Granada," and also on al-Amiri's printmaking. I spoke on the same topic, expanding on the relation between poetry and painting in general, and the ability of visual images to enrich the texts of these two poets. As I responded to the audience's comments and questions, I realized how brilliant the interpreters had been in clearly conveying my speech in

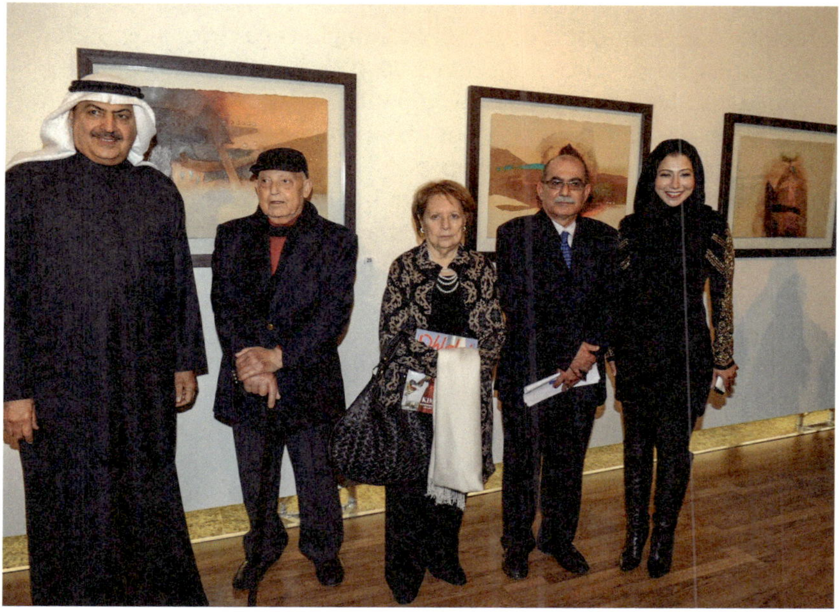

Rafa Nasiri's exhibition at the Financial Harbour Gallery, Manama, Bahrain 2013 – on the left Sheikh Rashid Al Khalifa

Spanish, for the audience seemed to closely follow and engage with what I said. Among what was requested of us was a brief summary of Iraq's visual art movement and the secret of its superiority. Rafa gave a comprehensive yet succinct overview, concluding with reference to the art of Jihad al-Amiri, who'd studied in Iraq and was an extension of this movement.

At the request of professors in the Faculty of Arts, Rafa held a one-day workshop for students in the university's graphic art studio. He spoke comfortably and energetically, demonstrating a practical application of the process he was known for in printmaking, and which he'd developed through his training in the printmaker Stanley William Hayter's French studio in 1968. I'll never forget how he stopped midday and told the participants, "Now excuse me while I swallow fifty dollars." He took out his pill and swallowed it, before continuing on with the workshop.

On our return, we spent two nights in Madrid in an apartment near the Museo del Prado. I received a message on my phone from our dear friend, writer and translator Bahira Abdul Latif Mohamed, who'd been living in Madrid since the mid-1990s. At the time she had obligations at the university, where she was preparing her dissertation on the relation of Jorge Borges to Arabic literature, and also lecturing. We agreed to meet the next morning at the entrance to the Prado, and walked over since it was so close to the hotel. Rafa was highly selective in this visit, searching out only the works that he'd long been connected to and that had enriched his artistic being throughout his life, particularly those of the great master Rembrandt. Once Rafa's eyes were happily satiated with these works, he moved on to Velázquez's wondrous work *Las Meninas*, and then we moved on to Goya. Rafa stood before his prints enchanted, as though seeing them for the first time. Then he said, "I'll suffice with that. You continue your tour and I'll wait for you in the courtyard." That was sufficient to break my heart. I walked away and roamed the vast space alone, accompanied only by my endless tears.

Bahira met us at the agreed time, crying out, "The scent of home!" She had only two hours to spend with us. I'd met Bahira during her work as a translator for al-Ma'mun Publishing House in the Ministry of Information and Culture, when she won wide acclaim for her brilliant translation of Rafael Alberti's book *The Lost Grove*. She was a shy young woman who looked at us from afar with a look of respect and appreciation, in light of her being from a younger generation. She left Iraq in the mid-1990s, and I still recall the sorrow with which our friend Naji al-Hadithi, head of al-Ma'mun Publishing House, spoke of her departure, saying, "Bahira's resignation means the press has lost one of its pillars."

When the internet entered our lives, Bahira communicated with Rafa and told us that she was living and working in Spain, and followed our news wherever we went. When we decided to go to Granada Rafa informed her, and she contacted us while we were there to set a time to meet in Madrid. We had two hours of snatched but effusive conversation in a nearby café. It was the first time I'd spoken with this brilliant intellectual. In Spain, she'd forged her path, becoming an accredited translator with the Ministry of Foreign Affairs, acquiring Spanish citizenship, and recently marrying a Spaniard. Up close I found her a warm and enchanting woman, sincerity beaming from her face. She slipped deep into your heart with her exceptional energy for friendship and cooperation.

At the end of our meeting, she asked me about Rafa's health and why he was walking with a cane. I told her it was nothing of concern. This was the beginning of a friendship that came to flourish, and we became even closer after I was left alone. She became one of the friends closest to my heart and mindset—and to my work—now that I lacked a companion, and among the most understanding and supportive during the first two years of that dark stage I passed through.

The next day we went to the Museo Reina Sofía, which had formerly been a hospital. It was a spacious building with long corridors and many large halls. Naturally, we weren't able to see it all in one day, so we sufficed with visiting certain wings to see masterpieces of modern art, focusing on artists of Spanish origin. To start with we stopped at Picasso's *Guernica*, rightly occupying a prominent space in its homeland. We stood there a long time, and I could practically read in Rafa's eyes his questioning whether Iraq would ever reopen its museum, or whether its artists would return from the diaspora. Then we moved on as Rafa viewed the works of the best Spanish modernists, stopping at the works of Miró, Chillida, and Tàpies. Whenever we found a seat in one of the halls, Rafa would sit down and lose himself in the magic of the art works.

On our last day in Madrid, Bahira asked Khalid Kaki, an Iraqi poet, musician, and translator living in the city, to join us until we left for the airport. We found him waiting for us beside the hotel with his fiancée in Plaza de Santa Ana. He was a wonderful companion and extremely kind and friendly. In the afternoon, we left for the airport to suffer another tortuous trip, and Rafa again refused to use the wheelchair. During our trip to Spain, Rafa would be energetic in the morning, but signs of exhaustion and pain would surface when we returned to the hotel to rest, and he'd decline going out in the evening. Except for the night of the lecture, he preferred to stay in the hotel. I'd attend the evening events without him, in the company of our friends Ali and Jihad.

Upon our return to Amman, Rafa resumed his testing. He underwent radiation therapy in addition to blood tests that showed the medication had lost its effectiveness following the fifth box, and that the percentage of disease in his body was rapidly increasing. Dr. al-Rabadhi asked him to discontinue it and return to chemotherapy, prescribing an additional injection he had on store in his clinic and which he said was a beneficial supplement. I wasn't comfortable with this procedure, but he assured me of its importance. I didn't notice any effect other than an additional cost, however, and whenever I asked about it he'd insist on it, until he discontinued it following the fifth dose, admitting it was not having any effect! This was only three months before Rafa's death, when his health deteriorated to its weakest state. Yet Rafa never lost hope and viewed his continued treatment as a sign of the possibility of improvement. All I could do was support his strong desire to live.

Dr. al-Rabadhi was always honest with me about the development of Rafa's disease, and while Rafa was undergoing treatment, he'd explain to me in his office how rapidly it was spreading through his bones. He always repeated that he didn't know how long Rafa's body would resist, especially when he'd have to lower the cortisone doses that gave him energy and vitality. I'd swallow the bitter truth and conceal it from Rafa, while holding onto hope.

In early 2012, as the months passed and his disease advanced, Rafa began creating an artist's book in which he documented his state with some degree of optimism. He was pleased with the new studio we'd recently moved to in Lweibdeh, with its spacious layout filled with daylight. We went every day, except in special cases when he needed to check in with the doctor. One day, his face bathed in the warm sunlight coming in from the door to the large balcony, he said, "The light here is strong and I need some time to grow accustomed to it."

So as to maintain his hand's flexibility, Rafa drew still lifes until he got used to the new space. He also began drawing portraits of visiting friends and would be delighted when he found that his hand still obeyed the commands of his early training, and every time he managed to capture the spirit of the person before him. Sometimes the portraits would take a few hours, as was the case with Maath Alousi, Mohammed Namir, Himat Mohamed Ali, and others. When he drew our dear friend Mahmoud Ahmed Uthman, it took two sessions, and he wasn't able to complete a portrait of Mohamed Kamel Arif at all, for he'd neither sit still nor hold himself back from talking. I was the last person he drew, and he didn't ask to do so until after a few months, surprising me one spring morning as we were having breakfast. I'd wanted to ask him when it would be my turn, but refrained, and then he surprised me by saying, "Today I'll draw your portrait!" The work took him five days to complete; the first portrait he'd drawn of me was in pen during our engagement and had taken him two hours.

Rafa had long loved drawing portraits of friends and would always select faces that appealed to him. He never hesitated to draw any face that attracted him, even if we were in a public event, or as happened once in a private gathering in Amman in the mid-1990s. It was a dinner party at the home of our friend Hind Oweis, may she rest in peace. Across from us sat three young female architects, among a limited number of guests in keeping with the size of the small and tasteful parlor. Suddenly Rafa requested a sheet of white paper from Hind and began sketching. I realized one of the women had appealed to him, and I was just about certain of his choice, due to her simple style and attractive features free of makeup, unlike her colleagues. My sense was right. When Rafa finished, he got up and came over to me, saying, "The drawing has to gain May's approval first." It was a splendid portrait of the young architect Hania al-Kabariti.

During this period, and perhaps due to an undisclosed submission to the facts of reality, Rafa worked consistently on the last of his artist's books. He began on May 16, 2011, and finished it, or abandoned it, on June 15, 2012. "Resist, he resists, resistance, I resist." These were phrases repeated across its handmade pages, amid clouds of bright colors, gold leaf, ink, and other mediums. The book consisted of twenty-two pages and a hard cover. It was dominated by a dark orange similar to the color of rust, lighter or darker and mixed with black or brown according to his mood. From deep within these strikes of color shone gold leaf, and amid this cacophony came his words of resistance, attempting to dissipate the dark heaviness hovering beneath them. At the climactic peak of this artist's book, among its previous peaks, the combatant reaches his end: a white page with a light sandy color on its corners indicating a space prepared for painting that was not completed. At the center of the two opposite pages, a horizontal stretch of turquoise is lined with pure white shining from the emptiness and flowing with the naturalness of the first creation. Perhaps he'd seen his beloved river flowing toward the absolute.

Also during this time, Rafa painted a series focusing on a recurrent theme that never left his mind or heart, and which he titled *Beside the River*. He began with large paintings, acrylic on canvas, and followed these with another series of watercolors and ink on paper, recalling in them his childhood and youth upon his first river in Tikrit. All of these works were distinguished by a purity of color and clarity of soul, and utter unification with the absolute. He didn't stop painting until two months before his passing. Rafa continued to pour life into his artistic work and gained strength from it, even as his body was being devoured by disease.

In early 2013, in February to be exact, Rafa was scheduled to hold a solo exhibition in Bahrain at the invitation of the Bahrain Cancer Society. He prepared a collection of paintings on canvas, and others on paper, under the title *Being in the Moment*. During his residency in China at the tender age of nineteen, he'd absorbed the morals, practices, and wisdoms of Eastern philosophies, and was greatly affected by what he learned from his teachers and his studies in China. In the final two years of his life, he turned to reading books on Zen and Tao, which he'd never distanced himself from, and his conviction that humans were in harmony with the universe and nature grew. This exhibition reflected the core of his concept of time. As he wrote in the exhibition text, "There is no future to existence; the past is neither here nor there. The present moment is all we have."

The exhibition was held in a new gallery on the top floor of Manama's Financial Harbor. It was a breathtaking space with an ample area, glass walls, and views of the sea. Although Rafa was still being treated with the pills, he appeared weak and wasn't able to stand for long periods of time; he spent most of the time seated on a chair in the gallery. Yet, the festive welcome he received from his friend Sheikh Rashid Al Khalifa, and our Bahraini and Iraqi friends and other lovers of art, in addition to the stunning appearance of his displayed works, filled him with great pleasure. Rafa had reached a pinnacle with this exhibition perhaps only surpassed by his final exhibition in Amman.

Upon our return, Dr. al-Rabadhi was convinced the pills had lost their efficacy, and we had no choice but to resume chemotherapy. We thus entered the most brutal stage of the disease and its debilitating effects, and Rafa's final months as he approached the end. In October 2013, among many times he was admitted to hospital, Rafa had to stay

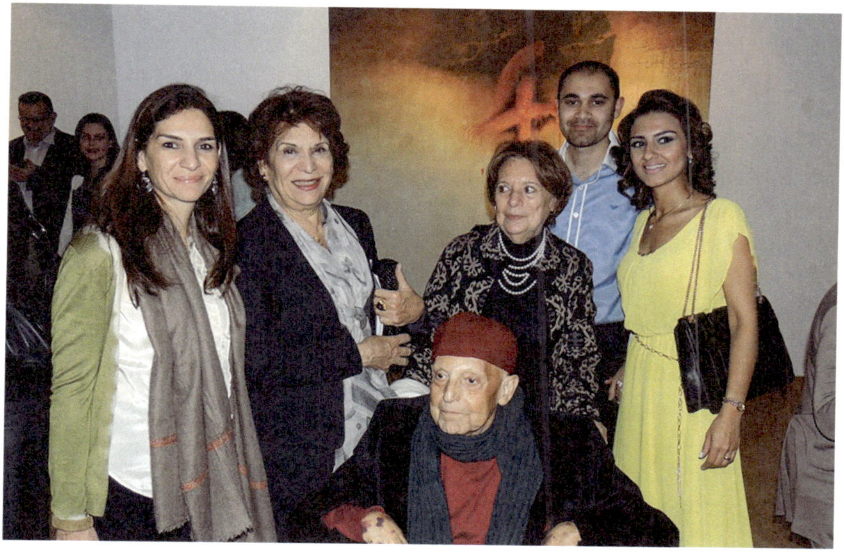

At the retrospective exhibition, *Rafa Nasiri: 50 Years of Painting and Printmaking*, with Princess Wijdan al-Hashemi, Princess Rajwa Ali, Mohammad Namir, and Basma Al-Ubaidy, Jordan National Gallery of Fine Arts, Amman, November 11, 2013

for almost two weeks. Naturally, I remained by his side day and night, attending to every detail large and small. His temperature would only go down with an IV.

During this stay I needed to write, in both Arabic and English, an introduction to the catalogue accompanying his retrospective scheduled to open on November 11 in the Jordan National Gallery of Fine Arts. Friends visited constantly to help as they could, and it was decided that Khalid Wahal would organize the exhibition and design its catalogue. I prayed that God would grant Rafa the opportunity to witness the celebration of his illustrious career. While still in the hospital, I at last completed the introduction and sat on the edge of his bed to read it to him before sending the text to print. Each time I raised my head to gauge his reaction, I'd see the fluttering of his silky eyes listening with love and appreciation.

Starting when I was young and throughout my life, I took charge of my affairs and those of my immediate family. When I married, this changed, due to the natural intertwining of our lives. The truth is that Rafa needed me as much as I needed him. We'd discuss everything, in perpetual dialogue, and only took decisions upon agreement, although I always made his choice a priority. We rarely disagreed. But when Rafa fell ill, I became the decision-maker for everything large and small. When Rafa found me meticulously managing our life affairs, including all of his, while simultaneously undertaking numerous professional and personal tasks, he seemed surprised but pleased, although he didn't openly express this. From time to time, he'd apologize for not being able to help me, and this would break my heart. I regularly treated a fungus he'd get on his fingers and toes, and when I sat down before him one day to treat it, he said, with some distress, "You're so generous with me!" I was astonished, as he'd always expressed his admiration for my ability to help others, so what should he expect when it came to him? I laughed and said, "Haven't you been generous with me?"

In July 2013, Rafa received an email from his favorite Chinese professor, Huang Yongyu, a world-famous artist, in which he invited us to his opulent Shanghai palace. "I'm ninety and do not have much time left. Come to Shanghai with your wife and be my guest." Rafa's eyes teared up as he said with all confidence, "We'll go in January, the weather will be marvelous in Shanghai."

Despite all this, we also had our joys that year. My nephew Mohammed shared with us his intention to ask for the hand of Basmah al-Obaidi, who'd been his colleague in the University of Jordan's School of Foreign Languages. She now lived with her family in Switzerland, and they'd met again over the internet. Rafa had long dreamed of such a day and congratulated him. "I want to see your son," Rafa told him. Basmah came from Switzerland with her uncle Haidar al-Darwish, and Rafa and Mohammed went to ask for her hand. Their official engagement was then finalized in Rafa's presence and a date was set for their marriage in October; Rafa wanted to host a proper wedding, but the bride and groom preferred to suffice with a dinner party. Rafa seemed well that day and was looking forward to taking part in the special occasion, but suddenly became very ill and was unable to attend. It was hard for me to go, and also hard for neither of us to attend the celebration we'd so long dreamed of for our beloved "son." I asked Mohammed to welcome the family and guests and told him I would join a bit later. It was a lovely celebration attended by the closest family members, young and old, and a select number of the bride and groom's friends. I spent an hour with them and then rushed back to Rafa.

When Rafa discontinued chemotherapy, he was no longer able to make the trip to Al-Khalidi Hospital, especially as he'd caught a microbe during his long hospital stay in October and this caused a lung infection and fever that persisted until the end. At this stage I was in dire need of assistance with his care and support of his mobility, as I was no longer physically able to undertake it alone. I sought the assistance of Basel Oliyan, director of Al-Sakha for Medical and Nursing Services, and with the great expertise he'd gained working at King Hussein Medical Center, he provided me with two professional nurses to stay with us day and night, providing all the necessary care through consultation with the doctor, and informing him of all developments. Rafa took comfort in returning to his beloved home.

Unfortunately, I noticed that this did not please Dr. al-Rabadhi, even though I brought it up with him beforehand. I don't know the reason, as he didn't express his opposition openly, but his behavior, which had always been kind, gentle, and comforting to us, changed completely. This surprised and pained Rafa. Following our last visit to the hospital for a blood transfusion, he asked me, "I saw a harshness I'm not used to in al-Rabadhi's eyes when he examined me. Why?" Rafa was extremely sensitive to negative situations and rough treatment, or even arrogant speaking in general. Harshness, coldness, and cruelty were wounding to him, and would keep him up at night. I told him I thought the doctor wasn't comfortable with the intervention of private nurses.

Naturally, I remained in constant contact with Dr. al-Rabadhi nonetheless, and he remained as responsive as we were accustomed to, although he didn't conceal his displeasure with the nurses. I began ignoring this, as home nursing greatly boosted Rafa's morale. Throughout Rafa's treatment, a warm and gentle friendship had developed between us and Dr. al-Rabadhi. He liked to chat with us when time permitted during Rafa's treatments in his clinic, and this increased our confidence in his medical expertise and vigilant care. I never noticed him taking any negative positions, and he gave me the freedom to contact him at any time, even when he was traveling, always helping me with his instructions.

In my last meeting with him, I went alone to his clinic to invite him and his family to attend Rafa's retrospective. He looked into my face, asking in disbelief, "Will Rafa really attend in the state he's in? If I were in his place, I would have stopped treatment some time back and submitted myself to death." I was shocked by this reaction, and by his tone and the stark look on his face. He was the one who'd insisted on treatment until the last moment. And where had his kindness, positive energy, and optimistic support gone? I replied calmly, and with a reasoning he would perhaps not accept, "I'm not surprised by what you've said, for you're a man of science with precise calculations. But let me remind you that Nobel prizes have been awarded in situations as bad as Rafa's. Thank God we've lacked such stern logic, for our life-long message as creative artists has been devoted to awakening the spirit of existence in the face of death. Rafa is an artist, and of the many skills that God granted him, he's done his best to deliver his creative message. This is not a mere exhibition, but rather a celebration of a half century's production by a major artist whose works have surpassed geographic boundaries. Friends and admirers of his art will come from around the world to honor him and his artistic legacy. Can you even begin to imagine what it means to him to attend this?" He kept looking into my face and did not reply. I do not know if I convinced him or not, but he surprised me by attending the opening in the company of his daughter, and he witnessed the large gathering and celebration of Rafa.

Despite the hope of survival dwindling every day, I began turning my back on everything I heard. I anticipated a miracle each time I found him with some energy, effusing vitality of an unknown source. One morning he woke up, had his breakfast, and bathed with the assistance of his nurse Abu Zayd. His face showed energy and cheer. At the time, Khalid, Sever, and Himat were busy setting up the exhibition. I suggested to Abu Zayd that we get Rafa out of the house and take him there while the weather was sunny and warm. He agreed enthusiastically, confirming that Rafa was in very good condition that day. I was certain Rafa was worried about the absence of his direct supervision, and the idea of going there pleased him.

At the gallery entrance we found ourselves facing his painting *Prayers for Baghdad* from 1985, which is 140 by 120 centimeters, with its gradations of brown mixed with red, white, and black, and a bird passing under an arch. This painting had graced the parlor in our Baghdad home, and I felt as though my heart would leap from my chest with its pounding. Each of us concealed our tumultuous feelings upon this magical meeting with the past. Our dear, lifelong friend Princess Wijdan al-Hashemi approached with her arms thrown wide open to greet Rafa. This made me cry, which I hid from the others alone in the next hall. Rafa thanked her and the museum director Khalid Khreis, a friend and artist, and expressed his delight with this institution in which he'd held a solo exhibition over thirty years earlier when it was first established.

The team had finished setting up the ground floor level and were working on completing the second. Rafa toured the first floor, passing by his brilliant academic sketches and prints he'd produced in China. Then he viewed the subsequent periods of his art production, and the paintings and prints he'd made in China, Portugal, Baghdad, Salzburg, London, Madrid, Amman, and Paris. In a soft voice he said to me, "Thank God, I've regained my past." On the second floor the team gathered around to greet him, delighted by this unexpected visit. They took him on a tour in his wheelchair, listening to his suggestions for switching the places of certain works, gesturing with his hands with all the energy we were accustomed to. I felt as though the spirit of a lion had possessed him.

As the date of the opening approached, friends began arriving from around the world, and they all came to check on Rafa upon their arrival. Dia, who followed Rafa's conditions closely from afar, was among the first in Amman, arriving about a week before the exhibition. Dia had previously undergone a similar situation and understood the horrors of this disease through all he'd suffered in the experience of his wife. He began frequenting Amman and visiting us in the studio, where he'd sit with Rafa as they discussed art projects and collaborations. This was how they always were when they met, whether in person or via phone calls, handwritten letters, or emails. They were allies, compatible in their approach and style of creative work, their artistic ambition, and their constant striving to promote the advancement of Arab and Iraqi art movements.

Upon his arrival, I found Dia rather somber, as he realized his companion may be nearing his end. Before going into his room, he asked me how Rafa was. "He's well," I told him, "as you'll see." I don't recall how long their meeting lasted, but I could hear their voices vying to talk as well as their laughing. When Dia came out, he told me, "I'm quite in shock. Rafa was competing with me on ideas and art projects and wants us to carry them out together." Then he asked me, in wonderment, how I'd maintained his morale to this degree. I told him, "With love for his glowing spirit that refuses to give in."

A few years after Rafa passed away, Dia sent me a touching email from Salzburg expressing how lonely he felt with the loss of Rafa:

> To: May Muzafar
> July 27, 2019
>
> Dear May,
>
> I arrived this afternoon in Salzburg, after passing by the Venice Biennale and all the exciting Arab work there. I suggested to Charlie, who's accompanying me, that we go to the museum of modern art in the late afternoon. Then we went to have coffee in a restaurant overlooking the city, but the fortress in which I learned printmaking so passionately from beloved Rafa was there before me, and our days here came back to me in all their detail. So I drank enough wine to allow me the pleasure of memories. Excuse my writing, but I want to thank you for having kept him alive in the memory of so many, and opened the door for those who don't otherwise know art history. As for me, I no longer have a friend to tease and argue with. I feel alone. My solace is in the efforts I make with the young artists who were his students.
>
> Most fondly,
> Dia

Also among the first to arrive was Modhir Ahmed, an internationally accomplished artist and Rafa's faithful student, who came from

Sweden. Rafa held great fondness for him and admired his art and pioneering practice, as well as his person and his refined manner. In our last visit to Bahrain in early 2013 for Rafa's solo exhibition, Modhir was in Qatar representing Rafa at their concurrent joint exhibition there and came to Bahrain to visit his teacher. In this visit to Amman, Modhir approached me with the idea of establishing an award in Rafa's name for young Iraqi printmakers. I told him that this was one of Rafa's dreams, but I wasn't currently in a position that would allow me to engage about such a serious endeavor. He assured me he'd take care of everything, and only wanted our approval.

Rafa had long dreamed of an award in Iraq's name and had submitted a proposal to the Ministry of Information and Culture to establish a graphic arts center and an Arab award. During our last visit to Kurdistan in the late 1980s, we walked around the Erbil Citadel, which was under restoration, with our friend Mahmoud Ahmed Uthman. We visited a beautiful old domed building that had been a public bath and had just been restored, and Rafa suggested that it be turned into a graphic arts center. Mahmoud got excited about the idea and tried to make it happen, but what subsequently took place prevented anything from happening, and all such dreams vanished into thin air. When Modhir proposed the idea to Rafa, he looked at him with a smile, and gave him the green light. We agreed he'd draft the award's framework and conditions to discuss later. After Rafa passed away, Modhir brought the topic up again and assured me he was holding to his promise. This was the first artistic decision I took alone, supported by my trust in Modhir and my reliance upon him. When I later shared the proposal with Dia al-Azzawi, he suggested it be an Arab award rather than Iraqi one, and so it was. This pioneering project came to fruition a year after Rafa's departure, and I set his birthday, March 24, as the date for granting the award.

On November 11, 2013, Rafa's nurses Abu Zayd and Abu Rami both helped me get Rafa ready and accompanied us to the exhibition. He seemed tense and stubborn about his attire and appearance, which he never neglected throughout his life. I'd prepared for him a formal suit with comfortable pants and covered the lower part of his body with a cashmere blanket. It wasn't cold out, but due to his physical weakness he always felt chilled. We arrived early, and the nurses took him around the ground floor halls before taking him up to the second floor, where he sat in an area that allowed everyone to greet him. Friends began arriving, both those residing in Amman and those who'd come from elsewhere. Among those who came to assist us was

Muhanad Nasiri, an architect residing in the Emirates and the eldest son of Rafa's sister. Arriving from France was Sabah, Rafa's closest brother, and from Iraq came his brother Maath, accompanied by his daughter Lina, who lived in Amman, with her husband Dhaif Abdul Majeed. The exhibition was held under the auspices of Princess Wijdan al-Hashemi, who arrived on time to find the museum's halls already filled with a large attendance. She approached him in his spot on the second floor, where Dia and Modhir were stationed by his side, and greeted him in a highly touching manner. I moved about between the floors, checking that everything was in place, and returning to greet arriving friends and visitors, answer questions, and sign the exhibition catalogue for Rafa. Modhir Ahmed broadcast a live recording of the event over the internet.

The following day I'd arranged a luncheon at the Amun Hotel for guests and locally based friends, numbering over fifty, and Rafa had planned to attend. That morning he awoke with a sense of satisfaction and satiation and told me he'd prefer not to take part. I felt it was the right decision, as the exhibition had both filled him with excitement and tired him. But I can't forget the disappointment on the faces of his nurses.

Among those who attended the exhibition was Sheikh Hassan Al Thani from Qatar, and a large Qatari delegation, and during the luncheon Sheikh Hassan left his place to come sit beside me. He praised me for the great effort that had been made to hold this exhibition and asked me about the fate of Rafa's works and how I'd maintain them. Noting what a great responsibility it was, and how much care was needed, he expressed the readiness of Mathaf: Arab Museum of Modern Art to undertake this mission, and to move the works in their entirety there. I hadn't expected this generous offer and was at a loss as to how to reply, for this was a major decision with which I had no experience. I had a vague sense of discomfort, and as I am wont to do, hesitated to give a clear response. I thanked him for his kindness and told him that I couldn't be separated from these works, for they were an Iraqi legacy, first of all, and a trust that Rafa was leaving in my care, and that I wanted to live in their midst. "You can visit us and check on them at any time," he said, and I laughed and asked him, "Would I get an entry permit?" And I told him I would run the idea by Rafa and get back to him. When I told Rafa, he expressed his gratitude for the initiative, but otherwise sufficed with a smile. He was aware that such an arrangement would never be as simple as stated.

At seven in the morning on Saturday, December 7, Rafa closed his eyes and passed away. He'd continued concealing his illness, not wanting to worry his siblings or close friends, until he'd appeared in a lovely interview with Ricardo Karam on the show "Other Talk." Ricardo held interviews with Iraqi figures in art, architecture, and science who'd left a strong mark on their scenes, and the program was broadcast in late 2012. The first episode was with Rafa, and at that time the signs of his illness had become clear, and friends who were not in Amman were alarmed to see it. That day I was contacted by one of our closest friends, Wijdan Maher, who lived in London, and she told me that the news had badly shocked Dia. When he realized what was happening, and I confirmed it when we met in Beirut at the *Art in Iraq Today* exhibition, he began frequenting Amman and spent a lot of time with Rafa in our new Jabal Lweibdeh studio. During one of his visits to our home we were joined by Wijdan and our beloved Maath Alousi, an architect visiting from Cyprus, as well as Ali Taleb, visiting from the Netherlands, and Faisal al-Jibouri, also an architect. I prepared a Baghdadi lunch for us and it was a pleasurable visit that brought Rafa much joy.

As his case progressed and Rafa had to frequent the hospital, our faithful friend Faisal al-Jibouri visited him daily, either alone or in the company of our great friend Ali Shabu, a former UN ambassador. Ali Taleb often accompanied them whenever he was in Amman, as did some family and other close friends. Rafa would enjoy his time with them and join in their laughter as much as possible, even if he was in discomfort. I'll never forget Faisal's great concern or the extraordinary efforts he made to help me day and night in the hospital or in our home, nor what it meant to me to have him by my side during my crisis following Rafa's death.

Throughout Rafa's illness, he always had a smile on his face and never complained. All Friday night, the night before he passed away, he was energetic and active. In the evening, after our guests had left, I fed him his dinner, and he asked me to find a lovely and entertaining film we'd seen before. This brought him pleasure, and we watched it together until after midnight. Then I tucked in his covers to help him sleep. I monitored him night and day, and even in the hospital I'd sleep on a sofa or a chair beside him. Despite the care given by the evening nurse, I wasn't at peace unless I checked on him several times to make sure he was covered, which could get heavy for him, or to have him drink some water, which he refused to accept from the nurse.

That night I checked on him twice before he finally woke up after six. I rushed to him, fearing he might be thirsty, and was surprised by the worried look in his eyes as he clung to my hand and asked me to stay with him. “Don’t go, I don’t feel well.” The nurse informed me that he needed oxygen. I contacted Dr. Said and he told me to call for an ambulance and said he was on his way. I called for an ambulance and returned to hold Rafa’s hand. He seemed pained and distressed. As I tried to reassure him, he cried out, “I can’t see!” I asked him what he meant, and he sternly replied, “I’m telling you, I can’t see anything!” A few minutes passed as he turned his head from right to left, and then he fell still. The nurse felt him and said, “Finished, Madame.” I asked what she meant and she repeated the phrase. At that very moment Dr. Said arrived, as did the ambulance and Abu Zayd, who was there to begin his shift at seven. But everything had truly ended and I was somewhere between shock and denial. Abu Zayd pulled the sheet to cover Rafa’s head, but I objected. I saw him as though he were sleeping, his face peaceful. I placed a few drops of water in his mouth and protected him by reciting the Koran’s opening verse and hugged his frail body.

Ever since leaving Iraq, we’d remained together wherever we went. Rafa began insisting on accompanying me anywhere circumstances would allow us to be together, and we only traveled alone on rare occasion. When Rafa closed his eyes, I promised him I’d remain with him. And in fact, I accompanied him and sat beside his corpse laid out in the mosque, awaiting his funeral prayer. I defied custom and remained sitting on the ground behind the men praying the noon prayer. I went with the men to the cemetery and I knelt at the edge of his grave until he was covered with earth.

Since my childhood I’ve been accustomed to seeing strange things in my dreams, people I don’t know or places to which I’ve never been. Some of them remain in my memory and others dissipate. Often these visions come true within the next few days, and some of the dreams are recurring, as though harbingers of the future. From time to time I dreamed that Rafa was packing his suitcase in preparation to leave, apologizing, “It’s time for us to separate, I want to take off freely as we agreed.” I’d have no option but to respect his will, as I’d promised myself at the start of our shared life. I’d wake up disturbed and thank God it had only been a dream.

A week or more before Rafa passed away, I dreamed we were on a trip together in the mountains of Lebanon, passing forests lining the road. Rafa asked the driver to make a brief stop, as he wanted to photograph the area. I warned him that his legs might not allow a mountain climb, but he didn’t reply. He walked away from the car with his camera, his eyes combing the site, and asked me to wait for him until he was finished. I followed him with my eyes as he disappeared into the depths of the forest. Worried, I went to look for him, but could find no trace. I called and called for him, but heard nothing save my own voice dissipating into space.